Living by Faith

TAKE GOD AT HIS WORD
AND HONOUR HIM BY TRUSTING HIM

92 devotions

Jan Philip Svetlik

In memory of David,
who encouraged me to write this book
and whose life of faith was a great example to me.

Living by Faith

Take God at His word
and honour Him by trusting Him

92 devotions

Jan Philip Svetlik

The Bereans Publishing Ltd.
United Kingdom
info@the-bereans.com
www.the-bereans.com

Believers Bookshelf Canada Inc.
Canada
orders@bbcan.org
www.believersbookshelf.ca

ISBN: 978-1-913232-47-4
All Rights Reserved
Copyright: © The Bereans Publishing Ltd.
2023

The Bereans Publishing Ltd.
United Kingdom
info@the-bereans.com, www.the-bereans.com

and

Believers Bookshelf Canada Inc.
Canada
orders@bbcan.org, www.believersbookshelf.ca

Original German publication:
Hmaidan.Media
Haiger, Germany

Cover design: David Lehnhardt

The reference to publications by authors who are mentioned or quoted from in this work need not imply that their theological views are shared by the author and publishers.

Printed in Germany

Table of Contents

Preface

What does it mean to live by faith? And what would be possible in my life if I were to trust God wholeheartedly, like a child? Have you ever asked yourself these questions?

This is especially relevant in our society, where health and security are most important and we're used to (or even obligated to) making sure everything is covered by some kind of insurance. Have we come to the point—just like the people of this world—where we trust in our own precautions more than the living God?

This matter is very important to God! He encourages us to live by faith. How does He do that? He shows us many men and women in His Word, whose impressive examples encourage and challenge—yes, even provoke—us to live by faith.

Isn't it depressing when we compare the great faith of these individuals in, for instance, Hebrews 11 and James 2 with our own little faith? Absolutely not! God doesn't want to overstrain us or push us over the edge into despondency, but rather to stir up our faith! He says to us: "Consider the outcome of their way of life, and imitate their faith" (Heb. 13:7). Words instruct, but examples spur us on!

In church history there were also countless believers who took God at His word, and their lives were characterised by their unconditional trust in Him. Occupying ourselves with their biographies on the one hand protects us from arrogance, and on the other hand it encourages us to let go of things more and more and to move on in faith.

The following pages should make tangible—using some examples of faith from both the Bible and church history—what it can mean to live by faith, to really trust God and to take Him at His word. Among other things, we'll see where the eye of faith is directed, what characterises great but also little faith, how the energy of faith manifests itself, and how faith proves itself in trials.

The aim of this book is to encourage you to live by faith, to trust God and to honour Him by doing so. Because when we trust God, we show that He's trustworthy—which then glorifies Him!

A tip for reading this book: it isn't intended to be read in one sitting. It would be better if you would meditate on the individual devotions and take time to consider the challenges at the end of each devotion in quietness and with prayer.

"There are no more eagles flying through the church sky today and therefore the smaller birds lack a yardstick to measure their size."

Friedrich Wilhelm Krummacher

Introduction

Faith has many facets: it believes the unbelievable, sees the invisible and does the impossible. In trusting by faith we bring the living God into the circumstances of life—and that changes everything! Why is that? Because faith helps us to see matters in the right perspective.

Faith is the great principle of divine life in us—from beginning to end. After having believed in the Son of God we were justified by faith. Now we live by faith, stand by faith and walk by faith. Faith gains us access to heaven and lets us enjoy now some of the things "no eye has seen, nor ear heard, nor the heart of man imagined, what God has prepared for those who love him" (1 Cor. 2:9).

Where do we find this faith in the Bible? Hebrews 11 is a good place to start. There we find an entire list of heroes of faith who in one way or another have trusted God and honoured Him in faith. But as the author places these tremendous examples before us, he makes a remarkable statement just a few verses earlier: "The just shall live by faith" (Heb. 10:38, NKJV). So, God first puts the principle for Christian life before us—to live by faith—and then, by using examples, shows us what characterises this faith and how it is manifested in practice.

And that's exactly what will occupy us on the following pages, where we will zoom in on several aspects of faith. How can confidence of faith, obedience of faith, energy of faith, works of faith and steps of faith become visible in the

Christian's life? We want to try to find answers to this question—and apply these to our lives.

Although faith has many facets, it's always directed at a Person: Jesus Christ, the Son of the living God. Paul wrote to the Galatians: "The life I now live in the flesh I live by faith in the Son of God, who loved me and gave himself for me" (Gal. 2:20). His was a living faith, day by day, hour by hour. He had his eye of faith directed at the Son of God, who was everything for him. That's why living by faith also means to make Jesus Christ the centre and goal of our daily lives.

> **"Looking to Jesus, the founder and perfecter of our faith."**
> (Hebrews 12:2)

God wants us to go through our daily lives in living fellowship with our Lord, continuously aware of the fact that we are dependent upon Him. As David aptly said: "For God alone, O my soul, wait in silence, for my hope is from him" (Ps. 62:5). That's the language of faith, which is focused on God and counts on Him in everything.

Soon the time will come when we don't need faith anymore. Why not? Because Jesus Christ will come to take us to be with Himself in heaven. Then we'll move from faith to sight (see 2 Cor. 5:7)—and we'll finally see who He is. Wonderful hope! Until then we should trust Him and rely on His promises: "Yet a little while, and the coming one will come and will not delay; but my righteous one shall live by faith" (Heb. 10:37–38).

> *Take some time and ask yourself the following questions: Is my life really characterised by a living faith? When I think back on yesterday: Did I live in conscious fellowship with God and really engage with Him?*

Notes:

....
....
....
....
....
....
....
....
....
....
....
....
....
....
....
....
....
....
....
....

Characteristics of Faith

What characterises faith and what does it produce in our lives? Hebrews 11:1 gives us the answer: "Now faith is the assurance of things hoped for, the conviction of things not seen" (Heb. 11:1). We'll now look at what that really means.

The Look Ahead

"Behold, I am coming soon, bringing my recompense with me, to repay each one for what he has done." (Revelation 22:12)

Faith looks ahead. The one who lives by faith doesn't doubt for a moment that what God says about the future will come to pass. The things we hope for are so certain for those who live by faith, it's as if they're a reality now. Faith works like a telescope, putting the future right before our eyes, so that we can enjoy it now. The trusting gaze at the wonderful hope waiting for us in heaven gives us strength and helps us to overcome present difficulties.

Furthermore, this look ahead in faith motivates us to bring sacrifices today. Why? Because faith looks at the reward! What motivated Abraham to live as a stranger in tents in Canaan? "He was looking forward to the city that has foundations, whose designer and builder is God" (Heb. 11:10). What moved Moses to suffer with God's people rather than enjoying the treasures of Egypt? "He was looking to the reward" (Heb. 11:26).

It is one thing to talk about something and to agree with it in principle, but it's a completely different thing to actually put it into practice. Take, for example, the Lord's promise that when we do something for Him and the gospel now, we'll receive a great reward. Is that a truth we just agree with, or do we lean on it in faith and act on it accordingly?

Charles Studd impressively showed in his life what it can mean to sacrifice things in order to have treasures in heaven. The famous former cricket player didn't put his trust in money and possessions, but made friends with the "unrighteous Mammon" to achieve God's ends (Lk. 16:9, NKJV). While serving as a missionary in China, the following happened:

> **Faith does not operate in the realm of the possible. There is no glory for God in that which is humanly possible. Faith begins where man's power ends.**
> (George Müller)

He was surprised when one morning he received a thick letter in the mail. The letter bore the watermark of Messrs. Coutts & Co, the Studd family's solicitor. As C.T. tore the envelope open, he realised that it had been two weeks since his twenty-sixth birthday, the day he was to inherit the money his father had left him. Sure enough, the envelope contained copies of stocks and bank deposits that now belonged to him.

When he added it all up, C.T. calculated that he had been left at least twenty-nine thousand pounds, enough money to live comfortably for the rest of his life. But that was not what he had in mind for the money. For two years now, he had been sure of what he wanted to do when he received the inheritance—he wanted to give the money to Christian charities. He thanked God that he was in Chungking, because he needed a British official to sign the papers giving his brother Kinny the necessary authority to dispose of the money.

Later that day C.T. found Mr. Bourne in his study.

"May I come in?" he asked.

"By all means, my good man. What can I help you with?" Mr. Bourne asked.

C.T. got straight to the point. "I received mail this morning. It was information about my inheritance, which I had almost forgotten about. Would you be able to draw up and sign some papers so that my brother can have power of attorney over the money? I wish him to give it away on my behalf."

C.T. watched as Mr. Bourne's face turned white. Mr. Bourne caught his breath and then spluttered, "But... but it would be quite a sum of money, wouldn't it? I mean, your father was a wealthy man."

"He was," C.T. agreed, "but he found the Lord just two years before he died, and I am sure he would approve of my giving it away. More important, I know my heavenly Father approves. There is no safer place for my money than in 'God's bank'. He offers one-hundredfold increase. Do you know anyone who offers better interest than that?"

"You... I... no!" the consul replied. "I won't let you do it. You need to think about this in the cold light of day." Then he softened his tone. "You will always need food and a roof over your head, and you might marry one day and have children. Think ahead a little. After all, you may like being a missionary now, but ten years from now, who can tell?"

C.T. was shocked. He never imagined that he would have to fight with his host to get him to sign the papers.

"But it's your duty to sign them," he said. "I am a British subject, and you are the resident consul."

Mr. Bourne threw up his hands and sighed. "Very well, but I am going to insist on this: take two weeks to think it over, and if you haven't changed your mind—and I am sure that when you think seriously about it, you will—then I will sign the documents for you."

C.T. went away satisfied that he had to wait only two weeks before he could carry out his plan.

In the following days C.T. settled on how the money should be divided up. He decided on four allotments of five thousand pounds each. The first allotment was for Dwight L. Moody, the man who had converted his father. C.T. wanted Moody to use the money to start a gospel work in Tirhoot, North India, where his father had made his fortune producing indigo dye.

The second allotment was for George Müller, a Prussian man who had emigrated to England and now ran Christian orphanages for the poorest children in Bristol.

C.T. chose George Holland to receive the third allotment. Holland was a zealous preacher who worked with the poor in Whitechapel, London. The fourth allotment was to go to Commissioner Frederick Booth-Tucker, General William Booth's son-in-law, who had advanced the Salvation Army into India.

C.T. divided the rest of the money up among other missions and Christian charities he admired.

Two weeks later C.T. was back in Mr. Bourne's office, asking him to draw up the papers. Although the consul was not happy about it, he agreed that C.T. had waited the agreed-upon two weeks.

On January 13, 1887, C.T. sent off the paperwork, glad that his money was now safely deposited in the "Bank of Heaven", as he called it.

(Geoff & Janet Benge, *C.T. Studd, No Retreat (Christian Heroes: Then & Now)*, YWAM Publishing)

> **Does the wonderful future, promised to you by God, influence your daily life? What are you willing to sacrifice in order to gather treasures in heaven? Is the heavenly interest more important to you than the interest you get from the bank? Take God at His Word and include Him and His promises in all of your life's decisions!**

Notes:

....

....

....

....

....

....

....

The Look Upwards

"I lift up my eyes to the hills. From where does my help come? My help comes from the LORD, who made heaven and earth." (Psalm 121:1–2)

Faith looks upwards. It opens our eyes to an invisible world: that is, it is fully convinced of the existence of invisible, spiritual and heavenly things and gives us certainty about them. After Paul contrasted the great and eternal glory waiting for us with the present and temporal trials and needs, he said: "We look not to the things that are seen but to the things that are unseen. For the things that are seen are transient, but the things that are unseen are eternal" (2 Cor. 4:18). Faith is therefore not aligned to a visible but an invisible world: "For we walk by faith, not by sight" (2 Cor. 5:7).

The most important thing is that faith has the living God in view. The psalmist said: "To you I lift up my eyes, O you who are enthroned in the heavens!" (Ps. 123:1). That's the language of faith, enjoying fellowship or intimacy with God and knowing He's always with us. Jesus Christ lived here on earth in the consciousness of this and said prophetically: "I have set the LORD always before me; because he is at my right hand, I shall not be shaken" (Ps. 16:8).

When we have God before our eyes, we receive courage to persevere in trials without giving up. Moses had the difficult task of appearing before Pharaoh several times and announcing God's judgment to this powerful ruler. What gave him the strength to do so? The author of the Epistle to the Hebrews gives the answer: "He endured as seeing him who is invisible" (Heb. 11:27). Because he had the great and invisible "I AM" before his eyes, he didn't need to fear the visible king.

Elijah also dwelt before God in faith. Suddenly he appeared before evil King Ahab, announced judgment and said: "As the LORD, the God of Israel, lives, before whom I stand, there shall be neither dew nor rain these years, except by my word" (1 Ki. 17:1).

We see a similar courage with Stephen in Acts 7. While the enraged Jews stood before him gnashing their teeth, he gazed intently into heaven, saw the glory of God and Jesus standing at God's right hand. Fearlessly he testified of his beloved Lord and thus became a tremendous example for a large army of Christians, who over the centuries have been encouraged by the boldness of his faith.

> **Rather let us look by faith to Christ at God's right hand, than at the mountain of difficulties before our eyes.**
> (Robert C Chapman)

Samuel Lamb was a man of faith who consciously lived in the invisible yet real presence of God. Twenty years of detention camps and brainwashing didn't harm this Chinese Christian's faith. Through his deep trust, he made a significant contribution to the underground church in China. In his biography we read the following impressive testimony when he was just in prison:

It was at this time that Samuel Lamb became so fully aware of the Presence[1]. He turned to look, almost expecting to see someone. He saw nothing, but in not seeing, he became all the more aware. He thought he heard the Presence say, "He shall give his angels charge over thee, to keep thee in all thy ways".

Though the Presence startled him, he felt he could almost reach out and touch the reality. He had been aware of the Presence before in his life—but never so markedly as now.

Samuel began singing softly:

> *When we walk with the Lord*
> *in the light of His Word,*
> *What a glory He sheds on our way!*

There was a Presence. Not some fancied phantasm but a tangible entity more visible to his spiritual eyes than to his physical eyes. Hallelujah!

The Presence reminded him, "Are not all angels ministering spirits, sent to serve those who will inherit salvation?" Praise the Lord of lords. Exalted be His name forever and ever! This awareness would follow Samuel through the anxious times awaiting him.

(Ken Anderson, *Bold as a Lamb*, Zondervan Publishing House)

---

1   Author's note: This is how he always referred to the comforting and encouraging awareness of the greatness of the Lord.

> How can you always put the Lord before you in your everyday life so that you don't waver when opposition comes? What can help you to keep your eyes open to the invisible world? When was the last time you confessed your Lord to unbelievers? How can you overcome the fear of men?

Notes:

....
....
....
....
....
....
....
....
....
....
....
....
....
....
....
....
....
....

Take God at His Word

God Does What He Promises!

"Blessed is she who believed that there would be a fulfilment of what was spoken to her from the Lord." (Luke 1:45)

Paul writes to the Romans: "So then faith comes by hearing, and hearing by the word of God" (Rom. 10:17, NKJV). This verse shows us the foundation of faith. It doesn't lie in man's wisdom, assumptions or speculations, but it is based on the living and unchangeable Word of God. Whoever believes takes God at His word—and is fully convinced that He does what He has promised. That's why faith is like an invisible hand taking hold of and standing on the promises of God. Our senses can disappoint us but never the Word of God!

The verb 'believe' is first used in the Bible in Genesis 15:6. There God promises Abram, over the age of 75 (and Sarai 65), and says: "'Look toward heaven, and number the stars, if you are able to number them.' Then he said to him, 'So shall your offspring be'" (Gen. 15:5). Humanly speaking it would be impossible for a couple that old to have children. But what is impossible with men is possible with God—"For all things are possible with God" (Mk. 10:27).

We're very much inclined to believe something because we think it's probable. But true faith begins there where probability stops, because it reckons with the living God and not with statistics!

How does Abram respond when he hears God's promise? He believes the Lord! Paul writes about this father of faith: "No unbelief made him waver concerning the promise of God ... fully convinced that God was able to do what he had promised" (Rom. 4:20–21). Because this patriarch took God at His word, he gained hope and confidence.

> **It is characteristic of faith to reckon on God, not simply in spite of difficulty, but in spite of impossibility.**
> (John Nelson Darby)

Is there a message for us in what Abram experienced? Absolutely: "For whatever was written in former days was written for our instruction, that through endurance and through the encouragement of the Scriptures we might have hope" (Rom. 15:4). Abram's God is our God. He doesn't change—and nothing is too hard for Him (see Gen. 18:14), or even too wonderful (Gen. 18:14, JND)!

The Bible contains many more examples where God promised something of which the fulfilment seemed entirely impossible for a long time. Take for instance Joseph. God promises him that one day all his brothers would bow down before him. Shortly after that matters seem to develop in an entirely different direction. Filled with hatred, the brothers take him and cast him into a pit and eventually sell him as a slave into Egypt. There he is wrongfully accused and thrown into prison. He spends at least two years in this prison cell. How often during this long period would he have thought of his dreams in which God had given such clear promises? "The word of the LORD tested him" (Ps. 105:19). There in prison his trust and his clinging to God's promises were put to the test in a special way.

Then suddenly something amazing happens: in just a few hours things take a 180-degree turn. Joseph is freed from prison and is suddenly promoted to be the second-most powerful man in Egypt. When the time appointed by God has finally come, his brothers travel to Egypt and bow before him, just as God had declared!

We see something similar with Moses: God promises him that he'll lead the people of Israel out of Egypt to take them to the land of Canaan. But first hardships only increase. The Israelites experience massive opposition and have to go through much suffering and many trials. Then finally the time comes: in a night never to forget they leave Egypt.

Shortly after that they stand at the shores of the Red Sea, with mountains left and right. From behind, angry Pharaoh's army is getting closer and closer. All seems hopelessly lost. But God intervenes! He fights for His people with an outstretched arm and destroys their enemies in the vast masses of water. Their fear changes to joy and they sing the first song mentioned in the Word of God.

When the Lord has promised us something, we should trust Him, even when the fulfilment seems without prospect and humanly speaking all hope is lost, because "God is not man, that he should lie, or a son of man, that he should change his mind. Has he said, and will he not do it? Or has he spoken, and will he not fulfil it?" (Num. 23:19).

Let's look at another example from church history:

Early one morning while he [Bakht Singh] was in Coonoor, he heard a voice saying, "Your eyes will see the king in his beauty and view a land that stretches afar," the words from Isaiah 33:17. The following two mornings he heard the voice again. Finally on the third morning, he asked the Lord, "Tell me the meaning of this verse."

"I want you to get ready to go abroad, to a land far off," he heard the Lord say. He went back to Jehovah-Shammah to share this with the brethren there, and they began praying about it with him. They too had peace that he should go abroad.

The Lord urged him to go quickly. During his daily Scripture reading while reading Ezekiel 8:1—"And it came to pass in the sixth year, in the sixth month, in the fifth day of the month..."—he understood that he should arrive in London on the fifth day of the sixth month. He would have to get a passport quickly—in just two days—and he would need money for the passage. Amazingly, he got his passport, but he still needed the money. Then a couple whom he had never met, a Mr. and Mrs. Devasahayam, came to see him. They said the Lord had told them to bring a special gift of money to Bakht Singh. God provided the money in time for him to get to the ship in Bombay.

When he arrived in Bombay, however, he was told that there was no room for him on the Veronica, the one passenger ship leaving that day and arriving in London on the fifth of June. But there was room for him on the Andes, which was leaving two days later and would arrive in London on the seventh of June. There was nothing else to do but take the later ship. As it turned out, the Veronica had engine trouble and was delayed getting to London, and the Andes, a much faster ship, arrived in London on the fifth of June.

(T E Koshy, *Bakht Singh of India, The Incredible Account of a Modern-Day Apostle*, IVP Books).

This occasion shows how the Lord precisely and wonderfully led him!

> *What circumstances sometimes bring you to the point where you doubt God's promises? Which encouraging Bible verses can help you to trust in God and His Word, regardless of the circumstances? Cling to God's promises, no matter where the wind blows!*

Notes:

....
....
....
....
....
....
....
....
....
....
....
....
....
....

Triumph before Victory

"By faith the walls of Jericho fell down after they had been encircled for seven days." (Hebrews 11:30)

The conquest of Jericho is a striking example of how faith, which trusts in the word of God and acts on it, rises above seemingly insurmountable obstacles.

It all begins with God's word. He makes a promise to Joshua before the conquest and says: "See, I have given Jericho into your hand, with its king and mighty men of valour" (Josh. 6:2). He doesn't say: "I will give Jericho into your hand", but "I *have* given Jericho into your hand". So he receives the firm promise that the victory is already his. It's now up to the people to realise that victory in taking possession of the city.

The Israelites receive clear directions from God as to how to act: march around the city, blow the trumpets and shout loudly! No normal person would have thought that this loud shouting or cheering (the Hebrew word can also be translated 'shouting in triumph' or 'shouting for joy') would cause the mighty walls of this city to collapse. But the secret to the victory lies in this cheering—because it's the shout of faith acting on God's word.

Living faith takes God at His word and already rejoices in the promised victory, although it's not even remotely visible. What does the LORD do in this situation? He answers to their trust in fulfilling His promise and making a wall that is so great that a woman can live in it suddenly collapse. Wonderful victory of faith!

H Forbes Witherby writes in relation to this:

Soldiers of Christ, our Lord, in heaven! Let us stir up our souls to faith. The Lord has promised the victory as He promised it to Israel. They believed Him, 'by faith the walls of Jericho fell down.' Faith grasps God's strength; 'all things are possible to him that believes.' Let the soldier of Christ, at his Lord's bidding, go forth to fight for Him, and let him be as assured of victory as was Israel, before whom, the ponderous walls fell down flat.

(H Forbes Witherby, *The Book of Joshua*)

How impressive the singing of Paul and Silas in prison must have been, when—although their backs were bleeding because of the beating with rods and their feet were fastened in the stocks—at midnight they sang hymns to the glory of God, listened to by their fellow prisoners. Then God gave an earthquake, loosed the iron chains of the prisoners and used His two servants to lead the cruel jailor from death to eternal life.

Today there are still "songs in the night" (Job 35:10) when we trust Him in all circumstances. Gladys Aylward, missionary to China, experienced in a special way how singing can be a means through which God saves. During the Second World War, when this brave woman was on the run with a large crowd of Chinese children fleeing the approaching Japanese soldiers, they arrived at a river that they couldn't cross. Humanly speaking it was just a matter of time before the enemy would find them and kill them without mercy.

But God is a fortress in the day of distress, and nothing is impossible for Him:

Again, night fell, and again the children slept on the riverbank. In this manner three days and three nights passed with no ferryboat in sight.

On the morning of the fourth day, the old Chinese farmer came to check on them. He told Gladys that the Japanese soldiers were advancing rapidly and that before the evening they would reach the river. "They kill all women and children who cross their path," he added gravely. After this dismal message, the old man returned to his hiding place. As he left, he advised Gladys, "Why don't you go back to the mountains with the children? You will be safer there. Here at the riverside not a child will remain alive."

> **There are three stages to every great work of God: first, it is impossible, then it is difficult and then it is done.**
> (Hudson Taylor)

Sualan came to stand close to Gladys. The girl noticed the growing doubt in Gladys' eyes. "Ai-weh-toh" [Gladys' Chinese name], she tried to comfort, "do you remember that you told us about Moses, when God told him to go through the Red Sea with the people of Israel? He went, and they arrived safely at the other side."

Gladys looked at Sualan incredulously with questioning eyes.

"Mother," the girl continued, "do you believe that this actually happened?"

"But child, do you think I would teach you something that I don't believe myself? It truly happened! It is written in God's Word!"

"Yes, I also believe it," Sualan answered. "And then you said that God is able to do the same with the Yellow River. Why don't we go through the water? Can't God make a path for us through the Yellow River?"

Gladys was shocked at Sualan's words. "Child," she cried in alarm, "I'm not Moses!"

"No, you are not Moses, but God is still the same God," Sualan answered with complete confidence.

"Yes, that He is. God is still the same powerful God!" replied Gladys with renewed hope.

Sualan called a few of the oldest boys and girls together, and along with Mother Gladys, they knelt at the riverbank. In childlike trust, Sualan prayed, "Lord, we are here. Thou seest us. We are waiting for Thee. We trust that Thou wilt open the Yellow River for us. No one can help us. Thou only art able to help us!"

Then Gladys bent forward, her face and hands on the ground. She cried and pleaded, "O my God, I am at the end of my strength. I cannot do anything for these children anymore. I am not worthy that Thou wouldst help us. But do it for Thine own glory, O Lord, for the honour of Thy Name! O God, help us! Do not let us perish! Rescue us; show Thy almighty power!

"Your life will be brighter than the noonday; its darkness will be like the morning. And you will feel secure, because there is hope."
(Job 11:17–18)

We are in Thy hand!" She continued pleading, "Lord, please, rescue us! Then the children will know that Thou alone art the Almighty God, that Thou art greater than all Chinese gods. Lord, deliver us! Our hope is in Thee alone!"

Then Gladys heard beautiful singing in her mind. Again, it was from Psalm 68: "Sing unto God, ye kingdoms of the earth; O sing praises unto the Lord" (v. 32). Was this the answer to her prayer? Powerfully it echoed in her soul, "Sing unto the Lord, sing unto the Lord!" Gladys called the children together and began to sing with them. They sang one psalm after another.

The little ones were very tired, but Gladys urged them on, "We have to sing, for if we sing we will be rescued!" Again and again, she started another verse, believing that this would lead to their deliverance.

At the riverbank, hidden in the reeds, a Chinese soldier was sitting. He, as the last military man on this side of the Yellow River, was keeping guard. He was the only one of the Chinese army left on the north bank. He had to remain there until the Japanese soldiers arrived, only then was he allowed to cross the river to the safety of the south. Time and again, the soldier scanned the land and the sky to see if the enemy was coming. He listened to the rushing water of the river. Then he heard something, far away. He heard a strange and wonderful sound. It was the sound of children singing! A little homesick, he thought of his youth, when they would also sing so beautifully in their small Christian congregation in Southern China. But here? Here at the Yellow River? Singing children at the Yellow River? No, that was impossible.

He walked back and forth behind the reeds, scanning the sky for airplanes and peering across the land to see if the enemy was approaching. It was quiet again at the river. Of course he had been mistaken. He sat down behind the reeds again, close to his boat, so he could flee when danger threatened. He thought about his youth. Listen! There was the sound again! Was that the sound of rustling reeds? Were the reeds singing so strangely? No! They were children's voices! Clearly, he heard the singing of a psalm. Was he dreaming? Children singing at the Yellow River? That was impossible! The soldier walked along the riverbank toward the sound. It was becoming clearer. For a few seconds it would be gone and then it was there again.

After a few hundred meters he suddenly stopped. At a little cove in the river a large group of Chinese children were sitting on the ground, and there was a woman with them. As he walked toward the group, the children suddenly shrieked, "A soldier, Mother! Mother, a soldier!"

Mother Gladys, sitting in the middle of the group, saw the Chinese solder and realised immediately that he was not the enemy.

"I heard children singing," the soldier said. "What are you doing here?"

"We are fleeing!" Gladys answered. "We have to cross the river, but the boats are not there anymore."

"How long have you been here?"

"For almost four days."

Speechless, the soldier stared at her. For four days on the riverbank with one hundred children waiting to be rescued!

"We come from Yang Cheng and are fleeing from the enemy."

"Who brought you here?"

"We walked for three weeks through the mountains to get to the river, and when we came here, it was too late."

"Were you alone with the children on this long journey?"

"No, I was not alone; our God was with us. With the Lord is deliverance from death. He is mighty to rescue us even now."

The soldier was moved at Gladys' speech, and looking seriously at her, he said, "You are a Christian then, and yet, you are not Chinese! Where did you get all these children?"

"I'm a missionary and must see to it that these children get safely to the other side of the river," she answered.

"The singing rescued you!" the soldier cried in amazement. "This afternoon I must go to the other side and remain there. I am the last patrol at the river. I heard singing children and then I found you. God saved you!"

The soldier took a few children along in his boat on the one and a half kilometre boat ride to the south bank. Soon two soldiers returned with a ferryboat. Joyfully, the children climbed aboard, excited about this new adventure.

On the boat ride to the opposite shore, one of the little boys said, "I think that the Lord Jesus saw how tired we were. So now we don't have to walk on a path through the river!"

"Yes! He saw that we were too tired to walk and that's why He sent a boat! Now we may sit down and rest," another child chimed in.

The boat had to make three trips. Mother Gladys was the last to embark. Totally exhausted, Gladys was unable to talk, but in her heart was a silent prayer of thanksgiving to God, who, had fulfilled His promise, "Unto GOD the Lord belong the issues from death." Yes, He had delivered from death.

Upon their arrival at the south bank of the Yellow River, Gladys stepped ashore with her children. At last they were safe! Timothy came to stand beside her and asked, "Mother, shall we now thank the Lord?"

"Yes... you do that, Timothy," she replied softly.

With a weak voice, Gladys asked the children to kneel down to thank the Lord for this great deliverance. Gladys knelt down with the children, but Timothy, standing in the middle of the group, prayed. Deeply moved the soldiers removed their caps and listened to Timothy's prayer. During this fearful journey Timothy had learned that the God of the Bible was the only One able to protect and deliver.

(M A Mijnders, *The Woman with the Book*, Bonisa Mission)

> **"Light shines brightest in a dark night.**
> **Thus it should be with our faith**
> **when we are surrounded by darkness."**

Unknown

> *What can you learn from the story of Jericho's conquest for your personal faith? What does the following quote from David mean for your life? "For by you I can run against a troop, and by my God I can leap over a wall" (Ps. 18:29). What can help you to trust God in seemingly hopeless situations? Is your life of faith based on calculating probabilities?*

Notes:

....

....

....

....

....

....

....

....

....

....

....

....

....

....

....

....

Giving and Receiving

Faith is not just accepting general truths of faith found in the Bible such as the Christian position or future prophetic events. Confidence of faith is evidenced in us relying upon the promises of the Word of God and the Son of God. This give us concrete choices.

There's no other subject the Lord Jesus spoke about more than money and possessions. This shows us how important it is to deal properly with these matters. We'll also see how this subject is closely connected to our spiritual growth, but more on that later.

Our Lord and Master Himself said to us: "It is more blessed to give than to receive" (Acts 20:35). This should be every Christian's motto! It's also remarkable to consider what promises the Lord gave to His disciples in connection with the subject of 'giving and receiving' which we can still rely on in faith today.

One of these promises that challenges our faith is: "Good measure, pressed down, shaken together, running over, will be put into your lap. For with the measure you use it will be measured back to you" (Lk. 6:38).

George Müller could testify to this at the end of his life: "I have been for fifty years, by God's grace, acting on the principle of Christian giving according to the Scriptures, and I cannot tell you the abundance of spiritual blessing I have received to my own soul through acting thus; that is, seeking to be a cheerful giver; seeking to give as God has been pleased to prosper me... Many beloved saints are depriving themselves of wondrous spiritual blessing by not giving as stewards what is entrusted to them. They act as if it were all their own, as if all belonged to them."

(From an address at a Mildmay Park Conference.)

Everything we own we only have by grace. God has entrusted us with money and possessions so that we can administer them for Him and use them for the promotion of the kingdom of God—as well as to make use of them for ourselves. The fundamental question we should ask ourselves is not, 'How much should I give?' but 'How much should I keep for myself?'

In 1 Kings 17 we find a widow who only has a handful of flour and some oil left. From out of nowhere the prophet Elijah appears and desires of her to make something to eat for him from the little she has left. At the same time he assures her that subsequently God would look after her, if she will only obey his words: an enormous test of faith! What does she do? She indeed uses all she has to look after the man of God.

How does God respond to this selfless devotedness? He opens the windows of heaven and subsequently we read: "The jar of flour was not spent, neither did the jug of oil become empty" (1 Ki. 17:16). Because this woman acted in faith and trusted the prophet's word, she experienced how God took care of her in a wonderful way. This story should encourage us to trust God more and to give Him alone the first place.

On the subject of giving and receiving there are countless examples in church history in which God has impressively demonstrated the fulfilment of His promises. Because the subject of 'money and possessions' was so central and important for the Lord Jesus, we want to look at some challenging experiences of faith in the course of this book, which should encourage us to take the Lord at His word in this area and act accordingly.

> **You can always give without loving, but you can never love without giving.**
> (Amy Carmichael)

The following incident took place in Essen, Germany, many years ago.

Albert Winterhoff, an evangelist, was walking through the streets of the city when the Lord suddenly said to him: 'Enter this house and give your money to this family.'

Albert was obedient and rang the doorbell. An old lady opened the door and asked: 'What do you want?'

'My Lord tells me to give you my money'. And then he preached the gospel in the home.

It turned out that this woman was caring for a sick person who was in dire need of medicine. When Albert had left the house and was about to cross the street, a man came up to him, gave him money and disappeared. Such experiences were not uncommon. God always rewards generosity!

(Andreas Steinmeister, *Das Leben Albert Winterhoffs* [The life of Albert Winterhoff], CSV)

> *Do you see yourself as the owner or the steward of what God has entrusted to you? What out of 'your' possessions could you make available to others? For example, would you willingly give your car or house to someone when there's a need? Are you looking for such 'opportunities' or would you rather avoid them?*

Notes:

....

....

....

....

....

....

....

....

....

....

....

....

....

....

....

....

....

....

Praying in Faith

Mary Slessor, who worked for the Lord in Africa, was once asked what prayer meant to her. She answered: "My life is one long daily, hourly record of answered prayer—for strength in mental overexertion and bodily weakness, for marvellous experiences of guidance, for errors and dangers averted, for enmity to the Gospel subdued, for food provided at the exact hour needed, for everything that goes to make up life and my poor service. I can testify, with a full and often wonder-stricken awe, that I believe God answers prayer. I know God answers prayer."

The Lord not only wants us to pray but also to do so in faith! We should ask in the expectation that God will or has already answered our prayer. That is why Jesus said to His disciples: "Whatever you ask in prayer, believe that you have received it, and it will be yours" (Mk. 11:24).

Our Lord and Master has set us an example: He had the certainty here on earth that His prayers would always be answered. That's why He said in public to His Father at the tomb of Lazarus: "Father, I thank you that you have heard me. I knew that you always hear me" (Jn. 11:41–42). In addition, Psalm 16 shows us prophetically the trust with which He prayed.

Lettie B Cowman very fittingly said:

Our too general neglect of looking for answers to what we ask, shows how little we are in earnest in our petitions. A husbandman is not content without the harvest; a marksman will observe whether the ball hits the target; a physician watches the effect of the medicine which he gives; and shall the Christian be careless about the effect of his labour?

Every prayer of the Christian, made in faith, according to the will of God, for which God has promised, offered up in the name of Jesus Christ, and under the influence of the Spirit, whether for temporal or for spiritual blessings, is, or will be, fully answered.

(Lettie B Cowman, *Streams in the Desert: 366 Daily Devotional Readings*, Zondervan)

When you pray, do not focus on the mountain to be moved, but on God who can move it.
(Unknown)

Sometimes God gives us the assurance on our knees that He has answered a prayer or prolonged supplication. This is a wonderful experience that James Fraser was also given to enjoy:

For several years he prayed that hundreds of Lisu families (mountain people in what is now China) would get converted. At some point he got the impression that the Lord was saying to him, "You have prayed long enough. When are you going to be willing to believe that your prayer is answered?"

He then prayed with faith and was sure he would be heard. He later wrote about it: "With full awareness of what I was doing and what it was going to cost me, I prayed, certain of the literal answer. I asked God for hundreds of Lisu families. In the peaceful, calm assurance of being heard, I got up."

And God actually answered his prayer. At the end of 1923, 129 families, probably about 600 people, had become Christians. Fraser wrote to his friends: "Perhaps some say: Your prayer has finally been answered. No! It was answered on January 12, 1915. Even then I was certain that I would be heard. The realisation has only now come."

(E Crossman, *James O Fraser, Der Bergsteiger Gottes* [God's Mountaineer], CLV)

> *How can you be sure that a prayer has been answered even though you don't see the answer at that moment? What can help you to pray more in accordance with God's will? What can hinder your trust that God will actually answer your prayer for a certain matter?*

Notes:

....

....

....

....

....

....

....

....

....

....

....

....

God Cares for His Children

"Do not be anxious about anything." (Philippians 4:6)

Again and again God asks us in His Word not to be anxious or worry. Why not? Because God has promised that He will take care of us!

The people of Israel experienced the care of God very concretely during their long journey through the wilderness. Therefore, looking back, Nehemiah could mention in prayer: "Forty years you sustained them in the wilderness, and they lacked nothing. Their clothes did not wear out and their feet did not swell" (Neh. 9:21). And what about us? We can rely on the faithfulness of God, who promised: "I will never leave you nor forsake you" (Heb. 13:5).

When the disciples entered a violent storm with their boat and the Lord was sleeping in the stern, they cried out: "Teacher, do you not care that we are perishing?" (Mk. 4:38). Years later Peter—who had also been in the boat—wrote to the believers: "Casting all your anxieties on him, because he cares for you" (1 Pet. 5:7)! He had come to know his Lord's care and that gave him hope and confidence.

God is the preserver of all people, especially believers (see 1 Tim. 4:10 JND). We are children and sons of God, sealed with the Holy Spirit, members of the body of Christ and redeemed with the blood of the Lamb. How much reason we have to trust that our Father will take care of us!

The unchanging Father of lights, from whom every good gift comes, knows every detail of our lives. He, who did not spare even His only-begotten Son, but gave Him up for us, will certainly give us everything we need, "So we can confidently say, 'The Lord is my helper; I will not fear'" (Heb. 13:6).

When he served the Lord in Africa, Charles Studd experienced in a special way how wonderfully God cares for His children:

It was early 1921, though C.T. had all but forgotten the importance of European time. He had been living in the Congo for five years now without a break, and he did not want one. "No," he told anyone who asked. "God told me to come to the Congo, and I'm not leaving until He tells me to!"

By now C.T. walked with a stoop, and all of his teeth were either broken or missing completely.

Some people trust the Lord to save their souls, but not to provide for their daily lives.
(Corrie ten Boom)

"Don't you want to go home and get a new set of teeth made?" people would ask him.

"If God wants me to have some new teeth, He can just as easily send someone to me as send me to them!" C.T. would reply.

His fellow missionaries laughed at this and remonstrated him for being impossible, but C.T. did not care.

...

In the rainy season of 1921, two sets of people came to Ibambi. The first comprised an Englishman and his three porters. The man strolled into C.T.'s hut one afternoon and greeted C.T. as one would greet an old friend.

*"My name is John Buck. I have come a long way to meet you, sir,"
he said.*

"Well, drink tea with me and tell me who you are," C.T. replied.

*"I suppose I should start at the beginning," the visitor said as he
sank into one of C.T.'s spare folding chairs. "I am a dentist, and
a year and a half ago God told me to go to the Congo and fix your
teeth. I applied to WEC (Worldwide Evangelisation for Christ)
to be a dentist missionary, but they rejected me because I was too
old."*

*C.T. studied John Buck's face, and, concluding that John must be
only half his own age, he laughed.*

*"Anyway, I still had my heavenly orders to fix your teeth, so I gave
up my business in London and sailed for Africa. I would have been
here sooner, but I took six months' work in Nairobi to earn the
money for the rest of the journey. So here I am."*

*For once in his life, C.T. was speechless. God had actually sent a
dentist halfway around the world to fix his teeth!*

*Over the next week John extracted C.T.'s remaining teeth and
molded a set of false teeth for him. C.T. was delighted. He could
sing much better with his new teeth.*

(Janet Benge & Geoff Benge, *C.T. Studd: No Retreat (Christian
Heroes: Then & Now)*, YWAM Publishing)

Isn't that great? This dentist will certainly receive a great
reward for his selfless sacrifice. Because he acted in obedience of faith, a wonderful testimony of God's care resulted.

"Oh, taste and see that the LORD is good!"

Psalm 34:8

> To what extent does the awareness that God is concerned for you and that He cares about you shape your life of faith? What can help you to better implement the exhortation: "Do not be anxious about anything"? What biblical passages come to mind in which you can recognise God's care for you?

Notes:

....

....

....

....

....

....

....

....

....

....

....

....

The Blessing of Giving

Everything we possess we have received by grace. Unfortunately, we sometimes forget this and imagine that we've earned it. Paul writes: "What do you have that you did not receive?" (1 Cor. 4:7). After the people had freely given for the building of the temple, David expresses a similar thought in prayer: "But who am I, and what is my people, that we should be able thus to offer willingly? For all things come from you, and of your own have we given you" (1 Chron. 29:14).

It's always refreshing and challenging to look at the lives of the first Christians: they sold their possessions and used the proceeds to bless others. How did God respond to this? He put the stamp of His blessing on the dedication of these disciples, so that immediately afterwards it says: "And with great power the apostles were giving their testimony to the resurrection of the Lord Jesus, and great grace was upon them all" (Acts 4:33). What a wonderful time!

A few years later, persecution broke out against the Christians in Jerusalem. At the same time, there was a great famine, which brought the believers there into even greater distress. Had they made a mistake by selling their possessions and giving up their financial security? No, absolutely not! They had made these sacrifices out of devotion to the Lord—and He did not abandon them now. He saw to it that the believers from the nations, through the ministry of the Apostle Paul, sent gifts to Jerusalem to meet the needs of the saints there (see Rom. 15:25–26), and for this

He even used poor brothers and sisters in the faith from Macedonia, who out of love gave from their great poverty (see 2 Cor. 8:1–5)! Indeed: "Great is [His] faithfulness" (Lam. 3:23).

This is how it should always be among God's people: those who have abundance should support those who need financial help. In this way, the needs are met and a certain 'balance' is created. But the flow of support need not always be in one direction. Perhaps at some point the formerly wealthy will find themselves in a situation where they themselves need financial help. Then it may be that the Lord will suddenly enable those who were previously recipients to provide the necessary support. As the apostle writes to the Corinthians, "Your abundance at the present time should supply their need, so that their abundance may supply your need, that there may be fairness" (2 Cor. 8:14).

This situation has also occurred many times in the history of the church. Rosalind Goforth, who as a missionary had no regular income and was dependent on gifts, had this experience because she was willing to open her hand for others. The following incident encourages us to let the Lord guide us more when He puts something on our hearts:

> **Also, what we receive from God, we are to put at His disposal.** (Oswald Chambers)

When busy in my home one day [the Goforths were on furlough in Canada], the thought of two dear friends of the China Inland Mission kept coming constantly to mind, and I [Rosalind] began to wonder if I should send them some money. Looking in my purse, I found that I had only fifty cents on hand. I put the matter out of my mind, with the thought that if the Lord wanted me to send them anything, He would provide a way. The afternoon mail brought a letter from a distant place in Ontario where, a year before, I had visited and spoken for a friend. The letter was from the treasurer of the Christian Endeavor Society for which I had spoken. He enclosed five dollars and said the money should have been given to me at the time I spoke for them but had been overlooked.

My first thought was to return it, as it would be dishonoring my friend to accept money for such a service, but then I remembered my friends for whom I wanted money, and I decided to send the five dollars to them. My husband, who returned the following morning, handed me another five to put with it, and the ten dollars was sent off.

In due course, a reply came from my friends, saying that the very morning my letter arrived, they both had been given the assurance that a certain sum would come, for which they had been praying… My letter brought the ten dollars, and another letter in the afternoon mail contained a sum which, in addition to mine, exactly equaled the amount they had been asking the Lord for.

(Rosalind Goforth, *How I Know God Answers Prayer*, Whitaker House)

**"Whoever brings blessing will be enriched,
and one who waters will himself be watered."**

Proverbs 11:25

> *How often do you ask yourself how you can financially support other Christians who have material needs? Do you sometimes give gifts to people because the Lord leads you to do so, without knowing the specific needs of the person?*

Notes:

....

....

....

....

....

....

....

....

....

....

....

....

....

....

....

....

....

....

....

The Intense Pleading of a Mother

"Beloved, if our heart does not condemn us, we have confidence before God; and whatever we ask we receive from him, because we keep his commandments and do what pleases him." (1 John 3:21–22)

It is God's intention to save entire families or households (see Acts 16:31). The examples of Noah, Rahab, the Philippian jailor and many others make this very clear. This knowledge should give us special boldness to pray more for family members who are not yet saved!

We can do this with perseverance on the one hand and with urgency on the other. The important thing is that it is done with faith! Sometimes while you are praying you already get the assurance that the request has been answered. On other occasions, God gives the certainty of an answer only after a long struggle in prayer. There are many examples of both from church history that encourage us to pray more with faith.

Let me tell you how God answered the prayers of my dear mother and my beloved sister (now Mrs. Broomhall), for my conversion. On a day which I shall never forget, when I was about fifteen years old, my dear mother was away from home. I decided to have a holiday; in the afternoon, I looked through my father's library to find a book with which to while away the unoccupied hours. Nothing attracting me, I turned over a little basket of pamphlets and selected a gospel tract that looked interesting. I said to myself, "There will be a story at the beginning and a sermon or moral at the close. I will take the former and leave the latter for those who like it."

I sat down to read the little book in an utterly unconcerned state of mind, believing that if there were any salvation, it was not for me. My distinct intention was to put the tract away as soon as it should seem tedious. I may say that it was not uncommon in those days to call conversion "becoming serious." Judging by the faces of some of its professors, it appeared to be a very serious matter indeed. Would it not be well if the people of God had always telltale faces, evincing the blessings and gladness of salvation so clearly that unconverted people might have to call conversion "becoming joyful" instead of "becoming serious"?

Little did I know at the time what was going on in the heart of my dear mother, seventy or eighty miles away. She rose from the dinner table that afternoon with an intense yearning for the conversion of her boy. Being absent from home, she had more leisure than she could otherwise secure; this afforded her a special opportunity of pleading with God on my behalf. She went to her room, turned the key in the door, and resolved not to leave that spot until her prayers were answered. Hour after hour did that dear mother plead for me, until at length she could pray no longer. She was constrained to praise God for that which His Spirit taught her had already been accomplished—the conversion of her only son.

In the meantime, I had taken up this little tract. While reading it, I was struck with the phrase "The finished work of Christ." The thought passed through my mind: "Why does the author use this expression? Why not say 'the atoning or propitiatory work of Christ'?" Immediately the words "It is finished" suggested themselves to my mind. What was finished? And I at once replied, "A full and perfect atonement and satisfaction for sin: the debt was paid by the Substitute; Christ died for our sins, and not for ours only, but also for the sins of the whole world." Then came the thought: "If the whole work was finished and the whole debt paid, what is there left for me to do?" And with this, as light flashed into my soul by the Holy Spirit, joyful conviction dawned on me that there was nothing in the world to be done but to fall down on my knees, accept this Saviour and His salvation, and praise Him forevermore. Thus, while my dear mother was praising God on her knees in her chamber, I was praising Him in the old warehouse where I had gone to read this little book at my leisure.

> It is the unbelief, that would not draw on Him, that refused to ask a blessing, and get it with a seal and a witness, that wearies God—not importunity, but, as I may say, the absence of it.
> (John G Bellett)

Several days elapsed before I ventured to make my beloved sister the confidante of my joy, and then only after she had promised not to tell anyone of my soul secret. When our dear mother came home two weeks later, I was the first to meet her at the door and tell her I had such glad news to give. I can almost feel that dear mother's arms around my neck, as she pressed me to her bosom and said, "I know, my boy; I have been rejoicing for two weeks in the glad tidings you have to tell me."

"Why," I asked in surprise, "has Amelia broken her promise? She said she would tell no one." My dear mother assured me that it was not from any human source that she had learned the news, and went on to tell the little incident mentioned above. You will agree with me that it would be strange, indeed, if I were not a believer in the power of prayer.

Nor was this all. Soon after, I picked up a pocket book exactly like one of my own. Thinking that it was mine, I opened it. The lines that caught my eye were an entry in the little diary, which be-

longed to my sister, indicating that she would give herself daily to prayer until God should answer in the conversion of her brother. Exactly one month later, the Lord was pleased to turn me from darkness to light.

(James Hudson Taylor, *A Retrospect (Updated Edition): The Story Behind My Zeal for Missions*, Aneko Press)

> **What can you learn from the experience of Hudson Taylor's mother and sister for your prayer life? What needs to happen for you to pray longer and more intensely for a cause again? What does it mean to fight in prayer for the salvation of souls?**

Notes:

....
....
....
....
....
....
....
....
....
....
....
....

The Blessing of Hospitality

In the New Testament, God often calls us to be hospitable. The writer of the Epistle to the Hebrews says: "Do not neglect to show hospitality to strangers, for thereby some have entertained angels unawares" (Heb. 13:2). How many blessings have come from believers opening their homes to others!

The biblical command is clear: "Seek to show hospitality" (Rom. 12:13). In the Old Testament we see a couple who did just that. Year after year they see a prophet passing through their village on his journey. The desire grows in their hearts to support this man. Finally, they build him a room on the roof of their house so that he can rest there in between his journeys. God wonderfully blesses their devotion: the woman becomes pregnant for the first time and a year later, by God's grace, the couple holds a baby boy in their arms (see 2 Ki. 4).

Of course, the Lord doesn't always reward hospitality in this way, but the divine principle remains: "Whoever brings blessing will be enriched, and one who waters will himself be watered" (Prov. 11:25)! Aquila and Priscilla, who may not have had children either, let Paul stay with them and certainly received no small blessing through this guest! They also opened their home to Apollos, for whom the time under their roof was very beneficial, and who subsequently became a channel of blessing to many. In addition, this couple also made their premises available to Christians who could meet there regularly.

Aquila and Priscilla, through their faith and dedication, have become role models for many. For this activity, they will undoubtedly receive a reward because God has promised this. The same is true for us: the Lord will reward every act of hospitality and remember every cup of water we pass on for the blessing of others for His name's sake (see Mk. 9:41)!

Robert Chapman's example of hospitality and charity is a wonderful testimony of someone who not only preached Christ but also really lived Him:

> **The gospel makes Christians, but you don't see it in their clothes, but in their works of love.**
> (Martin Luther)

Chapman at one point moved to a slum in Barnstaple (England) to reach out to the outcasts there. It was a scene of drunkenness, obscenity, disease and poverty, with rats in the alleys and dilapidated hovels. And yet he constantly ministered to these people and they were always welcome when they visited him at home.

Hospitality became an important part of his ministry. Chapman bought a house opposite his and asked the Lord to send guests of His choosing. He did not charge anything and no one was asked when they wanted to leave.

The guests were asked to put their shoes and boots outside the door every evening. The next morning they were polished. That was the way Mr Chapman washed his guests' feet. This hospitality of a bachelor taught the guests about a life of faith and service to the brethren.

(R L Peterson, *Robert C. Chapman—Der Mann, der Christus lebte* [The man who lived Christ], CLV)

> *Why is the ministry of hospitality among Christians so important? To what extent do you use the opportunities you have to be a blessing to others through hospitality? What does 1 John 3:17 mean in this context? How important is it to be aware that you're only the caretaker and not the owner of your home?*

Notes:

....

....

....

....

....

....

....

....

....

....

....

....

....

....

....

....

....

I Am There in the Midst of Them

"Where two or three are gathered together in My name, I am there in the midst of them." (Matthew 18:20, NKJV)

What a wonderful promise! The Victor of Calvary, who now sits glorified at the right hand of God, assures His disciples—and therefore also us—that He is in the midst of those who gather simply in His name here on earth. Every time we do this, we can expect Him to fulfil His promise.

At the beginning of the 19th century, Christians in many places left the large state churches because they became aware, when reading the New Testament, that all believers constitute a spiritual priesthood and can worship God in spirit and truth, and that not only a small, ordained group of people has this privilege (see 1 Pet. 2:5). At that time people also began to consciously forego human organisation and liturgy during meetings and instead trusted that the Lord would take over leadership through the guidance of the Holy Spirit—and God blessed this.

We can still do this today. If we trust in Jesus' wonderful promise: "Where two or three are gathered together in My name, I am there in the midst of them" (Mt. 18:20, NKJV), this will have an impact on our personal behaviour as well as on the way church meetings are conducted. It's easy to profess outwardly that we gather in the name of Jesus, but the question is: Do we really count on His presence and that He directs and guides everything? Do the brothers allow themselves to be used in true dependence on Him in what they say and do when we're gathered around Him? Do we consciously wait until the Holy Spirit leads someone to say something—even if that means that it might be quiet for a few minutes? Is everyone praying in silence for the Spirit's guidance and enjoying the presence of the Lord? Is the work of the Spirit hindered when the meeting is nearly over?

> **Earthly wisdom is doing what comes naturally. Godly wisdom is doing what the Holy Spirit compels us to do.**
> (Charles Stanley)

William Trotter describes from his own experience how wonderful it can be when Christians come together in the name of Jesus and trust in the guidance of the Holy Spirit:

How blessed were such seasons! There might be, and there were, intervals of silence; but how were they occupied? In solemn waiting upon God. Not in restless anxiety as to who was next to speak or pray; not in turning over the leaves of Bibles or hymn books to find something that we thought suitable. No; nor in anxious thoughts about those who were lookers-on, wondering what they would think of the silence that existed. God was there. Each heart was engaged with Him; and for any to have broken silence, for the sake of doing so, would have been felt to be an interruption indeed.

(W Trotter, *Five Letters on Worship and Ministry in the Spirit*)

It is relatively easy to organise meetings in which the schedule, the contributions and the speakers are arranged. It is, on the other hand, often not so easy for us to lean in faith on the promise of Jesus and consciously leave the guidance to Him. But this is exactly what God wants to encourage us to do!

When Charles Stanley, the evangelist, took part in such meetings for the first time, he was deeply impressed by the presence of the Lord and the guidance of the Holy Spirit. He writes about this:

I now come to an event that turned the whole current of my future course from that day to this.

I had heard that Captain W. and a few other Christians met on the first day of the week to break bread, like the disciples in Acts 20. One Lord's day morning, I went to see what this could mean. I found them gathered in an upper room, in Wellington Street, Sheffield. I sat behind, and naturally looked for the pulpit. There was no pulpit, but a table spread, or covered with a white cloth, and on it the bread and wine, in commemoration of the death of the Lord Jesus.

I then looked for the minister, or president; there was no such person. All the believers gathered were seated around the table of the Lord. A deep, solemn impression fell upon me: "These people have come to meet the Lord Himself." I have no doubt it was the Spirit of God that thus spake to me. It is impossible to describe the sense I had, for the first time, of being in the immediate presence of the Lord Jesus, according to that word, "For where two or three are gathered together in my name, there am I in the midst of them."

I could scarcely notice what was done, I was so overwhelmed with the presence of the Lord. No one can have any idea what this is, unless really gathered to His name. What a contrast to everything I had seen before, and yet how simple! It was like going back to that which was in the beginning of Christianity, before any priest was heard of to offer in the church a sacrifice for the living and the dead. I was much surprised to find, strange as this gathering together of Christians to break bread appeared to me, that it was exactly what we find in scripture. Instead of even a minister at the Lord's Table, I found the same simple liberty as described in 1 Corinthians 14:29-37. I was greatly struck with each worshipping before the Lord, in dependence on the Holy Ghost. I felt that was my place, deeply unworthy as I was of it. Well do I remember the thought, "This is my place, if even it were to be a door mat, for these Christians to wipe their feet on me."

After some weeks, I was named as one who desired to obey the Lord, "Do this in remembrance of me;" and, through grace, I took my place as one redeemed to God, at the Table of the Lord. Shortly after this, I experienced one morning, whilst we sat in silent worship, what I had never known before — the leading of the Spirit of God. It came as a gentle whisper from the Lord, "Read 2 Corinthians, chapter 1;" and very precious thoughts came into my soul on verses 3–5.

I felt agitated, so much so, that perspiration ran down my face and body. We had sat some time in silence. I felt bid to rise and read, but had not courage to do so. At length, Captain W., who sat at the other side of the room, arose and said, Let us read 2 Corinthians 1, and then he ministered the very thoughts the Spirit had laid on my heart. This was how I first learnt the leadings of the Spirit, in the midst of Christians gathered to Christ. This has been a matter of frequent occurrence for these many years.

(Charles Stanley, *Incidents of Gospel Work*, Believers Bookshelf USA)

> *How would you explain what it means to gather to the name of Jesus? What expectations do you have when you meet with other Christians? What does it mean to be guided by the Spirit of God in the meetings? How does that work?*

Notes:

....
....
....
....
....
....
....
....
....
....
....
....
....
....
....
....
....
....
....

The Power of Praying Together

"Again I say to you, if two of you agree on earth about anything they ask, it will be done for them by my Father in heaven." (Matthew 18:19)

This is a tremendous promise for corporate prayer! But it's linked to one condition: there must be unanimity when Christians pray together. On the one hand, we must be together in peace and love, and on the other hand, we must agree on what we want to pray for specifically. How can we achieve this unanimity? One example is by talking about specific prayer requests before praying and agreeing to bring them before the throne of grace together.

The first Christians prayed together with one accord. On the one hand, they were of one heart and soul, and on the other hand, they agreed on what they wanted to pray for specifically. They raised their voices to God with one accord and experienced the way the Lord answered their prayer. At that time, God's answer came when the earth shook, and the disciples were filled with the Holy Spirit and testified to the resurrection of Jesus with great power.

But how is it today? Are we of one mind when we pray together? Do we have peace and unfeigned brotherly love among ourselves? Do we exchange prayer requests and agree to pray specifically for them? Or do our corporate prayers only remind us of a liturgical gathering?

That the Lord's promise is still true for our time is made clear by the following incident, which a Christian had a few years ago in a gathering of believers:

We had a prayer meeting every Sunday before the 8 o'clock service. One Sunday, as we rose from our knees, a man next to us said, "Pastor, I would like you to pray for my boy. He is now twenty-two years old and has not been to church for years." The pastor replied, "We could spare a few minutes for that now." So we knelt down again and made earnest intercession for this young man.

Although this young man was not made aware of this, he came to church that same evening. Something in the sermon convicted him of his sin. He came to the sacristy with a broken heart and accepted Jesus Christ as his Saviour."

Not length but strength is desirable [in prayer]. A sense of need is a mighty teacher of brevity.
(Charles H Spurgeon)

On Monday morning, my friend who was in church ministry was present at the weekly board meeting. He said to the pastor, "Surely this conversion last night is a call to prayer for us—a call from God. Shouldn't we heed it?" "What do you mean?" the pastor asked. My friend said, "Shouldn't we for once choose the worst individual in our congregation and pray for him?"

By unanimous decision, they chose K as the worst they knew. Then they 'became one' in prayer for his conversion.

At the end of that week, when they were attending a weekend prayer meeting in the church hall and the name of that man was just on their lips, the door opened and in staggered K. He was quite drunk. He had never entered this particular meeting room before. Without thinking to take off his cap, he sank onto a chair near the entrance and buried his face in his hands.

The prayer meeting suddenly became a place of pastoral care. As he was—drunk—he sought the Lord who was seeking him. He never went back. Today he is one of the most blessed port missionaries in the country.

(*Der Kniende Christ* [The kneeling Christian], Herold Verlag)

> *What is the best way to agree on a cause to pray for at a prayer meeting? Why is it a special blessing that we can meet and pray together as Christians? Do you motivate others to pray together for specific matters, relying on the Lord's provision?*

Notes:

....

....

....

....

....

....

....

....

....

Prophetic Ministry

"Earnestly desire to prophesy." (1 Corinthians 14:39)

If we expect the Lord to be present in the Christian gatherings, then we should be there with the expectation that He will speak to us and, for example, give us answers to questions or put a finger on a sore spot in our lives. This is what prophetic ministry or prophecy is all about: God uses believers, under the guidance of the Holy Spirit, to say something that comes from Himself and speaks exactly into the circumstances of other believers.

1 Corinthians 14 makes it clear that prophetic ministry should characterise the meetings where the Word of God is preached. In this context Paul writes: "But if all prophesy, and an unbeliever or outsider enters, he is convicted by all, he is called to account by all, the secrets of his heart are disclosed, and so, falling on his face, he will worship God and declare that God is really among you. So, my brothers, earnestly desire to prophesy, and do not forbid speaking in tongues" (1 Cor. 14:24–25). The following example shows what this can look like in practice:

A few years ago, a young man, son of believing parents, attended a meeting—where Christians were gathered to hear the Word of God—for the first time in a long time. Although he had grown up in a Christian home, he had not been going to church meetings for the preaching of the Word of God for some time. One day, when he was travelling in another city, the thought came to him to go to the meetings of the believers there. He entered the room, sat down right at the back and looked at the faces. None of the Christians there knew him.

At the front, some men were seated and it was obvious that they were praying. After a short pause, a brother got up and read from Ezekiel 14:6–8. The following words hit the young man right in the heart:

"I ... will answer him myself. I will ... cut him off."

The brother who was preaching explained the verses and made some serious applications to the lives of the listeners. Through this the young man was led to repentance. He turned from his wrong ways and confessed his guilt before God and man.

(Andreas Steinmeister, *Wenn ihr zusammenkommt* [When you come together], Daniel Verlag)

Usually, however, prophetic ministry in the meetings is directed at the believers who are present. Through the preaching of the Word of God, the Lord would like to give answers to questions, guidance and—if necessary—correction.

> **Get into the habit of saying, "Speak, Lord," and life will become a romance.**
> (Oswald Chambers)

In the following I would like to share a personal experience that shows how concretely the Lord can speak into our circumstances through His living Word when we gather to His name.

Some time ago we had almost no money left in our household bank account. Because we work as missionaries, we have no regular income and no human assurance that money will come in again at some point. At that time, no one knew about our financial situation.

On a Wednesday evening, just before we met for prayer with the brothers and sisters of the local church, I received an email with a credit card bill, due a week later. The amount: 276 euros.

I stared at the amount on the screen and thought: How are we going to pay this bill, as we have almost nothing left anyway? Then I asked the Lord to help us and to speak into our circumstances through His Word in the meeting. Then I went to the prayer meeting.

First a hymn was sung. After a short break, a brother got up and read from Acts 27:27–28:15 about the shipwreck of the galley where Paul was a prisoner, which is rather unusual for a prayer meeting. I listened very attentively, expecting the Lord to speak to me through His living Word. At some point during the reading, the brother came to the following passage: "Then they all were encouraged and ate some food themselves. (We were in all 276 persons in the ship)" (Acts 27:36–37).

I could hardly believe it. I had been staring at the exact same figure on the screen in small faith only a few minutes before. That was no coincidence, I thought, while the brother read on. The passage ends with the words: "And so it was that all were brought safely to land" (Acts 27:44). No doubt the Lord wanted me to understand that I didn't have to worry about the 276 euros. I went home with a sense of deep peace in my heart. God sometimes speaks into our circumstances in a very concrete way!

The Lord did indeed do great things. In the following days, through the Lord's guidance, we received gifts again after a long time, for which we had prayed intensely. The bill was paid on time and once again we were amazed at the way God fulfils His promises at the right time!

> *Why is it that we so rarely have the experience described in 1 Corinthians 14:24–25? How can we put into practice the call to "prophesy" (1 Cor. 14:1)? When was the last time you made a real change in your life as a result of a word of ministry? With what expectation do you go to your local meetings?*

Notes:

....

....

....

....

....

....

....

....

....

Sow with Blessing and Reap in Blessing

"One gives freely, yet grows all the richer." (Proverbs 11:24)

How much of our money and possessions should we give to others? God doesn't give us a concrete answer to this. He leaves it up to our faith and our devotion. But Paul makes it clear that our reward depends on whether we act meanly or generously in this area: "The point is this: whoever sows sparingly will also reap sparingly, and whoever sows bountifully will also reap bountifully. Each one must give as he has decided in his heart, not reluctantly or under compulsion, for God loves a cheerful giver" (2 Cor. 9:6–7).

By the way, this principle also often applies to the experiences of faith that we may have. The more we're willing to let go, to continue on and to trust in God's care, the more we'll experience that God is faithful to His promises—and makes them come true in our lives.

Even children can have experiences in this area, as the following story makes clear: A little boy comes to Bethsaida, where the Son of God is preaching to 5,000 men plus women and children. Suddenly he hears that food is needed for the audience. The boy has five loaves and two fish with him—but what is that for so many people? Questions arise in his heart: Should he just keep the food for himself, so that at least he is satisfied himself, or would it be better to share it with others? He decides to give everything he has to Jesus.

The Lord doesn't let the boy's devotion go unrewarded: in His hands, the personal sacrifice of a child becomes a source of blessing for many. Thousands are provided with food—and the boy also goes home with a full stomach! God is true to His word: "Whoever brings blessing will be enriched, and one who waters will himself be watered" (Prov. 11:25).

This story shows us an important principle that runs through the entire Bible and is still true for us today: when we put the little we have at God's disposal, He multiplies it and uses it to bless others. The question is whether we actually believe this and then put it into practice! Sometimes, for example, the Lord is simply waiting for us to be willing to let go of material things and sacrifice them for the benefit of others, so that He can then show Himself mighty and bless the offering. It's in His hand "to make great and give strength" (1 Chron. 29:12).

In Luke 5, the Lord Jesus asks Peter to use his boat so He can preach the Word of God from it. Peter puts his possessions at the Master's service and shortly afterwards makes the greatest catch of his life. Upon the deep lake, God gives him a deep impression of the glory and greatness of the Son of God—an experience of faith that he certainly wouldn't forget for the rest of his life! He's so impressed by it that instead of clinging to the material blessings he leaves everything behind to follow his Lord and Master.

The wisest man of his time, Solomon, wrote: "Whoever is generous to the poor lends to the LORD, and he will repay him for his deed" (Prov. 19:17). This promise also applies to our time. Many believers who have really cared for poor people can testify to this.

Hudson Taylor wrote in his autobiography:

After concluding my last service about ten o'clock that night, a poor man asked me to go and pray with his wife, saying that she was dying. I readily agreed, and on the way to his house, I asked him why he had not sent for the priest, as his accent told me he was an Irishman. He had done so, he said, but the priest refused to come without a payment of eighteen pence, which the man did not possess, because the family was starving.

Immediately it occurred to my mind that all the money I had in the world was the solitary half-crown. Moreover, while the basin of water gruel I usually took for supper was awaiting me, and there was sufficient in the house for breakfast in the morning, I certainly had nothing for dinner on the coming day.

Somehow or other there was at once a stoppage in the flow of joy in my heart. Instead of reproving myself, I began to reprove the poor man, telling him that it was very wrong to have allowed matters to get into such a state as he described, and he ought to have applied to the relieving officer. His answer was that he had done so. He was told to come at eleven o'clock the next morning, but he feared that his wife might not live through the night.

"Ah," thought I, "if only I had two shillings and a sixpence instead of this half-crown, how gladly would I give these poor people one shilling of it!" But to part with the half-crown was far from my thoughts. I little dreamed that the real truth of the matter was simply that I could trust in God plus one-and-sixpence, but was not

yet prepared to trust Him only, without any money at all in my pocket.

My escort led me into a court, down which I followed him with some degree of nervousness. I had found myself there before, and at my last visit I had been very roughly handled, while my tracts were torn to pieces. I had received such a warning not to come again that I felt more than a little concerned. Still, it was the path of duty, and I followed on. Up a miserable flight of stairs into a wretched room, he led me; oh, what a sight presented itself to our eyes!

The crucial question is not how much we give, but how much we keep!
(Peter Maiden)

Four or five poor children stood about, their sunken cheeks and temples all telling unmistakably the story of slow starvation. Lying on a wretched pallet was a poor exhausted mother with a tiny infant, thirty-six hours old, moaning rather than crying at her side, for it too seemed spent and failing. "Ah," thought I, "if I had two shillings and a sixpence instead of a half-crown, how gladly should they have one and sixpence of it!" But still a wretched unbelief prevented me from obeying the impulse to relieve their distress at the cost of all I possessed.

It will scarcely seem strange that I was unable to say much to comfort these poor people. I needed comfort myself. I began to tell them, however, that they must not be cast down. Though their circumstances were very distressing, there was a kind and loving Father in heaven. But something within me said, "You hypocrite! Telling these unconverted people about a kind and loving Father in heaven and not prepared to trust Him yourself without a half-crown!" I was nearly choked. How gladly would I have compromised with my conscience if I had a florin (gold coin) and a sixpence! I would have given the florin thankfully and kept the rest, but I was not yet prepared to trust in God alone without the sixpence.

To talk was impossible under these circumstances. Yet, strange to say, I thought I should have no difficulty in praying. Prayer was a delightful occupation to me in those days. Time thus spent never seemed wearisome, and I knew nothing of lack of words. I seemed to think that all I should have to do would be to kneel down and engage in prayer, and relief would come to them and me together.

"You asked me to come and pray with your wife," I said to the man, "so let us pray." And I knelt down. But scarcely had I opened my lips with "Our Father who art in heaven" than my conscience said, "Dare you mock God? Dare you kneel down and call Him Father with that half-crown in your pocket?" Such a time of conflict came upon me then as I have never experienced before nor since. How I got through that form of prayer I know not, and whether the words uttered were connected or disconnected, I cannot tell, but I arose from my knees in great distress of mind.

The poor father turned to me and said, "You see what a terrible state we are in, sir; if you can help us, for God's sake do!" Just then the word flashed into my mind, Give to him that asketh thee, and in the word of a King, there is power. I put my hand into my pocket and, slowly drawing forth the half-crown, gave it to the man. I told him that it might seem a small matter for me to relieve them, seeing that I was comparatively well off, but that in parting with that coin, I was giving him my all. What I had been trying to tell him was indeed true—God really was a Father and might be trusted. The joy all came back in full flood tide to my heart; I could say anything and feel it then, and the hindrance to blessing was gone— gone, I trust, forever.

Not only was the poor woman's life saved, but I realised that my life was saved too. It might have been a wreck—would have been a wreck probably, as a Christian life—had not grace at that time conquered, and the striving of God's Spirit been obeyed. I well remember how that night, as I went home to my lodgings, my heart was as light as my pocket. The lonely, deserted streets resounded with a hymn of praise, which I could not restrain. When I took my basin of gruel before retiring, I would not have exchanged it for a prince's feast. I reminded the Lord as I knelt at my bedside of His own Word: He who giveth to the poor lendeth to the Lord. I asked Him not to let my loan be a long one, or I should have no dinner the next day; and with peace within and peace without, I spent a happy, restful night.

Next morning for breakfast, my plate of porridge remained, and before it was consumed, I heard the postman's knock at the door. I was not in the habit of receiving letters on Monday, as my parents and most of my friends refrained from posting on Saturday. So I was somewhat surprised when the landlady came in holding a letter or packet in her wet hand covered by her apron. I looked at the letter, but could not make out the handwriting. It was either a strange hand or a feigned one, and the postmark was blurred. Where it came from, I could not tell.

On opening the envelope, I found nothing written within, but a pair of kid gloves was folded inside a sheet of blank paper, from which, as I opened them in astonishment, a half-sovereign (gold coin) fell to the ground. "Praise the Lord!" I exclaimed. "Four hundred percent for twelve hours' investment; that is good interest. How glad the merchants of Hull would be if they could lend their money at such a rate!" I then and there determined that a bank which could not break should have my savings or earnings as the case might be—a determination I have not yet learned to regret.

I cannot tell you how often my mind has returned to this incident or all the help it has been to me in circumstances of difficulty in life afterward. If we are faithful to God in little things, we shall gain experience and strength that will be helpful to us in the more serious trials of life.

(James Hudson Taylor, *A Retrospect (Updated Edition): The Story Behind My Zeal for Missions*, Aneko Press)

> **What can you learn for yourself from Hudson Taylor's story? Why did the Lord Jesus speak so often about money and possessions? What is the connection between the way we deal with material things and the spiritual responsibility that God wants to give us (see Lk. 16:11)? And what does 1 Chronicles 29:14—where we see that what we can give back to God already belongs to Him—mean to you?**

Notes:

....

....

....

....

The Prayer of a Child

"Become like children ..." (Matthew 18:3)

You don't have to be an adult to pray in faith. On the contrary, adults often get in their own way by thinking too rationally and therefore have difficulty asking God for something with childlike trust. He responds to the faith of little children who simply trust Him and expect Him to hear prayer. Abigail Townsend experienced this when she spent time with George Müller in her early childhood years:

Once at Paul Street she said, "I wish Dod [she couldn't pronounce 'God' yet] would answer my prayers like He does yours, George Müller."

"He will, my dear."

Taking Abigail on his knee, he repeated the promise of Jesus: "Whatever you ask for in prayer, believe that you have received it, and it will be yours" (Mk. 11:24).

"Now, Abbie," he asked, "what is it you want to ask God for?"

"Some wool."

Clasping her hands together, Müller said, "Now, you repeat what I say: Please God, send Abbie some wool."

"Please Dod send Abbie some wool."

Jumping down Abigail ran out into the garden to play, quite sure that the wool would come.

Then she remembered that God didn't know what kind of wool she wanted, so she ran back to Müller.

"I want to pray again."

"Not now, dear, I'm busy."

"But I forgot to tell Dod the colour I want."

Taking her on his knee again, Müller said, "That's right, always be definite my child, now tell God what you want."

"Please Dod, send it wa-re-gated," said Abigail who possessed a wide vocabulary but couldn't pronounce her 'v's' any better than her 'g's'.

Next morning a parcel arrived addressed to Abigail containing a quantity of variegated wool. Her Sunday School teacher, remembering that her birthday was close although uncertain of the date, and remembering too that she was a keen knitter, had purchased some wool and sent it—not on her birthday—but on the right day to demonstrate to her delight that God hears and answers prayer.

(Roger Steer, *George Müller—Delighted in God*, Christian Focus Publications Ltd.)

> **What can you learn from this story for your own life of faith? What does it mean to become like children (see Mt. 18:3)? Why do we often value reason so highly when the Lord emphasises childlikeness? How can you encourage children to take God at His word?**

Notes:

....
....
....
....
....
....
....
....
....
....
....
....
....
....
....
....
....
....
....
....
....
....
....
....
....
....
....

The Victory of Faith

"Believe in the LORD your God, and you will be established; believe his prophets, and you will succeed." (2 Chronicles 20:20)

In the story of Jehoshaphat we're presented with a similar faith as we've already seen among the people of Israel at the conquest of Jericho (see 2 Chron. 20). There, the kingdom of Judah faces a powerful enemy army that vastly outnumbers them. What does the king do in this situation? He calls a fast. Then the people gather for prayer to seek God intensely in the face of this great need.

It's very interesting to see how the LORD responds: He answers through prophetic ministry—using a man to deliver a message to the people—and gives them the firm promise that they don't need to fight against the enemies because the LORD Himself will give them the victory. At the same time, He invites them to go out to meet this great army without fear. How do the Israelites react to this announcement? They take God at His word, fall down before Him and worship!

The next day Jehoshaphat encourages the people, saying, "Believe in the LORD your God, and you will be established; believe his prophets, and you will succeed" (2 Chron. 20:20). Solomon wrote: "A word in season, how good it is!" (Prov. 15:23). Outwardly, the circumstances are still the same. The strength of the enemy has not changed. But in the meantime, something very important has happened: God has made them a promise. Jehoshaphat and the people now have the word of God on their side—and that's what changes everything for them!

Because they firmly trust in God's promise, they go out to meet the enemy fearlessly and courageously. At the same time, they begin to praise God and rejoice loudly. This is faith that honours God—and God in turn honours this faith: "And when they began to sing and praise, the LORD set an ambush against the men of Ammon, Moab, and Mount Seir, who had come against Judah, so that they were routed" (2 Chron. 20:22). God intervenes, puts the enemies to flight and leads His people to victory!

Many men and women in church history have experienced the way God has given them prophetic promises in special situations, using His living Word. When believers rely on such promises and plead for their fulfilment with faith in prayer, the Almighty answers!

Charles E Cowman experienced this in Japan in an impressive way. After he had spent some time evangelising among the Japanese and some had come to faith, he became prayerfully convinced that he should build a large building where new converts could study the Word of God and thus grow in faith.

Not one dollar was in sight when he began the search for a suitable location. Small tracts of land were available, but every time he attempted to purchase one, some trivial thing occurred that completely blocked the way. The prayerful search continued until one day, Charles, Brother Kilbourn, and several others took a trip to the suburbs of Tokyo, where they found a field of waving grain.

The air was soft and balmy. Mount Fuji, with its snow-crowned summit, lay just beyond, and from the slight elevation, they could see miles of country. Here, without doubt, was God's own choice. Funds for its purchase came in answer to believing prayer—no great amounts, but small gifts from many saints scattered far and near.

Charles' ideas for plain but substantial frame buildings were similar to those of the early Quakers who believed in plain meetinghouses and not in lavish expenditures. Not without tests of faith were those buildings erected. The following incident gives a glimpse of one trial and its outcome.

The third payment for the building, $2,000, was due in three days, and there was only $72 in the mission treasury. This was barely sufficient to cover the cost of food needed for our large family of coworkers and students. The day before the payment was due, a steamer arrived from America. The foreign post usually brought a number of letters containing gifts, but this time only one letter came, and in it was a $5 bill.

The workmen were constructing the building, while the missionary and Japanese workers were closeted with God. We were at our wits' end but, thank God, not at faith's end, for faith generally begins at such tight places. Our last hope of help from America seemed to be gone, but as we continued in prayer, the burden on our hearts made a hasty exit as the promises of God rolled in until our mouths were literally filled with laughter.

It seemed that God had enabled us to lay hold of His promises. In the course of prayer, one of those present reminded the Lord that on one occasion He had met the need of his own by means of a coin in a fish's mouth. We prayed, "Lord Jesus, You still have fish at Your disposal. You can supply our need in this way even now, for You are still the same."

Another person quoted part of Mark 11:23: "and shall not doubt in his heart, ... he shall have whatsoever he saith." Thus, for several hours, one after another mounted up in faith until, at the end, there was a perfect blend, and prayer ended in praise. All watched, waited, and wondered how God was going to get to us the $2,000 before noon the following day. Faith burned brightly in every heart. A definite request had been registered in heaven. Faith claimed the great gift from God, and what was the result? Faith honours God and God honours faith. The clinging hand of his child makes a desperate situation a delight to him.

God's work done in God's way will never lack God's supply.
(James Hudson Taylor)

The next morning dawned bright and clear, and the army of Japanese workers was on hand early, singing as they worked, for this was payday. Nine o'clock came, then ten, still no answer. Noon arrived, and the simple dinner was served. One quoted Exodus 6:1: "Now shalt thou see what I will do." Each one present quoted some encouraging promise, and faith held fast.

At 5:00, about time for the workmen to quit, a messenger boy strolled up the walk, shouting, "Dempo! Dempo!" (Cablegram! Cablegram!). The band of missionaries stopped their work to listen to the message, which read, "Two thousand dollars at cable office." The donor was unknown to us.

"And Jesus himself drew near." Tears mingled with shouts of victory. God had not forgotten to be gracious. The little company

fell upon their knees and praised Him from the depths of their hearts for not permitting them to become a reproach among the unbelievers.

Who timed this to arrive just at the critical moment? Coincidence? The calculation on the basis of probabilities is too difficult. God! How unsearchable are His ways (Rom. 11:33). The feeling of His hand upon us gave us great peace, and such experiences are worth all that they cost.

God's hand was so evident during those days. We prayed daily, and the answers were marvellous. We hesitate in telling the public about some answers to prayer for fear that they might be tempted to think these were exaggerated.

(Lettie B Cowman, *Charles E. Cowman—Missionary Warrior,* The Oriental Missionary Society)

"Victories won by faith glorify God because no one can explain how they were achieved."

Warren Wiersbe

> *Why does God often make it so that His help comes at the last minute? Have you ever experienced praising God in the midst of a trial because you had faith that He would intervene? To what extent do you expect God to speak to you specifically through His Word and through prophetic ministry?*

Notes:

....

....

....

....

....

....

....

....

....

....

....

....

....

....

....

....

....

....

No Lack

"He who gives to the poor will not lack." (Proverbs 28:27, NKJV)

After the Lord has warned His disciples against the hypocritical scribes who wanted to look good before the people by showing off, He sits down opposite the treasury of the temple and watches how the people put in their offerings (Mk. 12:41–44). The rich give large sums, but for them—measured by their wealth—it is not a great sacrifice.

Suddenly a poor widow appears who attracts Jesus' attention. Although she only has two small copper coins left, she is willing to sacrifice both for God—she could have kept one for herself. The Son of God is clearly touched by this woman's trust and devotion, for He immediately calls His disciples and tells them what she has done. He doesn't tell them that they must do it just like that—as devotion cannot be forced—and yet He points out to them the exemplary behaviour of this widow. Unlike the rich, she held nothing back, but threw herself wholeheartedly into the arms of God.

Our Lord and Master still sits as an observer at the 'treasury' today. He sees not only how much we give, but also—and this is even more important—how much we keep back for ourselves! God judges the condition and motives of our hearts. It is relatively easy to give a lot when you have a lot. True sacrifice is shown by the fact that it really costs you something!

What follows now is not for the faint-hearted—and it challenges our faith! It's not that we must do it the same way. But just as with the scenario at the treasury, we can simply 'watch' and wonder at the faith of others.

> **If you give God everything you have, He will give you everything you need.**
> (Unknown)

The Indian evangelist Bakht Singh often had the experience that God acknowledges it when we, at His word, are ready to give everything for Him.

On another occasion, in Karachi, a man came to Bakht Singh in the year 1936 and told him that he had no money to pay his house rent. Bakht Singh invited him to sit down and he would pray for him. He went into his room and prayed, "Lord, this man has no money; what to do now?"

The Lord said to Bakht Singh, "You have 12 rupees in your suitcase, give it to him".

Bakht Singh knew that he had 12 rupees which he was keeping for his train fare to Ajmer, where he was invited to a convention. He had to leave after two days, so he said to the Lord, "I must go to Ajmer, how can I give this away to this man?"

The Lord said to him, "This is My money and not your money".

So Bakht Singh took that money and gave it to him: it was exactly what he needed, 12 rupees. The man was very happy.

The day came when Bakht Singh had to go to Ajmer. He was not sure what to do or where to go. At first he thought that he would go to his sister and look very sad, and then she would ask what the matter was. Bakht Singh thought that he would then say that he had to go to Ajmer. She would then give him the money to go there, but the Lord did not allow him to do that. Then a second thought came to him—he would send a telegram saying he was sorry that he could not go to Ajmer. The Lord however, reminded him that he had promised to go, therefore he should go. The Lord did not allow him to go to any one or cancel the plan.

By faith, Bakht Singh packed his suitcase and went to the railway station without having any money. He then went and stood in line at the booking office. As he was waiting, a man came to him and asked, "Are you Mr. Bakht Singh?"

Bakht Singh answered, "Yes".

The man gave him an envelope and said that it was for him: then he went away. When he opened the envelope, it contained exactly 12 rupees. Bakht Singh did not know who the man was. He disappeared before Bakht Singh could thank him.

(T E Koshy, *Brother Bakht Singh of India*, OM Books)

Such experiences are certainly extraordinary and require special faith. And yet they show us what is possible when we trust God wholeheartedly, because: "All things are possible for one who believes" (Mk. 9:23). By the way, the story of Bakht Singh is not an isolated case. Albert Winterhoff, an evangelist in Germany, experienced something similar:

After an evangelistic campaign he once received 50 Reichsmark and set off home with it. When he arrived at the railway station in Stuttgart, he saw an elderly woman sitting there, crying. The war had taken all her belongings and she didn't have enough to wear or anything to eat.

Albert went to her and told her about the Lord Jesus, who provides for soul and body. So, he gave her the 50 Reichsmark and his coat and prayed, "Lord, how am I supposed to get home now?"

"Jesus Christ is the same yesterday and today and forever." (Hebrews 13:8) *In faith he stood in the crowd at the counter and prayed to the Lord, "Now, O Lord, you must give, so that I may order my ticket".*

He had hardly finished praying when a man suddenly jumped up and rushed to him and said: "Brother Winterhoff, fancy meeting you here! I know you from the lectures you gave in ...". And turning to the counter, he ordered a 3rd class ticket to Hagen.

And so Albert received his ticket. Overjoyed, he thanked the great God to whom belong the silver and the gold, sat down on the train and travelled back to Hagen and then to Vogelsang.

(Andreas Steinmeister, *Das Leben Albert Winterhoffs* [The life of Albert Winterhoff], CSV)

"My God will supply every need of yours according to his riches in glory in Christ Jesus."

Philippians 4:19

Most of us are probably convinced that God provided for the widow in Mark 12 after she sacrificed everything she owned for Him. But how is it that very few seem to follow her behaviour, seeing the Lord presents her to us as an example? Devotion can't be forced, but we can encourage one another to be devoted to the Lord.

Notes:

....

....

....

....

....

....

....

....

....

....

....

....

....

....

....

....

Knock in Faith

"Ask, and it will be given to you; seek, and you will find; knock, and it will be opened to you." (Matthew 7:7)

There are situations in life when we pray with more urgency than usual. The Lord Jesus speaks in a parable of a man who suddenly receives a visitor but has nothing to eat in the house. See Luke 11:5–10. In order to entertain his guest, he is forced to turn to his friend with some urgency—and that at the most inconvenient time of day. In his distress, he knocks on his friend's door at midnight, gets him out of bed and asks him to immediately give him three loaves of bread.

> **Real supplication is the child of heartfelt desire, and cannot prevail without it; a desire not of earth nor issuing from our own sinful hearts, but wrought into us by God Himself.**
> (James O Fraser)

Through this parable, the Lord Jesus encourages us to pray with a certain urgency and emphasis. Figuratively speaking, we could call this 'knocking' too. If we live in fellowship with the Lord, we can 'knock with boldness on God's door' in prayer until it is opened to us!

Martin Luther often prayed with faith and boldly knocked on God's door. When his trusted colleague Melanchthon collapsed with severe fever and his condition continued to deteriorate, Luther rushed to Weimar to see his terminally ill friend who had changed beyond recognition. Luther was dismayed at the sight that met his eyes and spent some time in intense prayer at his bedside:

Filled with fear, [Luther] said: "O God, how the devil has shattered this instrument for me!" Then the faithful and manly friend approached his God in prayer for his much beloved friend, by throwing, as he, himself afterwards said, "the sack before the door, and by rubbing his ears with all the promises from His own Word".

He exhorted and commanded Melanchthon to be of good cheer, because God did not desire the death of the sinner, but needed further services from him; told him that he himself would rather depart now; had food prepared for him when he was gradually becoming convalescent, and upon his refusal to eat, threatened: "You will have to eat, or I will put you in the ban".

Gradually the patient improved in body and spirit. Luther could write to another friend: "We found him dead; by an undeniable miracle of God he lives".

(Julius Köstlin, *Life of Luther*, Lutheran Publication Society)

Luther clung to God's promises as best as he could and reminded Him of what He had promised in His Word. The Lord is pleased when He sees that we take Him seriously and lean on His Word in faith.

> **"My soul longs for your salvation;**
> **I hope in your word."**
>
> **Psalm 119:81**

> *Do you remind God of His promises and ask Him to make them real when you pray? Why does the Lord emphasise fervour as a condition for effective prayer in James 5? What do you want to pray for again, and that with urgency and emphasis? "You who put the LORD in remembrance, take no rest, and give him no rest" (Isa. 62:6–7).*

Notes:

....
....
....
....
....
....
....
....
....
....
....
....
....
....
....
....

Being Guided by the Holy Spirit

"If we live by the Spirit, let us also keep in step with the Spirit." (Galatians 5:25)

In the Acts of the Apostles we read several times that the Holy Spirit made it clear to Christians what they should do. The Spirit told Philip to go up to the Ethiopian eunuch to preach the gospel to him (see Acts 8). The Spirit told Peter to go with the three men who were waiting for him downstairs (see Acts 10). When Paul was in Antioch, the Holy Spirit sent him and Barnabas out on a missionary journey (Acts 13). Twice the apostle was prevented by the Holy Spirit from going in a certain direction (see Acts 16). Later, the Spirit used men of faith to tell Paul not to go to Jerusalem (see Acts 21).

These and other passages make it clear that the Spirit has a specific will and wants to guide us. Nevertheless, the guidance of the Holy Spirit is sometimes seen as something mystical or fanciful—perhaps also because in Christianity many things are declared to be guidance by the Spirit which really are only imagination or sentimentalism. But that shouldn't stop us from taking God at His word and trusting in the Spirit's guidance.

How concretely the Spirit can guide us is also shown by the following incident that Charles Stanley experienced:

Unbelief might be ready to say, that many of these apparent leadings of the Spirit were but incidental occurrences. In many cases this could not be. Take the following:

Many, many have never stopped at Romans 8:14 to ask: 'If then those who are led by the Spirit of God are the sons of God—and I am a child and heir—why am I not led by the Spirit of God? Why don't I know anything about what this verse encompasses?'
(Georg von Viebahn)

On one occasion I felt a very distinct call to go and preach at a place I had only seen once in my life: a town on the left-hand side coming from the Potteries to Derby. I did not know the name of the town, but it was vividly before my eye, and I felt assured that I must go there and preach Christ.

I described the town to a person from Staffordshire, and he told me at once the name of the place was Uttoxeter. I continued in prayer during that week; and on Friday I received a letter from Tenby, South Wales, enclosing a letter from Mrs. H., of Uttoxeter, asking the lady in Tenby if she knew my address, to forward an enclosed letter to me; which letter was an earnest request for me to go to Uttoxeter, and preach the gospel.

I immediately went, the word was owned, and a number were gathered to Christ. Was this a mere accident, on the day that I was called to go and preach at this, to me, unknown place? A Christian was also led to write a letter, to ask me to go?

Why should we doubt the presence and guidance of the Holy Ghost now, as He was manifestly present in the beginning? Jesus said, "And I will pray the Father, and he shall give you another Comforter, that he may abide with you for ever." Yes, He abides with us; and if we were more simple, we should know far more of His divine guidance in our path of service. It is just as ecclesiastical arrangements increase, that the direct guidance of the Spirit is set aside. We have little idea how much we lose by this.

(Charles Stanley, *Incidents of Gospel Work*, Believers Bookshelf USA)

> *Is the guidance of the Holy Spirit something mystical or is it a reality for you? Do you know situations in your life where you have been aware that the Spirit has guided you? What can help you to better recognise how the Spirit wants to guide you? The Son of God said about the Holy Spirit: "He will glorify me" (Jn. 16:14).*

Notes:

....

....

....

....

....

....

....

....

....

....

....

Seek First the Kingdom of God

"Seek first the kingdom of God and his righteousness, and all these things will be added to you." (Matthew 6:33)

The Lord Jesus encourages His disciples in the Sermon on the Mount to give the kingdom of God the highest priority. This means that God and His interests should be given the central place in our lives. We are to honour Him through practical righteousness, that means that we are to do what is in accordance with His will.

In 2 Corinthians 9:9 Paul makes it clear that God calls the giving of material things righteousness for which there will be reward one day. Furthermore, the Lord Jesus promised that if we seek first the kingdom of God and His righteousness, we will receive from Him all that we need to live.

In this way, the Son of God challenges His disciples in Matthew 6 to serve Him with their whole heart and to trust in the care of their heavenly Father for their present and future financial needs. Through these challenging words of the Lord, His disciples—and we too—are confronted with an important decision: Do we take Him at His word and act accordingly? It's also interesting to note that this instruction directly follows the warning about serving two masters. Could it be that our preoccupation with finances has become an idol?

The story of the widow who was told to feed Elijah, the man of God, illustrates this very well. She first prepares food for the man of God—although according to the human mind this would have left her and her son empty-handed. But God's promise, given through Elijah, is rock solid: "The jar of flour shall not be spent, and the jug of oil shall not be empty, until the day that the LORD sends rain upon the earth" (1 Ki. 17:14).

Because the widow takes God at His word, sets her priorities right and acts in obedience of faith, she experiences God's miraculous working, which she no doubt never forgot: "And she went and did as Elijah said. And she and he and her household ate for many days. The jar of flour was not spent, neither did the jug of oil become empty, according to the word of the LORD that he spoke by Elijah" (1 Ki. 17:15–16).

Now someone might ask: Does the Lord also require of me to sacrifice my last reserves? This may be the case in individual cases, but definitely not always. Perhaps you could ask yourself whether you would be prepared to do so if the Lord were to ask you. One thing is certain, however: the Lord wants us to consciously hand over the ownership of what is at our disposal to Him.

It all belongs to Him and He can dispose of it as He pleases. Only when we renounce everything we own can we be true disciples (see Lk. 14:33). We are therefore 'only' stewards of the things at our disposal and may use them in dependence on the Lord for the blessing of others—and enjoy them ourselves too (see 1 Tim. 6:17).

If we're willing to sacrifice things for others for the sake of the Lord, we'll also experience that God cares for us and gives us what we need. During the three years that the disciples followed their Master in His public ministry, they experienced God's faithful care every day. They were hosted by believers (see Lk. 10) and received gifts from women who served the Son of God with their possessions (see Lk. 8:1–3).

Even when He sent them out two by two without money to preach the gospel of the kingdom and heal the sick, they could say in retrospect that they had lacked nothing (see Lk. 22:35).

The Lord Jesus is no longer on earth. Have His promises or His care for us changed because of this? Not at all. On the contrary: He is now seated at the right hand of God, where angels, powers and authorities are subject to Him (see Heb. 1:3; 1 Pet. 3:22). To Him belongs the earth and its fullness, the silver and the gold, and the cattle on a thousand hills (see Ps. 24:1; Hag. 2:8; Ps. 50:10). How much more, therefore, should we lean on His promises and trust Him with our entire hearts that He will provide for us!

John Nelson Darby once said: "I have not seen the Lord leave those who have given themselves up to work, trusting Him: and I have seen distress of spirit and greatly hindered usefulness [in those] who, through their wives or own hearts, have turned to other things to help wife or family here. The most beloved and able witness was saved from great injury to his own spirit and usefulness, by its making him thoroughly miserable, and it did hinder him."

Obey God and leave all the consequences to Him!
(Charles Stanley)

Seeking the kingdom of God often involves personal sacrifice, for if it's our top priority, we'll put personal desires and interests on the back burner. This may mean, for example, that we give up material things or a luxurious life so that His kingdom may expand and grow. But not just that: we should also expect resistance and persecution if we consistently stand for the interests of God, because: "Indeed, all who desire to live a godly life in Christ Jesus will be persecuted" (2 Tim. 3:12).

Carl Brockhaus experienced exactly that. In 1850 he gave up his teaching profession and devoted himself entirely to working for a Christian association that was active in evangelism in Germany. During this time, he came to know the Word of God better and better and consistently applied what he had understood in his life.

He began to preach the gospel of grace without legalistic additions, as well as the perfect position of believers in Christ. The believers from the Christian association didn't agree with this and so he was forced to leave. This meant poverty and deprivation for him and his family—he had 13 children.

When he spoke of this time in later years, he never tired of telling his children about God's care during that time. When he was in short supply for his family after leaving the association, the thought occurred to him whether he should not look for a job again, at least half-time, in order to earn a living. His brother-in-law, Julius Löwen, offered him a job in his business. But he didn't come to a decision and asked the Lord for wisdom and guidance.

One morning an envelope was delivered, in which were five taler and a little note, on which it said: "No soldier gets entangled in civilian pursuits" (2 Tim. 2:4). From the handwriting and the postage stamp he recognised that the unsigned letter came from a member of the Brüderverein, from whom he hadn't heard any kind words since he had left them.

A few days later he met him in the street and said: "I thank you very much for the great service you have done to me in sending your letter. You have freed me from the indecisiveness about the matter whether I should look for some job or devote all my time to the Lord's work."

The brother was very surprised and told him that one night he thought of him very often, and that the concerns about his fate kept him awake. Then the thought came to his mind: You need to send him something. First, he didn't want to, but the Lord left him no peace until he got up and prepared the envelope for him. He had planned to write a short message, but then this passage came to his mind and he wrote that on the piece of paper.

(Arend Remmers, *Gedenket euer Führer* [Remember your Leaders], CSV)

How wonderfully the Lord provides for us when we set our priorities right in dependence on Him and firmly trust in Him and His faithful promises!

What Bible verses do you associate with what Carl Brockhaus experienced? What does it mean practically for your life to seek first the kingdom of God? Trust that the Lord will give you what you need if you put His interests first! Do you believe that God won't owe you anything?

Notes:

....

....

....

....

....

....

....

....

....

....

....

....

....

....

....

....

....

Praying and Fasting

"This kind cannot be driven out by anything but prayer."
(Mark 9:29)

The words of the Lord Jesus make it clear that there are sometimes particular situations and problems in which, in addition to prayer, it is also good to fast, i.e. to consciously abstain from food. Our Lord and Master Himself showed us how to do it: after He began His ministry with prayer and then fasted for 40 days in the wilderness, we read shortly afterwards that He revealed the power of God in the synagogue by casting out a demon.

Paul also fasted often—especially before important decisions (see 2 Cor. 11:27; Acts 14:23). Throughout the centuries, many believers have experienced that God blesses prayer and fasting in a special way when it is done in faith. Among them are the Waldensians, the Huguenots, men like David Brainerd, Jonathan Edwards, George Whitefield and many others.

The question we need to ask ourselves is: Do we believe that God acknowledges this in a special way or not? Let us look at a faith experience that Amy Carmichael had in connection with the casting out of a demon. The following is what she wrote in her autobiography:

We heard of an old man who was possessed by an evil demon. As in India, so in Japan, people might live in the country for years and never once even hear of, much less come across, this kind of thing. It was in the purpose of God that it should come my way, therefore it was so. The man who, as the people believed, was possessed by the Fox spirit lived in a street near our house. He was in a very desperate condition. When we were told of this, words I had read often came to me as if they were new: "All power is given unto Me ... These signs shall follow them that believe; in My Name shall they cast out devils."

Misaki San [Amy's language teacher and friend] and I read these words together and we prayed, and waited upon the Lord. Then, full of confidence that the power of the Lord would cast out the Fox spirit, we asked if we might see the man. We were taken to an upstairs room where he was confined. He was strapped and bound to two heavy beams laid crosswise on the floor. His arms were stretched out as if for crucifixion. His body was covered with burns. Little cones of powdered medicine had been set on his skin and lighted. They burned slowly with a red glow.

That alone, one would have thought, was enough to make him mad; but it had not been done till all other means known by his people had been tried in vain. The idea was that the fire would drive out the Fox spirit. We had been told that he was possessed by six Fox spirits; but that was nothing to what the man had who said, "My name is Legion, for we are many".

> **I think we should see a great deal more of His work made manifest if there were more prayer and fasting.**
> (Walter T P Wolston)

With confidence, then, we told the old man's wife and the relations who crowded round, that our mighty Lord Jesus could cast out the six Fox spirits. But the moment we named our Saviour it was as if a paroxysm of rage filled the poor man, he raved and cursed and struggled to get at us. The men in charge of him held him down and covered his face with a cloth. We were hurried out of the room.

The poor wife followed us to the door. She spoke not one word of reproach, but she must have felt reproachful. As for me I was utterly bewildered and ashamed. It was as if the Name that is above every name had been shamed. What should we have done—stayed and said, "I command thee in the Name of Jesus Christ to come out of him"?

As we turned to go a sudden quickening of faith was given, and, my Japanese sister interpreting for me, I asked the wife to let us know when her husband was delivered from the power of the Fox spirit, "for our God will conquer, and we shall go home and pray till we hear that He has".

Within an hour a messenger came to say that the foxes were gone, the cords were off. He was asleep.

Next day he asked to see us. He was sitting quietly with his wife, a well man. Except for the unhealed burns there was nothing to show what had been. He sent for flowers and someone brought a branch of pomegranate in flower. He gave it to me, and I don't think I ever see a pomegranate flower without seeing that old man's face, so courteous and so calm.

(F Houghton, *Amy Carmichael of Dohnavur*, Christian Literature Crusade)

What was the core problem of the disciples who were not able to cast out the demon although the Lord had given them the power to do so (Mk. 6:7)? Why is it explicitly mentioned in the New Testament that certain demons can only be cast out through prayer and fasting? What incidents from the Bible can you think of in which people both prayed and fasted and in which God responded? Why is fasting preached so little today, even though it was practised by many biblical and church history role models?

Notes:

....

....

....

....

....

....

....

....

....

....

....

....

In the Shadow of the Almighty

"He who dwells in the shelter of the Most High will abide in the shadow of the Almighty. I will say to the Lord, 'My refuge and my fortress, my God, in whom I trust.'" (Psalm 91:1–2)

The presence of God is the safest place there is. Many believers in the Old Testament and in church history can confirm the experience of the psalmist who wrote: "God is our refuge and strength, a very present help in trouble" and "in the shadow of your wings I will take refuge till the storms of destruction pass by" (Ps. 46:1; 57:1). This applies first of all to inner crises and temptations that we encounter but it can also be the case with external dangers.

Shadrach, Meshach and Abednego experienced God's miraculous rescue in the fiery furnace when the Son of God protected them by His presence. Daniel was saved by God from the lions' jaws; "no kind of harm was found on him, because he had trusted in his God" (Dan. 6:23). Many years later, in Africa, David Livingstone experienced how God saved him from the attack of a lion—carrying the marks of that attack with him throughout his life.

The devil often whipped up the people to attack the Son of God. But God held His hand over Him and preserved Him. Once the people of Nazareth led Him to the edge of a mountain to throw Him down from there; "But passing through their midst, he went away" (Lk. 4:30). Another time the Jews tried to seize Him in the temple. But what happened? "No one laid a hand on him because his hour had not yet come" (Jn. 7:30). God answered the prayer of His servant who had said, "Preserve me, O God, for in you I take refuge" (Ps. 16:1).

The salvation of the Lord can vary greatly. Sometimes it seems spectacular; other times it may hardly be noticed. Evangelist D L Moody had a very special experience of God answering prayer and giving salvation.

On another occasion, one Saturday evening he found in a house a jug of whiskey, which had been stored there for a carouse the following day. After a rousing temperance lecture, Mr. Moody persuaded the women of the house to permit him to pour the whiskey into the street. This he did before departing.

Early the next morning he came back to fetch the children of the place to Sunday school. The men were lying in wait for him to thrash him. It was impossible to get away, for he was surrounded on all sides, but before they could touch him, Mr. Moody said, "See here, men, if you are going to whip me, you might at least give me time to say my prayers".

The request was unusual; perhaps it was for that very reason that it was granted. Mr. Moody dropped upon his knees and prayed such a prayer as those rough men had never heard before. Gradually they became interested and then softened, and when he had finished they gave him their hands, and a few minutes later Mr. Moody left the house for his school, followed by the children he had come to find.

(J Wilbur Chapman, *The Life and Work of D. L. Moody*, Moody Press)

The story of David Brainerd, who saw it as his ministry to bring the gospel to unreached Indian tribes in North America, is also impressive. He was a man of prayer who often spent many hours on his knees. To this day, he is an example to many Christians through his unwavering devotion:

> **The shadow of the Almighty removes all gloom from the shadow of night—once covered by the divine wing, we care not what winged terrors may fly abroad in the earth.**
> (Charles H Spurgeon)

"It is also told of Brainerd that one day he decided to visit an Indian tribe known to be extremely xenophobic and murderous. Some friends of his strongly advised him not to risk his life. But Brainerd knew he was being called by God and said goodbye to his friends, who expected to have seen the last of him.

With a small travelling tent and his few belongings, he soon reached his destination and pitched his tent just outside the tribe's main village to prepare himself in prayer for the first encounter.

Little did he know, however, that a hostile Indian had long since observed him and had rushed to the chief to inform him and his warriors of his discovery. A council of war was immediately held and a party of the bravest warriors sent out to kill and scalp the white man who had dared to tread on their territory.

This tribe was in the habit of attacking its enemies not openly but from ambush, and so they crept up to Brainerd's tent and waited for him to step out so that they could kill him with their arrows. But they had to wait a long time, and when some hours had passed, they sent three or four men to spy what the white man was doing in the tent.

They saw through an opening that he was on his knees talking to someone. They were so astonished that they did not dare harm him. To their horror, they saw a rattlesnake suddenly crawl into the tent and move towards the kneeling white man. It reared up in front of him and was about to sink its poisonous teeth into his neck, but suddenly turned away from its victim and slithered out of the tent on the opposite side.

"You came near when I called on you; you said, 'Do not fear!'"
(Lamentations 3:57)

The astonished Indians crept away silently to tell the chief this extraordinary story. But Brainerd, unaware of all this, got up from his knees, picked up his Bible and set out to preach the gospel to these feared Indians.

To his great astonishment, the chief and his warriors were already coming to meet him, not to kill him, but to receive him as a long-sought friend—as one who lived under the protection of a great God. Brainerd preached the gospel to these men with great joy, and in the days that followed he saw the entire tribe transformed by the gospel of the Lord's saving grace and obeying the gospel in simple faith.

(W Bühne, *Das Gebetsleben Jesu* [Jesus' Prayer Life], CLV)

"On his knees the believer is invincible."

Charles H Spurgeon

> *How would your life change if you would let go more and live in trust in the living God? What spurs you on? The throne of grace is the safest place when the enemy attacks!*

Notes:

....
....
....
....
....
....
....
....
....
....
....
....
....
....
....
....
....
....
....
....
....
....
....

When the Lord Calls

"Jesus said, 'Truly, I say to you, there is no one who has left house or brothers or sisters or mother or father or children or lands, for my sake and for the gospel, who will not receive a hundredfold now in this time, houses and brothers and sisters and mothers and children and lands, with persecutions, and in the age to come eternal life.'" (Mark 10:29–30)

Every Christian has the task of proclaiming the gospel in his or her environment—and there are different ways of doing this. We're all called to do the work of an evangelist. And where does this ministry begin? On our own doorstep!

But it doesn't have to end there. We should not forget that in many parts of the world there are still billions of people who have never heard the true gospel. Moreover, many brothers and sisters in distant lands are longing to learn things from God's Word that we may have heard as children in Sunday school.

On the one hand, the Lord said to the man who had been delivered from the legion of demons, "Return to your home, and declare how much God has done for you" (Lk. 8:39). On the other hand, He also told His disciples: "Go into all the world and proclaim the gospel to the whole creation" (Mk. 16:15). We should not play one off against the other but agree with both—and do what the Lord shows us personally.

The Son of God said to His disciples: "If anyone comes to me and does not hate his own father and mother and wife and children and brothers and sisters, yes, and even his own life, he cannot be my disciple" (Lk. 14:26). The love we are to have for Him should surpass any other relationship. Now, when the Lord calls someone to serve Him in a distant land, it often means leaving behind loved ones as well as the luxuries to which one has become accustomed. But when God calls, there is only one thing to do: give Him the first place and be obedient.

It is interesting to note, by the way, that the Lord Himself placed the spiritual family above the natural family by giving the will of God the first place in everything. That's why it is once said, when His relatives sought Him, "And he answered them, 'Who are my mother and my brothers?' And looking about at those who sat around him, he said, 'Here are my mother and my brothers! For whoever does the will of God, he is my brother and sister and mother'" (Mk. 3:33–35).

When the Lord calls to a task and, at some point, the time comes to tell your parents or friends about it, the thought that you will soon be separated from each other for a long time is often not easy. But the awareness of being in the will of God and having the Lord by our side helps us to overcome these tensions. He is already waiting for us in the place where He has called us (see Acts 7:3).

When the Lord called Amy Carmichael to go as a missionary to a faraway land, it was not easy for her to say goodbye to her family. But she also experienced the Lord's help and the way He made His promises come true in her life.

Amy had long been preoccupied by the thought that fifty thousand people died every day in the darkness of paganism. Again and again she had heard the call ringing through everything: "Come over and help us!" She had resisted the call from the pagan land and prayed for peace. Her plea was only half answered, and that made her think.

But one evening, on January 13 1892, in her quiet time, she heard again and again the word: "Go!" It was a call she couldn't escape. She wrote about it to her mother on January 14:

My precious mother,

Have you given your child unreservedly to the Lord for whatever He wills?

...

He is no fool who gives what he cannot keep to gain what he cannot lose.
(Jim Elliot)

Oh may He strengthen you to say "Yes" to Him if He asks something which costs.

Darling Mother, for a long time as you know the thought of those dying in the dark—50,000 of them every day, while we at home live in the blazing light—has been very present with me, and the longing to go to them, and tell them of Jesus, has been strong upon me. Everything, everything seemed to be saying "Go", through all sounds the cry seemed to rise, "Come over to help us".

Every bit of pleasure or work which has come to me, has had underlying it the thought of those people who have never, never heard of Jesus; before my eyes clearer than any lovely view has been the constant picture of those millions who have no chance, and never had one, of hearing of the love which makes our lives so bright. ...

I went to my own room and just asked the Lord what it all meant, what did He wish me to do, and, Mother, as clearly as I ever heard you speak, I heard Him say,

"Go ye."

I never heard it just so plainly before; I cannot be mistaken for I know He spoke. He says "Go", I cannot stay.

Mother, I feel as if I had been stabbing someone I loved. It is Friday now, I could not finish this yesterday, and through all the keen sharp pain which has come since Wednesday, the certainty that it was His voice I heard has never wavered; though all my heart has shrunk from what it means, though I seem torn in two, and just feel one big ache all over, yet the certainty is there—He said to me "Go". Oh, nothing but that sure word, His word, could make it possible to do it, for until He spoke, and I answered, "Yes, Lord", I never knew what it would cost.

These are the verses He gave me, when He spoke to me: "If any man will come after Me, let him deny himself, and take up his cross, and follow Me." "For whosoever will save his life shall lose it, and whosoever will lose his life for My sake shall find it." "He that loveth father or mother more than Me is not worthy of Me."

"To obey is better than sacrifice."

Many difficulties have risen in my mind, they seem very great, the "crooked places" seem very crooked, but it seems to me that all He asks is that we should take the one step He shows us, and in simplest, most practical trust leave all results to Him.

Mother, I know that very few of our friends will think I am right. Those who don't know the Shepherd's Voice themselves will be quite sure I am very wrong and mistaken, but He has said, "Walk before Me, and be thou perfect." He knows, and He won't let me dishonour Him by making a mistake and following my own fancy instead of Him. If it is so, He will show it to me, but if it is His will, I must do it.

There isn't much of gladness in this letter, I'm afraid, but I don't feel anything except sore at the pain this must bring to my loved ones.

Goodbye, my Mother. May He come very near to you and strengthen and comfort you.

Your own Amy.

...

From her mother to Amy, in firm clear handwriting, dated January 16th, and marked on the back in Amy's writing, "First letter received—praise the Lord"!

> *My own precious Child,*
> *He Who hath led will lead*
> *All through the wilderness,*
> *He Who had fed will surely feed...*
> *He Who hath heard thy cry*
> *Will never close His ear,*
> *He Who hath marked thy faintest sigh*
> *Will not forget thy tear.*
> *He loveth always, faileth never,*
> *So rest on Him today—for ever.*

Yes, dearest Amy, He has lent you to me all these years. He only knows what a strength, comfort and joy you have been to me. In sorrow He made you my staff and solace, in loneliness my more than child companion, and in gladness my bright and merry-hearted sympathiser. So, darling, when He asks you now to go away from within my reach, can I say nay? No, no, Amy, He is yours—you are His—to take you where He pleases and to use you as He pleases.

...

So, my precious child, I give you back into His loving arms, saying from the depths of my being, "Take her, dear Lord—Thou wilt take the most loving care of her, use her in Thy service and for Thy glory now and where Thou pleasest."

(F Houghton, *Amy Carmichael of Dohnavur*, Christian Literature Crusade)

The Lord then guided Amy wonderfully over the next few years, and when she later served Him in South India, He provided brothers and sisters to assist her, and made her a spiritual mother to many believers. The stamp of God's blessing that rested on this work can still be seen today when you visit Dhonavur in the state of Tamil Nadu.

God not only calls; He also gives wonderful promises that encourage us to set out and trust Him firmly. He promises us a hundredfold reward (10,000% interest) and assures us that He will not fail us nor forsake us (see Heb. 13:5).

> *"Have I not commanded you?*
> *Be strong and courageous.*
> *Do not be frightened, and do not be dismayed,*
> *for the LORD your God is with you wherever you go."*

Joshua 1:9

Are you ready to go should the Lord call you to serve in a faraway land? What shows that someone loves the Lord Jesus more than their own parents? Are you ready to let your children, grandchildren or good friends go if it is God's will?

Notes:

....
....
....
....
....
....
....
....
....
....
....
....

The Power of Prayer

"The effective, fervent prayer of a righteous man avails much."
(James 5:16, NKJV)

This statement has encouraged many believers to pray more and more intensely. But in what context does James actually write this verse? He writes it in connection with God's great answer to Elijah's prayer. Elijah longed to see revival among God's people. This deep desire drove him to prayer. He begged God to close the heavens so that the people would finally wake up and turn to the LORD with all their hearts.

God had already announced through Moses that He would make the heavens like iron if the people turned away from Him (Lev. 26:19; Deut. 11:17). He had confirmed this statement to Solomon (1 Ki. 8:35). Now Elijah asks the Lord to make His word come true. The prophet's prayer is answered and heaven remains closed for three years and six months. God answers the plea for the revival and restoration of His people!

After the people have turned back to God, we find Elijah again in earnest prayer. Seven times he bows down to the earth, puts his head between his knees and asks God to give rain again—just as He had said He would if His people repented: "When I shut up the heavens so that there is no rain, or command the locust to devour the land, or send pestilence among my people, if my people who are called by my name humble themselves, and pray and seek my face and turn from their wicked ways, then I will hear from heaven and will forgive their sin and heal their land" (2 Chron. 7:13–14). How does God respond to this? He acknowledges the prayer of faith, fulfils His promise and unlocks the windows of heaven!

The Word of God encourages us to pray for revival among God's people. We can be sure that even today God will respond to sincere humiliation and give revival if we pray intensely and persistently with faith. There are numerous examples of this in church history:

> *The great revival movement that happened in America in the 18th century began with intense and sustained prayer. George Whitefield and John Wesley were both men who prayed a lot. Whitefield began 1739 with other believers with a love feast where he spent the whole night in prayer, thanksgiving and singing.*

It is men of prayer who have moved the arm of Omnipotence in all ages.
(John Nelson Darby)

> *This wasn't a one-off event, for just a few days later he wrote in his diary: "We remained in fasting and prayer until three o'clock, and then parted with a firm conviction that God would do great things among us". The Lord had given them this conviction on their knees, and that is exactly what happened: Thousands came to faith in the following years, while many gave themselves to prayer.*

(Benedict Peters, *George Whitefield—Der Erwecker Englands und Amerikas* [George Whitefield—The Revivalist of England and America], CLV)

The biography of Charles Cowman tells of how many believers experienced the miraculous work of God in Japan in 1917.

Japanese workers spent three full days waiting on God before those meetings. Far off in the quiet country, in an abandoned farmhouse, they waited and prayed until all felt that God had heard them and they returned with faces shining. God came in mighty power in the first service. The workers were drawn together in tender love; there were no divisions to be found anywhere. I wish you could have heard them singing "Crown Him Lord of All!" It was like a great wave of praise surging up against the pillars of the throne of God.

Later Cowman wrote about this time: "We don't want anything new in revivals. We want the old elements: the living Spirit of God, the living Word of God and the old gospel."

(Lettie B Cowman, *Charles E. Cowman—Missionary Warrior,* The Oriental Missionary Society)

Of the many other miraculous revivals that God has brought about in the course of church history, only the one in Kilsyth (Scotland) is mentioned here. It took place under the ministry of William Burns, who later worked with Hudson Taylor. It was preceded by the earnest prayers of people in Kilsyth who humbled themselves under the mighty hand of God and pleaded with great desire and fervour for His mighty work. The revival began on the morning of Tuesday 23 July, 1839.

The night before the Word of God was proclaimed, many gathered for prayer, wrestling for several hours for the salvation of souls. They became firmly convinced that their prayers had been answered and the next morning they came with the expectation of experiencing the glorious work of God.

When a young preacher spoke, God worked with special power. The whole audience began to weep. Many found peace with God. Many 'revival meetings' were held night after night for months, in the church and in the marketplace.

At times 3,000 or 4,000 people came together to hear the Word of God. The whole town was cleansed of immorality and the drinking of alcoholic beverages stopped. Many houses and shops became places of prayer.

We can be sure that even today God will give us a new revival in some places if we humble ourselves before Him and ask Him fervently and persistently for it.

> **The native soil of revival is prayer circles.**
> (Charles H Spurgeon)

*"If my people who are called by my name
humble themselves, and pray and seek my face
and turn from their wicked ways,
then I will hear from heaven
and will forgive their sin and heal their land."*

2 Chronicles 7:14

> *Do you still believe that God can bring revival locally? Do you trust Him to do so? What have you resigned yourself to over time and what do you reach out for in prayer? What does it mean to humble yourself before God? "Put me to the test … if I will not open the windows of heaven for you and pour down for you a blessing until there is no more need" (Mal. 3:10). Is the God of past revivals still the same God today?*

Notes:

....
....
....
....
....
....
....
....
....
....
....
....
....
....

God's Tools for Revival

"Fear not, Daniel, for from the first day that you set your heart to understand and humbled yourself before your God, your words have been heard, and I have come because of your words." (Daniel 10:12)

During the Babylonian captivity we find another praying man who took God at His word and relied on His promises in faith. Daniel, the greatly beloved, humbled himself under the sinful condition of the people, acknowledged their sins and begged God for mercy. This is exactly what God had been waiting for. He heard His servant's plea and responded to his humiliation by bringing about a miraculous revival which is described in the Book of Ezra.

"God opposes the proud but gives grace to the humble" (Jas. 4:6). The fulfilment of this divine promise is very clear in Nehemiah. When this faithful man humbled himself under the failure of the people and acknowledged their sins, he then became God's chosen instrument to rebuild the walls of Jerusalem.

> **Every great movement of God can be traced to a kneeling figure.**
> (Dwight L Moody)

Many Christians don't know how many times God has brought about revivals in different places in the course of church history. The revivals in Herrnhut (1727), in New England (1730), in Wales (1904), in Assam (1905), in Hinghwa (1909) and in many other places all began with intense prayer, to which God responded by a mighty working of His Spirit. Brokenness, humiliation, burning hearts and healing of broken relationships were often the miraculous results.

T E Koshy writes in his biography about the life of Bakht Singh, who was a servant of God in India:

From 1936 onwards, the Lord brought about mighty revivals in many villages, towns and cities. From the north of India, Punjab (now part of Pakistan), to Kerala in the south, the fire of revival broke out and spread to more than 70 places in the course of ten years. Tens of thousands turned to the living God. India had never experienced such a mighty revival before, and has not since.

In a way, the Lord began answering the prayers of many of His servants who loved and prayed for the people of India, such as Praying Hyde, in the North, Lady Ogle from England, Amy Carmichael, Pandita Ramabai and many others both in India and abroad. At the turn of the century, a company of missionaries met together at Southern Hill station, Kodaikanal, and decided that the time had come to pray definitely for a ministry to awaken the Indian church. They issued a prayer circular and sent it to Britain, America and Australia to mobilise believers for intercession.

A prayer movement began and gathered strength. John Hyde, from his arrival in India in 1892, devoted himself more and more to intercessory prayer. Praying Hyde, with a group of friends, spent days and nights in prayer for an awakening throughout India, in all its provinces.

(T E Koshy, *Brother Bakht Singh of India*, OM Books)

The following incident also shows that God blesses persistent prayer for revival in a special way:

In the month of May 1938, prior to his going to Madras and Kerala for three-month gospel campaigns, the Lord burdened Bakht Singh and members of his team to go from Poona to the Pandita Ramabai Mukti Mission at Kedgaon for a time of all night prayer. At the Mukti Mission, the staff, children, and adults, numbering about three hundred, mostly women, joined the special time of all-night prayer which lasted for 19 consecutive nights except for only two days' break in between.

Bakht Singh divided the saints into various groups, with each group praying earnestly for revival in different parts of India and other parts of the world. They all persevered in prayer, interceding for a mighty work of God. As a result of these nights of prayer, the Lord worked in many parts of South India, particularly in Madras, eventually establishing 'Jehovah-Shammah' and other assemblies based on New Testament principles. Through these experiences, the Lord taught Bakht Singh the secret of the power of all-night prayer.

(T E Koshy, *Brother Bakht Singh of India*, OM Books)

To some readers, these experiences may sound like stories from another planet. But the fact is that the Lord miraculously responded to the persistent pleading of these believers and the effects are still evident in India today!

"I think it will be found that all important movements among the people of God have been the result of united heart-felt prayer."

Charles H Mackintosh

> *What is stopping Christians today from praying for revival as intensely as they did in the examples mentioned above? What is stopping you from praying for the Lord to bring about a Spirit-led revival in your area? Ask Him to give you others who have the same concern on their hearts!*

Notes:

....

....

....

....

....

....

....

....

....

....

....

....

....

....

....

....

....

....

Put Me to the Test

Towards the end of the Old Testament, at the time of Malachi, the Jews who had returned from captivity were in a very poor spiritual condition. They were in the right place outwardly but had a disastrous inward attitude. Both the people and the priests had lost confidence in the promises of God.

For example, God said in His Word: "Honour the LORD with your wealth and with the firstfruits of all your produce; then your barns will be filled with plenty, and your vats will be bursting with wine" (Prov. 3:9–10). But because the people didn't believe God and honour Him with their wealth, they didn't experience the fulfilment of this promise. Instead, the Jews were very selfish and wallowed in self-pity. How did God respond? He closed the heavens and withheld the blessing from above.

Was all now lost? Not yet. The LORD turned again to the people and challenged them to test Him and see if He was really true to what He had promised: "Bring the full tithe into the storehouse, that there may be food in my house. And thereby put me to the test, says the LORD of hosts, if I will not open the windows of heaven for you and pour down for you a blessing until there is no more need" (Mal. 3:10). How many believers responded to this challenge at that time?

Now for a change of scene. It's more than 2,400 years later. Christianity is in the state presented in the letter to Laodicea (Rev. 3:14–22); lukewarmness, complacency and lack of faith are becoming more and more widespread. There are still those who are purely outwardly in the right place—separated from nominal Christians and those who no longer want to practise biblical principles.

> **For fifty years I have looked up to the Lord to give me what I need, and never for a moment have I thought where the money would come from. I have never known, nor do I now know, where the money will come from for the next fortnight. But I know God, and I know He will provide.**
> (William MacDonald)

But what is their inner spiritual condition? Do they really still take God at His word? Do they believe that He will still make good on His promises of financial sacrifice in the 21st century if they are willing to let go and trust Him wholeheartedly? Or is such an attitude rather called unrealistic or even unspiritual?

We can all ask ourselves where the great power and the great grace that God gave to the first Christians have gone. Has He changed? Or is it not rather that our practical condition is reflected in the words that the Lord Jesus said to His disciples 2,000 years ago: "One who is faithful in a very little is also faithful in much, and one who is dishonest in a very little is also dishonest in much. If then you have not been faithful in the unrighteous wealth, who will entrust to you the true riches?" (Lk. 16:10–11)? Are we owners or stewards of the things that are at our disposal?

It's very interesting to note that during the revivals in church history, believers were so moved by Christ and heavenly things that they were often willing to sacrifice material things.

Andrew Miller writes about the beginning of the revival movement in the 19th century:

It was no uncommon thing at this time to find valuable jewellery in the collection boxes, which was soon turned into money, and given to the deacons for the poor. But this quiet way of disposing of a little finery did not satisfy the devoted spirits at Plymouth. They parted with all that was considered worldly in dress, books, and furniture. These free-will offerings were collected, and when the stripping time seemed nearly at an end, the accumulation was so great that it was necessary to sell them by auction.

...

After classifying the articles, and selling a number of the smaller things in lots the whole extended to six hundred lots, and were three days in selling.

...

The following quotation is from the last letter we received, and given on the testimony of more than one witness.

"Respecting the quantity of goods, jewels, books, furniture, etc., given up and sold during early days at Plymouth, there was no call of any particular kind, no special need for which it was done. It was quite simply and freely, as desiring to express their then indifference to the world, their separatedness to the Lord, and their waiting for His coming from heaven."

(Andrew Miller, *The Brethren*)

> *How can this attitude become evident in your life? The Lord Jesus told His disciples: "Sell your possessions, and give to the needy. Provide yourselves with moneybags that do not grow old, with a treasure in the heavens that does not fail, where no thief approaches and no moth destroys. For where your treasure is, there will your heart be also" (Lk. 12:33–34). What do these words mean to you today?*

Notes:

....

....

....

....

....

....

....

....

....

....

....

....

....

....

The Peace of God and Prayer

"Do not be anxious about anything, but in everything by prayer and supplication with thanksgiving let your requests be made known to God. And the peace of God, which surpasses all understanding, will guard your hearts and your minds in Christ Jesus." (Philippians 4:6–7)

This is probably one of the most challenging exhortations for us in the New Testament: "Do not be anxious about anything". How difficult it often is for us to put this into practice! But that is exactly what the Lord wants from us. We should bring our worries to Him in prayer and then leave them with Him—and not carry them around with us.

If we really cast our worries on the Lord in confidence, then the peace of God will take the place in our hearts that was previously filled with worries. This peace that reigns at the throne of God is unshakeable, and it is this peace that He wants to give us, regardless of the size of our worries and needs.

The following example shows how it can look in practice to bring your worries to the Lord in an emergency and then firmly trust that He will take care of them:

Any concern too small to be turned into prayer is too small to be made into a burden. (Corrie ten Boom)

We were conducting meetings in Battersea, London, and at the close of the service were leaving the Tabernacle with Mr. David Thomas, a London dry goods merchant, who was also the founder of the movement in which we were working. Suddenly his son, panting and breathless, rushed up the steps, saying, "Father, the store is on fire."

The attitude of Mr. Thomas amazed me. Instead of becoming excited as most people would, he quietly asked, "Are the firemen at work?" On being assured that they were, he put his hand on my shoulder, saying, "Let us pray about this." The prayer he prayed was as simple as anything I have ever heard. Standing there on the steps leading to the street he said, "Lord, it is not my store, it is Thine. Put Thy hand upon that fire and do it now, for Jesus' sake."

Then quietly he said, "Now let us go to supper." "But, sir," half a dozen voices cried, "what about the fire?" To which he replied, "Didn't we commit it to the Lord? If we were to go, what more could we do? He will take care of it."

We went to his home for supper and the fire was not mentioned again until halfway through the meal his son came in and Mr. Thomas enquired, "Well, what happened?" "Happened?" replied the young man, "It seemed as though a miracle happened. When I left the store to come to you it looked as though nothing could save it from being completely burned out, but when I returned, in some mysterious manner the flames had been arrested. The firemen themselves cannot understand it. It looks like an act of God."

I shall ever praise God for that definite fact of faith on exhibition.

(Harry E Jessop, *The Ministry of Prevailing Prayer*, Kessinger Publishing)

> *How can you tell that you have really unburdened all your worries to God in prayer and left them there? What can help you to worry less? "You keep him in perfect peace whose mind is stayed on you, because he trusts in you" (Isa. 26:3).*

Notes:

....

....

....

....

....

....

....

....

....

....

....

....

....

....

....

....

....

....

The Lord Is Coming!

"Behold, I am coming soon." (Revelation 22:12)

What a mighty promise! The Lord Himself, the Creator of heaven and earth, the Sustainer of all things, the great "I Am", the First and the Last, the shining Morning Star: He will come Himself, "with a cry of command, with the voice of an archangel, and with the sound of the trumpet of God" (1 Thess. 4:16), to take us to Himself in the eternal glory of the Father's house.

In a fraction of a second our corruptible body will be replaced by an incorruptible one as we go to meet the Lord in the air. Then we will be with Him forever. Wonderful, glorious hope!

> **If you have no longings for Christ's appearance, no desires for His speedy return, surely your heart is sick and your love is faint!**
> (Charles H Spurgeon)

God presents this great hope to us so that we may live in the daily expectation of it. We are not only to know passively that the Lord will come again someday, but we are to count on His coming every day.

When Hudson Taylor first grasped the truth about the Lord's coming in faith, it had concrete consequences for his practical life. He writes about this:

The effect of this blessed hope was a thoroughly practical one. It led me to look carefully through my little library to see if I had any books that were not needed or likely to be of no further service. I examined my small wardrobe to be quite sure it contained nothing that I should be sorry to give an account of should the Master come at once. The result was that the library was considerably diminished to the benefit of some poor neighbors and to the far greater benefit of my own.

I also found I had articles of clothing which might be put to better advantage in other directions. It has been very helpful to me from time to time through life, as occasion has served, to act again in a similar way. I have never gone through my house from basement to attic, with this object in view, without receiving a great increase of spiritual joy and blessing.

(James Hudson Taylor, *A Retrospect (Updated Edition): The Story Behind My Zeal for Missions*, Aneko Press)

George Müller said regarding this wonderful truth: "When it pleased God in July, 1829, to reveal to my heart the truth of the personal return of the Lord Jesus, and to show me that I had made a great mistake in looking for the conversion of the world, the effect that it produced upon me was this: From my inmost soul I was stirred up to feel compassion for perishing sinners, and for the slumbering world around me lying in the wicked one, and considered, 'Ought I not to do what I can for the Lord Jesus while He tarries, and to rouse a slumbering church?'"

> **"You know the time, that the hour has come**
> **for you to wake from sleep.**
> **For salvation is nearer to us now**
> **than when we first believed."**

> **Romans 13:11**

> *Do you really expect the Lord to return very soon, or do you think it will take at least another ten years? How does it show in your life that you really expect Him to come soon? What concrete effects does this hope have on your life?*

Notes:

....

....

....

....

....

....

....

....

....

....

....

....

....

....

....

....

....

....

....

Striving in Prayer

"I appeal to you, brothers, by our Lord Jesus Christ and by the love of the Spirit, to strive together with me in your prayers to God on my behalf, that I may be delivered from the unbelievers in Judea." (Romans 15:30–31)

Often we pray for specific issues because we are aware of needs and wants. Surely the believers in Rome also prayed for Paul because he asked them and gave them a specific request, but there are also situations where we do not know the exact needs or wants of others and God still wants us to pray for them at the right time. Sometimes, through the Holy Spirit, He suddenly puts a prayer request on our hearts to pray for spontaneously. When we feel a burden to pray for someone we should definitely do it as soon as possible.

Here are two examples that underline this:

One night at midnight Mrs. Ed Spahr was awakened and burdened for missionary friends Rev. Jerry and Mrs. Rose in Dutch New Guinea [now part of Indonesia] working among stone-age culture people. She was so burdened for him she prayed and next morning wrote a letter telling of it.

Later it was learned that he received prayer letters from five prayer partners in five continents saying they prayed for him on that specific occasion. By adjusting the dateline and time span it was seen that they all prayed at the same time—at that very time Mr. Rose was standing with his arms tied behind his back and a huge "stone-age" savage standing before him with a spear ready to pin him to the ground. As five prayer partners on five continents prayed, another man in the tribe (there were no Christians in the tribe at the time) spoke to the man and he walked away.

...

Isabel Kuhn tells how she and her husband were experiencing great opposition in a heathen village in South China. The people were deeply convicted but could not break from their sinful customs.

Then something happened. "The last two days, without any explanation that we could discover, a sudden and astounding change took place," she wrote. Glorious victories were gained and quarrels settled. They did not know it, but a letter giving the explanation was already on the way. She had noted the date in her diary and said to her husband, "I am sure someone in the homelands is specially praying for us." Two months passed, and then a letter. "John," she said, "you read this while I get my diary." This is what he read:

A persistent spirit brings a man to the place where faith takes hold, claims and appropriates the blessing.
(Edward M Bounds)

'I must write and tell you what happened today. All morning I could not do my housework because of the burden on me concerning Three Clan Village. So finally I went to the telephone and called Mrs. W. She said she had been feeling the same way and suggested we call Mrs. J. and all go to prayer together. We did so, each in her own kitchen. We spent the morning in intercession for three quarrelling clans. We feel God has answered. You will know?'

The date in the diary corresponded exactly with the victory gained in Three Clan Village.

(J Oswald Sanders, *The Power of Transforming Prayer*, Our Daily Bread Publishing)

> ***Do you have an awareness that God has given you a prayer burden for someone or something? What experiences have you had in this regard? Be sensitive to the working of the Spirit in you and obey His voice when He asks you to pray for a specific matter!***

Notes:

....

....

....

....

....

....

....

....

....

....

....

....

....

Never Alone!

"Behold, I am with you always, to the end of the age."
(Matthew 28:20)

God's promises are like an anchor for the soul. They give us support and security in the storms we go through. This is especially true when we're lonely and there's perhaps no one around us who understands us or who can just sympathise with how we feel.

When God gave Moses a commission, He also gave him the promise: "I will be with you" (Ex. 3:12). Moses then set out and did mighty things "by the hand of the angel who appeared to him in the bush" (Acts 7:35). Later, when the man of God gave the staff to Joshua, he received the promise, "Just as I was with Moses, so I will be with you. I will not leave you or forsake you" (Josh. 1:5).

Gideon, who was to deliver the people from the Midianites, and Jeremiah, who had the difficult task of prophesying among the people of God, also heard the words of the LORD: "I will be with you" (Jud. 6:16; see Jer. 1:8). When God calls us to do something, we can be sure that He will be with us until we have fulfilled the commission.

The Son of God gave His disciples the command to go into all the world and make disciples of all nations. Immediately afterwards He assured them that He would be with them (see Mt. 28:20). In the Gospel of Mark it is said: "And they went out and preached everywhere, while the Lord worked with them and confirmed the message by accompanying signs" (Mk. 16:20). Wonderful! The Lord was involved—and He did not abandon them!

Over the centuries, many Christians have found deep comfort and encouragement in the words of Jesus: "Behold, I am with you always". In this context, the story of John Paton, who firmly relied on this promise of the Lord, is impressive:

His courage came through his personal fellowship with Jesus. The beauty of this fellowship reached its highest and deepest forms when

> **Courage is fear that has said its prayers.**
> (Karle Wilson Baker)

Christ's promises reached a troubled missionary hovering on the edge of eternity. The promise was given directly in the context of the Great Commission: "Go therefore and make disciples of all nations ... And behold, I am with you always, to the end of the age" (Mt. 28:19–20). More than any other promise, this promise gave John Paton, in all his dangers, the certainty that the Lord Jesus Christ was very near and was really at his side.

After the measles epidemic, which killed thousands in the islands and for which the missionaries were blamed, he wrote:

During the crisis I felt calm and firm of soul, standing erect and with my whole weight on the promise, "Lo, I am with you." Precious promise! How often I adore Jesus for it and rejoice in it! Blessed be His name.

The power of this promise was that Christ was real to Paton in crisis situations. It was far greater than any other scripture or prayer:

Without that abiding consciousness of the presence and power of my dear Lord and Saviour, nothing else in all the world could have preserved me from losing my reason and perishing miserably. His words, "Lo, I am with you I, even unto the end of the world," became to me so real that it would not have startled me to behold Him, as Stephen did, gazing down upon the scene.

I felt His supporting power, as did St. Paul, when he cried, "I can do all things through Christ which strengthened me." It is the sober truth, and it comes back to me sweetly after twenty years, that I had my nearest and dearest glimpses of the face and smile of my blessed Lord in those dread moments when musket, club, or spear was being directed at my life. Oh the bliss of living and enduring, as seeing "Him who is invisible!"

(John G Paton, *The Story of John G Paton: Or Thirty Years as a Missionary Among South Sea Island Cannibal Tribes, An Autobiography*)

> **What reasons does God give you in His Word for not being afraid when He sends you to a new place? What does it mean when God says He is with someone? Do not be afraid when God calls you! "My presence will go with you, and I will give you rest" (Ex. 33:14).**

Notes:

....
....
....
....
....
....
....
....
....
....
....
....
....
....
....
....
....
....
....
....
....
....
....
....
....
....
....
....

Have the Requests of God on Your Heart

"And this is the confidence that we have toward him, that if we ask anything according to his will he hears us. And if we know that he hears us in whatever we ask, we know that we have the requests that we have asked of him." (1 John 5:14–15)

It often happens during their prayers that believers get the conviction that the Lord has put a certain request on their hearts. As they make this request in prayer, they get peace that God will surely hear it, but only if they have a clear conscience, live in fellowship with the Lord, submit to His will and make Him the centre of their lives (1 Jn. 3:21–22; John 15:7). As David wrote in Psalm 37, "Delight yourself in the LORD, and he will give you the desires of your heart" (Ps. 37:4).

Amy Carmichael applied the words of 1 John 5:14–15 to her life in a very practical way. She longed, as she prayed, to speak out the requests that came from God Himself, and then to see Him answer those prayers. When she was a missionary in Japan many years ago, she had this experience several times. She did not pray at random, but let herself be guided by the Spirit of God:

The first place in Japan which I really loved was Hirose, a large, almost purely Buddhist village. The eight or nine Christians there, fruit given to Matsuye workers, were scattered in that dark village like stars in the night. Before going for the first time I spent a day alone with God. The thought had come, if only I could be sure of what He wanted me to ask for, then I should have no doubt in asking for it. So I wanted to take time to know His mind.

At last I seemed pressed in spirit to ask for a soul, one soul. Next day Misaki San and I set forth together. One young silk weaver gave up a day's weaving that she might have time to listen and understand. She crossed the line that evening. That joy is alive in me now.

A month passed and we went to Hirose again. This time it was laid on my heart to ask for two souls. Three others joined in this prayer. When we reached the village the young silk weaver, saved in November, brought another. She had just found peace when we were called to go to an old woman who wanted to hear. She also turned to the Lord. These we left in loving hands, for there was a dear old Christian there who was a true under-shepherd, and in Japan, unlike India, no one was turned out of the house because of being a Christian.

A fortnight later we went again. Four souls had been laid on our hearts. By this time our fellow-workers in Matsuye were much with us in prayer. The rickshaw ride was through deep snow, and we arrived cold and tired. Very few came to the meeting. The Christians felt four too many to ask for. And where were they? We did not know.

Next day we were out visiting most of the day. We found no one the least interested. One could almost see the devil, one could almost hear him laugh. And then came the thoughts, the wiles which cling, and twist, and entwine one. "So much for being sure of the Shepherd's Voice. Next time better wait and see, before telling everybody. You can't expect conversions every time you come. It's quite presumptuous. Fancy going back to Matsuye empty-handed! What a pity you told them about the four." But worst of all was the fear that I had missed His will after all. It looked very like it.

The afternoon, upon which I had unconsciously counted so much, was gone; I was at the very end of my resources. Prayers and pleadings alike seemed to rebound like balls hitting a stone wall. The listeners sat and gazed and smiled, and felt nothing. With a sort of blind longing to rush away into the darkness and lose oneself in the snow, and forget, I was rising to bow myself out of what seemed like a prison of mocking spirits, when there was a sudden sense of a presence gone, and a Presence come.

We sat down again, and a hush rested upon us. Then almost without preface one of the women who had been listening carelessly before, said quietly, "I want to believe." While we were talking to her, a young man, her son, came in and knelt down. Within half-an-hour, mother and son were both Christ's.

To faith that which is unseen becomes as near and as real as though present to sight (v. 1); yea, much more so; because there is deception in seen things; but there is no deception in things communicated by the Spirit to the heart.
(John Nelson Darby)

Then we came away, and as we passed one of the Christians' homes, we went in to tell them. They said they had one more waiting for us at the preaching room: would we go to see her at our honourable convenience? She was another brought by our first, and she, too, trusted the Lord Jesus, and was saved.

By this time all the Christians had assembled. We told them we knew God's fourth must be somewhere, and one man exclaimed, "Why, it must be my wife. She wants to be a Jesus-person, but she is away at her own village." Early next morning a message came to say the wife had unexpectedly returned. We went to see her. Before her family and relations she confessed her desire to be a Christian, and there and then she too "was illuminated." And they all, with one consent, praised the Lord.

These four were the first birthday gifts I ever had from heathendom. That day was December 16th, 1893.

Towards the end of January, 1894, we went to Hirose again. For a fortnight the pressure that I could not resist, had been on me to ask and receive according to 1 John 5:14–15 eight souls from among the Buddhists of Hirose—that was the petition then. And once again Matsuye stood behind us in prayer.

We found the Christians very happy about the one, two, and the four, but they were not prepared for this. To pray for things and not receive them "would be a very bad happening; better just pray for a blessing, then there would be no disappointment". We offered to stay longer so as to give God more time to find the eight, but they said they could not arrange for more meetings. No, better be content with a blessing. But

> Whoso hath felt the Spirit of the Highest,
> Cannot confound, nor doubt Him, nor deny.

So we read the great prayer promises with the group of Christians, and the dear old under-shepherd said slowly "You are a Jesus-walking one; if His voice speaks to you, though it speaks not to us, we will believe." And then, opening their Bibles at Jeremiah 32:27 and 17, they kept them open there, and prayed. Before they left the room we were all of one mind.

It would take too long to tell how the eight were given. It was like watching an invisible Hand at work. The last was a proud old grandfather who for fifty years had been a slave to sin. Kneeling *before all he prayed, "Honourable God, deign to forgive me, deign to wash." It was nearly midnight (meetings are late in Japan), but it felt like the dawn of the morning, so happy and fresh of heart were we.*

And afterwards? I wonder if you feel the almost breathless feeling that was mine as I prepared to go to Hirose in February. Would sixteen be the number laid on me to ask? No, there was no number at all laid on my heart. I think the Christians were surprised. They had been so keyed up with the joy of the eight that they were ready for anything; but instead of that we were led to have a time of prayer with them all, Christians and any Buddhist friends who had come with them.

At the end they separated into two groups. The Christians drew together into a corner and prayed, and the Lord hearkened. I do not know how many turned to Him for the first time that night. I only know that the Christians were too full of joy for speech, and we parted in a sort of singing silence.

(F Houghton, *Amy Carmichael of Dohnavur*, Christian Literature Crusade)

Critics may claim that Amy Carmichael put pressure on God through her behaviour. Why is this not true? Why can we become God's co-workers when we pray? How can you reach the point of having the requests that come from God on your heart?

God Is Faithful!

"And now I am about to go the way of all the earth, and you know in your hearts and souls, all of you, that not one word has failed of all the good things that the LORD your God promised concerning you. All have come to pass for you; not one of them has failed." (Joshua 23:14)

God wants us to take His Word and promises seriously. How can we show Him that we do? By reminding Him again and again in prayer, with confidence, what He has promised. The psalmist did this and said: "Remember your word to your servant, in which you have made me hope. This is my comfort in my affliction, that your promise gives me life" (Ps. 119:49–50).

We also see this in connection with the people of Israel: God had given them the promise that He would one day restore them and make them the centre of blessing on earth. Despite this—or rather, precisely because of this—Isaiah challenges them to remind the LORD of His promises: "You who put the LORD in remembrance, take no rest, and give him no rest until he establishes Jerusalem and makes it a praise in the earth" (Isa. 62:6–7).

David also took God at His word in this way. When he received a promise from God through the prophet Nathan, he prayed afterwards: "And now, O LORD God, confirm forever the word that you have spoken concerning your servant and concerning his house, and do as you have spoken. ... For you, O LORD of hosts, the God of Israel, have made this revelation to your servant, saying, 'I will build you a house.'

Therefore your servant has found courage to pray this prayer to you. ... Now therefore may it please you to bless the house of your servant, so that it may continue forever before you. For you, O Lord GOD, have spoken, and with your blessing shall the house of your servant be blessed forever" (2 Sam. 7:25, 27, 29).

Solomon then takes up God's promises to David in prayer and says: "Now therefore, O God of Israel, let your word be confirmed, which you have spoken to your servant David my father" (1 Ki. 8:26).

> The days of a Christian's life are like so many Kohinoors [a large diamond] of mercy threaded upon the golden string of divine faithfulness.
> (Charles H Spurgeon)

God likes it when we remind Him in prayer of His faithfulness to His promises and ask Him to make them come true. That's why it's not impudent or disrespectful, but a sign of living faith when we pray, "You have said," and then present God with His promises. We must take Him seriously—and calmly trust in His Word! "My soul longs for your salvation; I hope in your word. ... You are my hiding place and my shield; I hope in your word" (Ps. 119:81, 114).

When the well-known missionary David Livingstone made his first trip to Africa, some friends accompanied him to the ship to bid him farewell.

Because they loved him, they were worried about his safety in the foreign country. One of them tried to persuade him at the last minute not to make the journey. Livingstone, however, was convinced that it was God's will that He should go. He opened his Bible and read the words of Jesus to his friends who were worried about him: "I am with you always, to the end of the age"! Then Livingstone said, "This, my friends, is the word of a man of honour. Let us therefore go."

Many years later he was invited to speak at Glasgow University. There he asked the audience the following question: "Do you want me to tell you what was the greatest help to me during all those years of exile among people whose language I didn't understand and whose attitude towards me was always uncertain and often hostile? It was the word of Jesus: 'I am with you always, to the end of the age'. On this word I risked everything, and I was never disappointed!"

Once we're in glory and look back on our lives, we will say with full conviction: "Not one word of all the good promises that the LORD had made ... had failed; all came to pass" (Jos. 21:45).

> *To what extent do you pray for God to make His promises a reality in your life? What are the reasons that prevent you from taking God at His word and taking steps of faith? God says: "I am watching over my word to perform it" (Jer. 1:12).*

The Direction of Faith

The Giver of the Promise

"When they lifted up their eyes, they saw no one but Jesus only." (Matthew 17:8)

Living faith does not only focus on the promise of God, but it has God Himself before its eyes. I not only believe in the promises of the Bible, but I put my trust in the living God, the Author of the Holy Scriptures. Faith trusts that He is worthy of that trust. Trusting God is the most rational, healthy and logical thing a person can do.

Jeremiah speaks of this very thing when he says: "Blessed is the man who trusts in the LORD , whose trust is the LORD" (Jer. 17:7). For us, this means that we not only rely on the words and promises of Jesus, but that we make Him the focus of our trust! We have Him before our eyes—that gives us courage and strength! Strength does not lie in faith, but in the One towards whom faith is directed.

Several times in the Word of God, Abraham is presented to us as an example of faith. That's why it is very instructive to see what his faith was focused on. Paul writes about this in his epistle to the Romans: Abraham believed "the God ... who gives life to the dead and calls into existence the things that do not exist" (see Rom. 4:17). At the age of 99, the patriarch came to know God as the Almighty (Gen. 17:1). This new knowledge of his Creator strengthened his faith and directed his gaze away from himself and towards the great El-Shaddai.

In Job we see something similar: after having received a deep impression of the greatness and glory of God, he said, "I had heard of you by the hearing of the ear, but now my eye sees you" (Job 42:5). What does he conclude from this? "I know that you can do all things, and that no purpose of yours can be thwarted" (Job 42:2).

The more the Giver of the promise is before our eyes, the more we will lean in faith on what He has promised! Therefore, we should be very occupied with the greatness, the power and the sovereignty of God. This will help us to grow in faith, to trust God more and to have more confidence in Him.

David was the man after God's own heart in the Old Testament. He had a deep awareness of the greatness of God and said, "Great is the LORD, and greatly to be praised, and his greatness is unsearchable" (Ps. 145:3). He also desired to see God and to have His beauty before his eyes (see Ps. 27:4). He knew how crucial the right direction of vision is, which is why he wrote: "Those who look to him are radiant, and their faces shall never be ashamed" (Ps. 34:5).

> **You do not need a great faith, but faith in a great God.**
> (James Hudson Taylor)

If an Old Testament man could speak like that, how much more should it be the case with us! Why? Because we know that a glorified Man is now at the right hand of God. With the eyes of our heart we can already see Him in faith, as it is written: "We see ... Jesus, crowned with glory and honour" (Heb. 2:9). That is why we are expressly encouraged to do just that: "Looking to Jesus, the founder and perfecter of our faith, who ... is seated at the right hand of the throne of God" (Heb. 12:2).

The secret of our failure is that we see people instead of God. The Roman Church trembled when Luther saw God. The "great revival" broke out when Jonathan Edwards saw God. Scotland was overcome when John Knox saw God. The world became one man's church when John Wesley saw God. Great multitudes were saved when Whitefield saw God. And He is "the same yesterday, today and forever".

(*Der kniende Christ* [The Kneeling Christian], Herold Verlag)

Particularly in the Book of Isaiah, it is emphasised again and again that God is unique and incomparable—in contrast to the idols that people have invented. When the people of Israel at the time of Elijah ran after one of these idols, the rain god Baal, the eternal Creator revealed that He stands high and exalted above all gods. How did He do that? By dropping fire from the sky and then opening the windows of heaven—whereupon torrential rain fell.

Watchman Nee once had a special experience in this regard when he preached the gospel in China together with other preachers:

The holiday celebrations in the Chinese village of Mei-hua were in full swing. Families made ceremonial visits and burned incense to their ancestors. Men laughed and gambled. Huge feasts were prepared and offerings were made to the household gods. And at night, fireworks lit up the sky.

Watchman Nee and six other young preachers tried to share the gospel with the noisy holiday crowds. They spread out around the town and preached on the street corners. A few villagers stopped to listen, but most people hurried by. Finally on the ninth day, Li Kuo-ching, the youngest preacher and a new believer himself, cried in frustration to the crowd, "What's wrong? Why won't you believe?"

A villager shrugged. "Why should we? We have our own god, Tawang [Great King]. His feast day is two days away. And for 286 years Ta-wang has sent sunshine for his feast day without fail. He's very dependable."

"Then I promise you," cried Li, "our God, who is the true God, will make it rain on Ta-wang's feast day."

Immediately, the villagers were interested. It was like a game, a contest. "Agreed!" they cried. "If it rains on Ta-wang's feast day, then your Jesus is indeed God. We will be ready to hear about Him."

The news of Li's challenge spread rapidly all over the village. When Watchman Nee heard it, he was horrified. Li was young and inexperienced. He had put God's honour to the test in a reckless way. What if God did not choose to make it rain on the feast day? If it did not rain, no one would listen to them preach about Jesus in the future.

But that night as the young men prayed, Watchman sensed God speaking to him: "Where is the God of Elijah?" In the Bible, Watchman remembered, the prophet Elijah had challenged the priests of Baal to a similar contest. Both Elijah and the pagan priests had built altars and sacrificed an animal. Elijah even poured buckets of water over his sacrifice. But only Elijah's God, the one true God, had sent fire to burn up the sacrifice.

Now all seven young men got excited. They felt sure that the God of Elijah whom they preached would send rain on Ta-wang's feast day.

When the little band of preachers woke up on the feast day of Ta-wang, sunshine streamed through the windows. Watchman was tempted to pray, "Oh, Lord, please make it rain!" but the still, small voice just said, "Where is the God of Elijah?" So instead of begging God, the young men just settled down to eat their breakfast. As they bowed their heads to thank God for the food, rain pattered on the window tiles. As they finished their first bowl of rice, it was coming down in a steady shower. As they began their second bowl of rice, the rain had become a downpour.

At the first sign of rain, some of the villagers said, "Jesus is God! There is no more Ta-wang!" But Ta-wang's worshippers insisted on carrying their idol in a parade anyway. Surely their god would stop the rain on his feast day! But by this time the streets were flooded, and the parade marchers stumbled and slipped. Down went the idol, cracking its jaw and left arm as it fell.

By now the whole village was eager to listen to the gospel. Satan's power had been broken when the idol fell.

(Dave & Neta Jackson, Hero Tales, Vol. 2, Castle Rock Creative, Inc.)

"For who is God, but the Lord?
And who is a rock, except our God?—
the God who equipped me with strength
and made my way blameless."

Psalm 18:31–32

> *In what ways does God show today that He is absolutely unique and incomparable? How often do you think about the greatness, the power and the sovereignty of God? How can you make the Lord the centre of your confidence?*

Notes:

....

....

....

....

....

....

....

....

....

....

....

....

Abraham's Eye of Faith

With the creatorial power of the Eternal in mind, Abraham believed the God "who gives life to the dead and calls into existence the things that do not exist" (Rom. 4:17). What is special about his faith is the deep trust that God is able to bring life out of death—although up to that point no human being had ever been raised from the dead.

We have it much easier today because we know the end of this story. Moreover, we know that God the Father raised His unique Son from the dead through His glory (Rom. 6:4). This exact divine power has also worked on us. Paul calls it "the immeasurable greatness of his power toward us who believe, according to the working of his great might" (Eph. 1:19).

Creation is a testimony to the eternal power of God (see Rom. 1:20). It gives us a glimpse of what the Almighty is able to do. When we look at the things God has created, it should encourage us to trust Him in every situation of our lives. As the psalmist aptly says: "I lift up my eyes to the hills. ... My help comes from the LORD, who made heaven and earth" (Ps. 121:1–2).

> My eye is not on the density of the fog, but on the living God who controls every circumstance of my life.
> (George Müller)

When we see our problems and difficulties in the light of God's greatness, we gain hope and confidence, for the need is not greater than the helper.

George Müller had a clear view of precisely this. He didn't look at the circumstances, but at the One who is above the circumstances and rules over everything. Once, when he was on his way to America by ship, the following happened:

Although the Atlantic was rough, the ship remained on schedule until running into thick fog off Newfoundland. Captain Dutton had been on the bridge for twenty-four hours when George Müller appeared at his side.

'Captain, I have come to tell you that I must be in Quebec by Saturday afternoon.'

'It is impossible,' said the captain.

'Very well,' said Müller, 'if your ship cannot take me, God will find some other way—I have never broken an engagement in fifty-two years. Let us go down into the chart-room and pray.'

Captain Dutton wondered which lunatic asylum Müller had escaped from.

'Mr Müller,' he said, 'do you know how dense the fog is?'

'No, my eye is not in the density of the fog, but on the living God who controls every circumstance of my life.'

Müller then knelt down and prayed simply. When he had finished the captain was about to pray, but Müller put his hand on his shoulder.

'Do not pray. First, you don't believe He will answer, and second, I believe He has and there is no need whatever for you to pray about it.'

Captain Dutton looked at Müller in amazement.

> **"Some went down to the sea in ships, doing business on the great waters; they saw the deeds of the LORD, his wondrous works in the deep."**
> (Psalm 107:23–24)

'Captain,' Müller continued, 'I have known my Lord for fifty-two years, and there has never been a single day that I have failed to get an audience with the King. Get up, captain, and open the door, and you will find the fog is gone.'

The captain walked across to the door and opened it. The fog had lifted.

(Roger Steer, *George Müller, Delighted in God*, Christian Focus Publications)

> *How often do you think about the Creator when you think about creation? What examples from God's Word can you think of that God would use to strengthen our faith in connection with things He created or cares for?*

Notes:

....

....

....

....

....

....

....

....

Everything Is Possible for the Believer

In the Gospel of Mark we find two very interesting statements of Jesus that are closely connected: "All things are possible with God" (Mk. 10:27) and "All things are possible for one who believes" (Mk. 9:23).

Why is everything possible for one who believes? Because they count on the living God, for whom no single thing is impossible! Faith connects us with the Almighty, for whom there are no limits.

Charles H Mackintosh writes about this:

There is no limit to the blessing which we might enjoy, could we only count more fully upon God. "All things are possible to him that believes." Our God will never say, "You have drawn too largely; you expect too much." Impossible. It is the joy of His loving heart to answer the very largest expectations of faith.

(Charles H Mackintosh, *Notes on Deuteronomy*)

In what context does the Son of God make this powerful statement: "All things are possible for one who believes"? He directs these words to a father who asks Him to heal his son who is tormented by a demon. This should encourage all parents who pray for their children! We can trust the Lord to save them from evil influences and to protect them from the power of the devil.

But we can also apply the words of Jesus to our ministry. When He gives us a commission, we should trust and be sure that He will give us all that is necessary to accomplish the task—even if He has to move mountains to do it.

Edward Dennett has aptly said:

No one goes to warfare at his own charges at any time. His name, indeed, when rightly borne and used, carries omnipotence with it. Thus when the seventy returned to the Lord, they said, "Lord, even the devils are subject, unto us" (not "through," as rendered, but) "in Thy name." "Yea," replied the Lord, "behold, I give unto you power to tread on serpents and scorpions, and over all the power of the enemy." The mission and the power for its accomplishment are thus intimately connected; only faith, faith in activity, is the essential condition for the use of the power.

This truth needs to be earnestly insisted upon at the present time, if there is to be a revival, or recovery, before the Lord's return. It is written, "all things are possible to him that believeth"; we read the words, do not doubt them, and yet we seldom think of the possibility of their being verified in our own experience. A saint of olden time knew the secret when he wrote, "Lord, give what Thou commandest, and then command what Thou wilt."

We are immortal until our work on earth is done.
(George Whitefield)

Even so, for it is only by the Lord's own power that the smallest of His precepts can be translated into practice; while it is equally true that His largest behests are as easy of performance as the smallest, inasmuch as adequate power is ever at the service of faith.

(Edward Dennett, *The Name Above Every Name*)

John Paton, who worked as a missionary among South Sea cannibals, could tell you a thing or two about it:

Over and over this faith sustained him in the most threatening and frightening situations. As he was trying to escape from Tanna at the end of four years of dangers, he and Abraham were surrounded by raging natives who kept urging each other to strike the first blow.

[From John Paton's autobiography:]

My heart rose up to the Lord Jesus; I saw Him watching all the scene. My peace came back to me like a wave from God. I realised that I was immortal till my Master's work with me was done. The assurance came to me, as if a voice out of Heaven had spoken, that not a musket would be fired to wound us, not a club prevail to strike us, not a spear leave the hand in which it was held vibrating to be thrown, not an arrow leave the bow, or a killing stone the fingers, without the permission of Jesus Christ, whose is all power in Heaven and on Earth. He rules all Nature, animate and inanimate, and restrains even the Savage of the South Seas.

(John Piper, *Filling up the Afflictions of Christ*, Inter-Varsity Press)

**"Open your mouth wide,
and I will fill it."**

Psalm 81:10

> *What does it mean that everything is possible for the believer? Why is God honoured when we trust Him? What expectations can you have of God? Are there requests you have not made to God before because they seemed "too big" or "too bold"?*

Notes:

....

....

....

....

....

....

....

....

....

....

....

....

....

....

....

....

....

....

God Is Able!

"Looking up, they saw that the stone had been rolled back—it was very large." (Mark 16:4)

Faith not only clings to the Word of God but clings to God Himself! The Apostle Paul not only knew what he had believed, but he could also say with deep conviction, "I know whom I have believed" (2 Tim. 1:12).

Through the wonderful experiences of faith that the apostle had with his Lord, he gained the boldness to present the riches and glory of God to other believers. He assured the Philippians in view of their financial needs: "My God will supply every need of yours according to his riches in glory in Christ Jesus" (Phil. 4:19). Finally, he encouraged the men who were in great distress with him on the high seas, saying, "So take heart, men, for I have faith in God that it will be exactly as I have been told" (Acts 27:25).

Again and again the apostle speaks of things that God is able to do (see Eph. 3:20; 2 Cor. 9:8; Rom. 11:23; 14:4; 16:25; Phil. 3:21; 4:13). With God's omnipotence and sovereignty in mind, he writes to Timothy, "I am convinced that he is able to guard until that day what has been entrusted to me" (2 Tim. 1:12). God always has the power to make the promises He has given to us a reality in our lives.

In 2 Corinthians 9:8 Paul says, "God is able to make all grace abound to you, so that having all sufficiency in all things at all times, you may abound in every good work". Charles Stanley often had this experience. He repeatedly experienced the way God gives the means needed at the right time to carry out a mission for Him. Here is an example that the evangelist tells himself:

Our high and privileged calling is to do the will of God in the power of God for the glory of God.
(James I Packer)

I had gone down to Hull to collect a few accounts. At the time I was only in a small way of business, and as I was pretty sure to collect the same, I had not taken money with me.

I was at a meeting for prayer and reading the Word, with a few Christians from different places, at eleven o'clock on the Saturday morning. As we were reading, the Spirit of God laid it on my heart that I must go to Scarborough to preach. I went into a room alone, and looked to the Lord in prayer that I might be assured of His will in the matter. He gave me distinct assurance that I must go.

This was a long journey then, via York, and I had not money to take my ticket. But then the Lord knew that. I took my bag, told the friends I was staying with, that I felt distinctly called to go to Scarborough, though I had never been there, and only knew the name of one person there, and I had not money to pay my fare. I named this to no one.

But when God gives faith, it is faith. I left the house, and walked until I was just stepping up to the booking office, when A. J. cried out behind me, "We have just heard you are feeling led to go to Scarborough to preach tomorrow. A brother, Mr. H., desires to have fellowship with you, and has sent you, [I think it was £3] to pay your expenses."

On the way we had a slight collision, exactly at the corner of the carriage where I sat, which was broken through. None of us were injured beyond a shaking. I thought this was surely a token that the Lord would have me speak the Word to some one.

I got into conversation with a young man who was, I judged, going home to die of consumption [tuberculosis]. I found him somewhat anxious about his soul, but thought he had a great work to do before he could be saved. I believe God blessed the message to his soul. "It is finished" was a wondrous new truth to him.

As we drew near to Scarborough, his mother who was with him, was so delighted with the joy and peace of her son, that she begged I would make her house my home whilst I stayed in Scarborough. I thanked her very much, but said I could not do so, as I had just been making a request to the Lord that would hinder me from accepting her kind offer.

As I only knew one name in Scarborough, I had been asking the Lord to bring him to the station, and show me which was he. At last, the train stopped. A gentleman came, and looked very earnestly at me. And the Lord said to me, "That is he." Still I hesitated to speak, and got out of the carriage. He continued to look at me. I thought, how foolish I am to pray, and not to believe God, so I said: "May I ask, Is your name Mr. L.?" "Yes, it is," he said; "is your name Stanley, of Sheffield?" "Yes, it is," I said; "but how do you know my name?" He said, "Mr. J., of Hereford, was expected by this train, to preach tomorrow; and this is the last train, and there is not one in the morning. And as I was feeling disappointed, my eye caught you, and it was just as if a voice had said to me, "That is Stanley of Sheffield: I have sent him."

(Charles Stanley, *Incidents of Gospel Work*, Believers Bookshelf USA)

> *How can you experience that God always gives the means at the right time so that we can fulfil the orders He gives us? Why are there so many places in the Bible where it is said that God can do things? How well do you know the One you have believed and how can you grow in His knowledge?*

Notes:

....

....

....

....

....

....

....

....

....

....

....

....

....

....

....

....

....

Faith Based on Divine Revelation

"When Abram was ninety-nine years old the LORD appeared to Abram and said to him, 'I am God Almighty; walk before me, and be blameless'." (Genesis 17:1)

It is of the utmost importance for our practical life of faith that we keep in mind how God has revealed Himself to us in the New Testament and how we relate to Him.

Abraham knew God as the Almighty who has the power to fulfil all that He has promised. Today we have even more knowledge about the Creator than was the case with Old Testament believers: we know God as the Father of our Lord Jesus Christ and know that He is also our God and Father. He is the unchanging One from whom every good gift comes, the God of all grace who will bring us safely to our heavenly destination, and the only wise God who has a perfect plan for our lives.

Furthermore, we know that the eternal Son of God now sits on the throne as the glorified Man—at the right hand of the Majesty on high. He is the Head in heaven to whom we are inseparably united as His body.

Church history shows us many men and women who have taken steps of faith based on the revelation of God in His Word.

George Müller had the desire that God would prove anew through his life that He has not changed and that the promises of His Word are still fully valid. One day he read Psalm 68:5: "Father of the fa-

therless and protector of widows is God in his holy habitation". In relation to this he wrote in his journal:

By the help of God, this shall be my argument before Him, respecting the Orphans, in the hour of need. He is their Father, and therefore has pledged Himself, as it were, to provide for them, and to care for them; and I have only to remind Him of the need of these poor children, in order to have it supplied. My soul is still more enlarged respecting Orphans. This word "Father of the fatherless," contains enough encouragement to cast thousands of Orphans, with all their need, upon the loving heart of God.

> **"From of old no one has heard or perceived by the ear, no eye has seen a God besides you, who acts for those who wait for him."**
> (Isaiah 64:4)

(George Müller, *A Narrative of some of the Lord's Dealings with George Müller*, J Nisbett & Co.)

The following story, which Abigail Townsend experienced as a little girl with George Müller, shows how concretely God acknowledged Müller's faith.

Early one morning Abigail was playing in the garden on Ashley Down when Müller came out and took her by the hand.

'Come and see what our Father will do.'

He led her into the long dining room with the plates, cups and bowls all laid on the table. According to the account (which may have got somewhat distorted before being written down) there was nothing but the empty dishes on the table. The children were standing waiting for breakfast.

'Children, you know that we must be in time for school,' said Müller. Lifting his hand he prayed, 'Dear Father, we thank Thee for what Thou art going to give us to eat.'

Then they all heard a knock at the door. The baker stood there.

'Mr Müller, I couldn't sleep last night. Somehow I felt you didn't have bread for breakfast, and the Lord wanted me to send you some. So I got up at two o'clock and baked some fresh bread, and have brought it.'

Müller thanked the baker and praised God for His care.

'Children,' he said, 'we not only have bread, but fresh bread.'

Almost immediately they heard a second knock on the door. This time it was the milkman.

'Mr Müller, my milk cart has broken down outside the orphanage. I would like to give the children the cans of fresh milk so that I can empty the waggon and repair it.'

Müller thanked the milkman and the children enjoyed their breakfast.

(Roger Steer, *George Müller, Delighted in God*, Christian Focus Publications)

> **"I do not know how He will bring me through,**
> **but this I do know,**
> **that Jesus, as His Word promises,**
> **will bring me through wonderfully."**

Friedrich Traub (*1873 †1906)

> *What consequences does the awareness that God is your loving Father have for your life of faith? What titles of God in the New Testament show you what He wants to give you? How can you encourage your brothers and sisters in the faith to trust God more?*

Notes:

....

....

....

....

....

....

....

....

....

....

....

....

....

....

....

....

....

....

The Eye of Faith in Prayer

"Those who look to him are radiant, and their faces shall never be ashamed." (Psalm 34:5)

It's very interesting to see the look of faith with which men of God prayed in the Old and the New Testament. Often, at the beginning of their prayers, they focused their mind's eye on the greatness, the power and the glory of God before presenting their requests to Him.

An example of this is Hezekiah. God gives him a wonderful testimony in His Word when He says: "He trusted in the LORD" (2 Ki. 18:5). When the king is threatened by the mighty power of the Assyrians, he prays: "O LORD, the God of Israel, enthroned above the cherubim, you are the God, you alone, of all the kingdoms of the earth; you have made heaven and earth. Incline your ear, O LORD, and hear; open your eyes, O LORD, and see; and hear the words of Sennacherib, which he has sent to mock the living God" (2 Ki. 19:15–16). That very night, God answered this prayer and sent an angel that killed 185,000 enemy soldiers and delivered Hezekiah from his distress.

A few years later, when the army of the king of Babylon besieged Jerusalem, the LORD told Jeremiah to buy a field. Not only that, but the prophet was to announce to the people that houses, fields and vineyards would be bought again in this land. See Jeremiah 32:7–15.

Humanly speaking, the fulfilment of this promise was completely hopeless at that time. Nevertheless, Jeremiah prays with faith and says: "Ah, Lord GOD! It is you who have made the heavens and the earth by your great power and by your outstretched arm! Nothing is too hard for you. ... O great and mighty God, whose name is the LORD of hosts, great in counsel and mighty in deed, whose eyes are open to all the ways of the children of man, rewarding each one according to his ways and according to the fruit of his deeds. You have shown signs and wonders in the land of Egypt, and to this day in Israel and among all mankind, and have made a name for yourself, as at this day" (Jer. 32:17–20).

How does God respond to this trust? He takes up the faith of His servant and says: "Behold, I am the LORD, the God of all flesh. Is anything too hard for me?" (Jer. 32:27).

Jehoshaphat is another example of the same prayerful attitude. One day he is threatened by a huge army that wants to take the Promised Land from the people of Israel. In faith, he looks to the faithfulness and sovereignty of God and says: "O LORD, God of our fathers, are you not God in heaven? You rule over all the kingdoms of the nations. In your hand are power and might, so that none is able to withstand you. Did you not, our God, drive out the inhabitants of this land before your people Israel, and give it forever to the descendants of Abraham your friend?" (2 Chron. 20:6–7).

> **We have to pray with our eyes on God, not on the difficulties.**
> (Oswald Chambers)

Because this man has the greatness and power of God before him, he can pray with boldness: "O our God, will you not execute judgment on them? For we are powerless against this great horde that is coming against us. We do not know what to do, but our eyes are on you" (2 Chron. 20:12). The LORD's answer is wonderful: "Do not be afraid and do not be dismayed at this great horde, for the battle is not yours but God's. ... You will not need to fight in this battle. Stand firm, hold your position, and see the salvation of the LORD on your behalf" (2 Chron. 20:15, 17). That's exactly what happened!

In the New Testament, too, we find valuable examples that spur us on to confident prayer. The prayer life of the first Christians is a real goldmine for anyone looking for exemplary prayers. What do they do when the Jews threaten them? They raise their voices to God with one accord and pray: "Sovereign Lord, who made the heaven and the earth and the sea and everything in them" (Acts 4:24).

The disciples turn their eyes to the great Ruler who sits on the throne and has everything under control. He is the Almighty who rules sovereignly and has everything at His command. How does God respond to this? He makes the earth tremble—and blesses the believers with great power and grace (Acts 4:31–33)!

August Hermann Francke, who founded several orphanages in Halle at the beginning of the 18th century, once found himself in great financial need.

Another time I stood in need of a great sum of money, insomuch that an hundred crowns[2] would not have served the turn, and yet I

---

2   Publisher's note: Old British coin; in today's value around £30 or $37.50. So, 100 crowns is around £3,000 or $3,750.

saw not the least appearance how I might be supplied with a hundred groats[3] . The steward came, and set forth the want we were in. I bade him come again after dinner, and I resolved to put up my prayers to the Lord for His assistance. When he came in again after dinner, I was still in the same want, and so appointed him to come in the evening.

In the meantime a friend of mine had come to see me, and with him I joined in prayers, and found myself much moved to praise and magnify the Lord for all His admirable dealings towards mankind, even from the beginning of the world, and the most remarkable instances came readily in my remembrance whilst I was praying. I was so elevated in praising and magnifying God, that I insisted only that exercise of my present devotion, and found no inclination to put up many anxious petitions to be delivered of the present necessity.

At length my friend taking his leave, I accompanied him to the door, where I found the steward waiting on one side for the money he wanted, and on the other a person who brought an hundred and fifty crowns for the support of the hospital.

(David McIntyre, *The Hidden Life of Prayer*, Christian Focus Publications)

---

3   Publisher's note: Old British coin. There are 15 groats in a crown, so today's value would be around £2 or $2.50. 100 groats therefore is around £200 or $250.

What can help you to pray with more confidence and courage of faith? In what areas have you seen God reward the courage of faith? Think about all the things you can be thankful for—and don't forget to praise God when you pray!

Notes:

....

....

....

....

....

....

....

....

....

....

....

....

....

....

....

....

....

....

....

Coming to Conclusions with Faith—The Love of God

When we are faced with great challenges or massive difficulties, the question we have to ask ourselves is from what perspective do we look at things? Do we look at the size of the problem or the greatness of God? When assessing the problem, do I start with my inability or with God's omnipotence? The right focus makes all the difference!

It's very interesting to see how Abraham reacts when he gets the promise from God that he and Sarah will have a son despite their old age—which, humanly speaking, was impossible. In judging the circumstances, he doesn't start with his own inability but with God. That's why it says: "He did not weaken in faith when he considered his own body, which was as good as dead" (Rom. 4:19).

We see the same faith in Sarah: instead of looking at the circumstances, she looks at God's faithfulness—and believes the One who made the promise (see Heb. 11:11).

Living faith draws conclusions about the circumstances and challenges of life based on what it knows about God, not the other way around. The Apostle Paul did this more than once. In Romans 5 he writes: "God shows his love for us in that while we were still sinners, Christ died for us. Since, therefore, we have now been justified by his blood, much more shall we be saved by him from the wrath of God" (Rom. 5:8–9). If God already loved us when we were still sinners, how much more can we expect that He has only the best intentions for us and will save us from the wrath to come, now that we stand before Him as the justified—washed in the blood of Jesus!

Then the Apostle goes one step further and says: "For if while we were enemies we were reconciled to God by the death of his Son, much more, now that we are reconciled, shall we be saved by his life" (Rom. 5:10). When we were still enemies of God, Christ reconciled us to God through His death.

But now He, the Risen and Living One, to whom all authority in heaven and on earth has been given, sits at the right hand of God as a glorified Man. If He has already obtained such a mighty blessing for us through His death, how much more may we now count on His help, knowing that He intercedes for us as our great High Priest and daily ministers to us (see Heb. 7:25)!

> There is no place that inspires so much confidence as Golgotha. The air on this holy hill heals the trembling faith.
> (Unknown)

Sometimes it happens that someone begins to doubt God's love because of suffering and trials. What are they to do then? In such situations we have to look with the eyes of the heart to the cross again. There God demonstrated His love in an unsurpassable way. What does faith conclude from this? "If God is for us, who can be against us? He who did not spare his own Son but gave him up for us all, how will he not also with him graciously give us all things?" (Rom. 8:31–32). If God hasn't withheld from us the most precious thing He has, then He will surely give us everything else that's good for us!

It is precisely because God loves us unconditionally that we can know that He has only the best intentions for us. Even though we may not understand much of what is happening now, one thing is certain: "We know that for those who love God all things work together for good" (Rom. 8:28).

During the Second World War, when H L Heijkoop was an inmate in a concentration camp in Vught near Eindhoven, he lost consciousness several times. He was then, by God's control, admitted to the sick barracks, where it became apparent that he had developed a stomach ulcer. From a human point of view, his condition was very precarious. He had been losing weight ever since he was arrested, and it was exacerbated by an onset of fever and reduced food intake.

Although he didn't rebel against the Lord inwardly, he wondered why he had to go through all this. When he was later freed by God's grace and was allowed to look at his files, he found out that he was supposed to have been sent to a notorious German concentration camp. A brother he knew who had been sent there had died within a month. But the Lord had guided Heijkoop to have fainting spells and a stomach ulcer at just the right time, so that he could not make the journey because of his illness.

When we one day look back on our lives from glory, we will say with admiration: "Oh, the depth of the riches and wisdom and knowledge of God! How unsearchable are his judgments and how inscrutable his ways!" (Rom. 11:33).

"If we really believe in God's love and omnipotence, we do not need to be afraid that we will not get something that He has intended for us."

Watchman Nee

> *What impact do the words in Romans 8:31–32 have on your life of faith? How can you be of help to other believers who are going through suffering and doubting God's love? What experiences have you had that underline God's promise in Romans 8:28? If you have trusted God in the matter of eternity, then you should also trust Him in the matters of daily life!*

Notes:

....

....

....

....

....

....

....

....

....

....

Coming to Conclusions with Faith—The Goodness and Faithfulness of God

In Psalm 81:10 God says to His people: "I am the LORD your God, who brought you up out of the land of Egypt. Open your mouth wide, and I will fill it". First He reminds them of what He did for them in Egypt, and then He tells them to expect great things from Him. In other words, He says, 'Look at the great things I've already done for you'.

In many instances, the Lord Jesus encourages His disciples to trust in the goodness of God. On one occasion He does it by contrasting divine goodness with human goodness and says: "If you then, who are evil, know how to give good gifts to your children, how much more will your Father who is in heaven give good things to those who ask him!" (Mt. 7:11).

The goodness of people depends on their changeable moods. This isn't the case with God: "Every good gift and every perfect gift is from above, coming down from the Father of lights, with whom there is no variation or shadow due to change" (Jas. 1:17). He is great in goodness (see Ps. 86:5, 15)—and He loves to give! "For as high as the heavens are above the earth, so great is his steadfast love toward those who fear him" (Ps. 103:11).

When we have this wonderful truth before us, we can say with confidence: "You are good and do good" (Ps. 119:68). And because we know God in this way, we may conclude and say like David: "The LORD is my shepherd; I shall not want" (Ps. 23:1).

We're also shown that the Roman centurion, who had great faith, came to a similar conclusion. He says, in effect, to the Lord: 'If I can give orders and people obey me, then it should be no problem at all for You, who are much greater, to give an order to diseases, which then have to obey it and leave' (see Lk. 7:7–8).

Faith is strengthened in fellowship with God and grows through the experiences we have with Him. We see this especially in the life of David. When he was about to confront the giant Goliath, he says with conviction: "The LORD who delivered me from the paw of the lion and from the paw of the bear will deliver me from the hand of this Philistine" (1 Sam. 17:37).

In many Psalms, the man after God's heart describes the answers to prayer that he has experienced. Based on this experience, he trusts God to do great things in the future and says: "For by you I can run against a troop, and by my God I can leap over a wall", and "The LORD is my light and my salvation; whom shall I fear? The LORD is the stronghold of my life; of whom shall I be afraid?" (Ps. 18:29; 27:1).

It's also remarkable how Peter reacts when he sees his Master walking on the sea. He immediately realises that if the Lord can do this, He also has the power to make him walk on water. Therefore, he asks with bold faith: "Lord, if it is you, command me to come to you on the water" (Mt. 14:28). Immediately he hears the voice of the Lord calling him and saying: "Come"!

In the Epistle to the Hebrews we find another important point. There, the writer concludes that we can say certain things because of God's promises: "He has said, 'I will never leave you nor forsake you'. So we can confidently say, 'The Lord is my helper; I will not fear; what can man do to me?'" (Heb. 13:5–6).

> **The more complete our faith is, the stronger we stand in composure, the more we surrender to God's will and trust Him to do what is right in due time.**
> (August H Francke)

If God is able to bring life out of death, then He is still able to revive believers today in ways that we might not have thought possible (see Eph. 3:20)! Therefore, in faith we can pray with the psalmist: "Will you not revive us again, that your people may rejoice in you?" (Ps. 85:6).

David Brainerd, a missionary to the Indians, had God's greatness clearly in mind—and therefore expected great things from Him. How did he express this? Through prayer! His diaries are an impressive testimony of how much time he spent in prayer and with what devotion he lived before the face of God. In this way he became an example for many Christians:

William Carey read Brainerd's life story and was so moved by it that he went to India as a missionary, as did Henry Martyn. Payson read it as a young man of twenty and said that nothing in his life had made such a deep impression on him as the story. Murray McCheyne read it and was struck to the core. The prayer and total commitment of this one man, David Brainerd, did more in the great missionary revival of the nineteenth century than any other power.

The hidden life, a life lived in fellowship with God, trying to get at the source of all power, sets the world in motion. Prayer without faith is nothing but a worthless shell; but with faith it contains the seed for a harvest of millions.

When we depend on an organisation, we get what organisations can achieve. If we depend on education, we get what education can give us. When we depend on people, we get what people can bring about; but when we depend on prayer, we get what God is able to do.

(Lettie B Cowman, *Alle meine Quellen sind in dir* [All my springs are in You], Gerth Medien)

> *What other examples are there in God's Word where believers have judged circumstances in the light of God's greatness? In what areas do you find it difficult to see your circumstances in the light of God's greatness? What kind of example are you setting for others through your practical life of faith?*

Notes:

....

....

....

....

....

The Example of Jesus

In Hebrews 11 we are shown many heroes of faith who have honoured God through faith in certain situations in their lives and whom we can take as examples. But then we are introduced to the One who far surpasses them all: Jesus Christ—the founder and perfecter of faith (Heb. 12:2). The words: "I will put my trust in him" (Heb. 2:13) are like a caption of His unique life, which was at all times characterised by perfect faith.

Again and again, we see Him lifting up His eyes to heaven, having the Lord of heaven and earth before His eyes (Mt. 11:25). He trusts in the sovereignty and power of His Father for the salvation of souls and His preservation in the dangers He faces daily. In Gethsemane He falls on His face and cries out: "Abba, Father, all things are possible for you" (Mk. 14:36). Shortly thereafter He says to Peter: "Do you think that I cannot appeal to my Father, and he will at once send me more than twelve legions of angels?" (Mt. 26:53).

As a dependent human being, He prays and says: "Preserve me, O God, for in you I take refuge" (Ps. 16:1). He has no doubt that His Father hears—and answers—His prayers. At the grave of Lazarus, He says with unshakable trust in God: "Father, I thank you that you have heard me. I knew that you always hear me" (Jn. 11:41–42).

He entrusts Himself to the guidance and power of the Holy Spirit and allows Him to lead Him day by day. The Word of God is a lamp to His feet and a light to His path (Ps. 119:105). He lives by every word that comes from the mouth of God and trusts in its power when the devil tempts Him in the wilderness.

His wonderful trust is also shown in the fact that He always patiently waits for God's time. It is written: "Whoever believes will not be in haste" (Isa. 28:16). We see this in the life of the Son of God: He waits for divine direction and the right time before going to the Feast of Tabernacles (Jn. 7) and also before going to answer Martha and Mary's cry for help (Jn. 11).

> **Our model is the Jesus, not only of Calvary, but of the workshop, the roads, the crowds, the clamorous demands and surly oppositions, the lack of peace and privacy, the interruptions.**
> (C S Lewis)

He lives in the deep consciousness that His Father is always with Him, and also testifies to this before people by saying: "He who sent me is with me. He has not left me alone", "Yet I am not alone, for the Father is with me", "I have set the LORD always before me; because he is at my right hand, I shall not be shaken" (Jn. 8:29, 16:32; Ps. 16:8). The awareness of God's presence fills Him with joy and takes away His fear even in the valley of the shadow of death (Ps. 16:9, 23:4).

Moreover, He knows that God will help Him and that He will therefore not be put to shame (Isa. 50:7). He does not show vague hope, but says with conviction of faith: "He who vindicates me is near. ... Behold, the Lord GOD helps me", "Surely my right is with the LORD, and my recompense with my God" (Isa. 50:8–9, 49:4). Yes, through faith His heart is so filled with the glorious future that He endures the cross for the sake of the joy that lies before Him (Heb. 12:2).

He trusts God during His life, in death by committing to Him His Spirit, under the judgment of God by vindicating His holiness (Ps. 22:3), and in relation to His resurrection. How unshakable is His trust when He says: "Therefore my heart is glad, and my whole being rejoices; my flesh also dwells secure. For you will not abandon my soul to Sheol, or let your holy one see corruption. You make known to me the path of life; in your presence there is fullness of joy; at your right hand are pleasures forevermore" (Ps. 16:9–11).

Faith is a constant and unwavering gaze on Christ.
(Martin Luther)

What an example for each of us! We should follow Him, "looking to Jesus, the founder and perfecter of our faith" (Heb. 12:2).

Incidentally, the Word of God calls us in many places to sing hymns to the glory of God—even in the time in which we are currently living. How could it be otherwise, with such a wonderful Lord! The following incident shows how wonderfully God can use singing for His glory:

It was Christmas Eve, 1875, and Sankey, the famous singer in Moody's crusades, was travelling up the Delaware River on a steamer. It was a beautiful, starlit evening. A large number of passengers were gathered on deck. Someone asked Sankey to sing a hymn. Leaning against one of the ship's great chimneys, he raised his eyes to the starry sky in silent prayer. He wanted to sing a Christmas carol, but almost against his will he was driven to sing "What a Friend we have in Jesus".

Silence reigned. The words and melody sounded in the singer's powerful voice across the deck and the silent river. The audience was deeply touched. After the hymn had faded away, a man with a weather-tanned face approached Sankey and asked, "Did you once serve in the Union Army?"

"Yes," Sankey replied, "in the spring of 1862."

"Do you remember standing on guard on a bright moonlit night?"

"Yes," replied Sankey, most astonished.

"Me too," said the stranger, "but I served in the Confederate army. When I saw you standing, I said to myself: 'This fellow won't get away from here alive!' I raised my rifle and took aim. I was standing in the shadows, completely covered, while the full moonlight fell on you.

At that very moment, you raised your eyes to the sky, just as you had just done, and began to sing. Music, and hymns in particular, have always had a great power over me. So I lowered my rifle.

'I want to wait until he finishes the hymn', I said to myself, 'and shoot him afterwards. But the song you sang then was the same as the one you have just sung. I could clearly hear the words: 'When the enemy's power threatens us and many a storm blows around us...'

When you finished singing, it was impossible for me to shoot you. 'The God who can save this man from certain death must be truly great and mighty', I thought, and had to drop my arm as if paralysed.

Since that time I have travelled far and wide in the world, but when I saw you standing there praying, just as I did then, I recog-

nised you. I was struck to the core by your singing. Now I ask you to help me find healing for my wounded soul."

Deeply moved, Sankey wrapped his arms around the shoulders of the man who had once been his enemy. And that night the stranger found Jesus Christ as his personal Saviour.

(Lettie B Cowman, *Alle meine Quellen sind in dir* [All my springs are in You], Gerth Medien)

> **What can you learn concretely for your life of faith when you think about the life of Jesus? What other passages in the Bible show us something of His confidence in faith? Why is singing praises so important for Christians and how does it affect our life of faith?**

Notes:

....

....

....

....

....

....

....

....

....

The Measure of Faith

Great Faith

"Truly, I tell you, with no one in Israel have I found such faith."
(Matthew 8:10)
"O woman, great is your faith!" (Matthew 15:28)

We live in a world of mistrust of God and hostility towards Him. Against this dark background, the living faith based on the Almighty and His unchanging Word shines all the brighter—and gladdens the heart of God! "Without faith it is impossible to please him" (Heb. 11:6).

God rejoices when we have great faith, because we honour Him when we have great trust in Him and when this trust is shown concretely in our lives. In the Gospels, the Lord Jesus speaks of great faith twice: once in connection with a Roman centurion and a second time in connection with a Canaanite woman. From both we can learn important lessons for our life of faith.

The Centurion's Faith

"Lord, I am not worthy to have you come under my roof, but only say the word, and my servant will be healed." (Matthew 8:8)

The servant of a Roman centurion falls ill and is at the point of death. The commander in chief turns in faith to the Son of God and sends elders of the Jews to Him, asking Him to come and heal the servant.

As soon as he learns that Jesus has complied with his request and is setting out to meet him, he takes another step of faith: he sends his friends to the Lord with a new message. They are to tell Him that He doesn't need to come to his house, because he himself feels unworthy to receive Him. Instead, he asks the Lord—in the place where He is—to simply speak a word and heal the sick person by the power of His word from a distance.

Two things distinguish this man's faith: he trusts in the power and majesty of the Son of God and at the same time gets an impression of his own nothingness. He is therefore deeply impressed when Jesus turns to him in grace. John Nelson Darby has aptly said: "Faith always makes humble, because it exalts the object of faith". Unfeigned faith, which thinks big of God and is impressed by His greatness, also always gives man the right place.

It's interesting to see how the centurion argues. He concludes from what he has recognised of the greatness of the Son of God in faith what the solution to the problem is. His faith in the powerful and effectual word is based on faith in the Person who speaks the word. If he, as the Roman commander, can command his servants to do things, then Jesus can certainly do them, since He is much more powerful! In other words, he says: "Servants wait for my command, but illnesses for yours".

The Lord admires the great faith of this man. During His public ministry, He hadn't found such living and expectant faith in the entire nation of Israel. We can be sure that living faith, which trusts God with much, still causes joy in heaven today!

The centurion doesn't need to see the Son of God in the flesh in order to believe. While the Lord is absent, this man simply trusts in the effectual power of His word and doesn't need any visible signs and wonders. This is where the application to our lives comes in: although the Lord Jesus is no longer on earth today, we still have His living and effectual Word in our hands through which He speaks to us—and which is like a hammer that shatters rocks (see Jer. 23:29).

Great faith comes from recognising how great the Son of God is and trusting that nothing is impossible for Him who has all things at His disposal. A simple faith can often be a very great faith.

> **A little faith will bring your soul to heaven; a great faith will bring heaven to your soul.**
> (Charles H Spurgeon)

T E Koshy writes in his biography about the life of Bakht Singh:

For two years he kept on reading the Bible. During his second reading, he came to the verse in Hebrews 13:8: "Jesus Christ the same yesterday, today, and forever." He had been suffering from nasal catarrh for many years. He had consulted the best English doctors, but they were not able to help him. His eyesight, too, had become very weak. So he prayed, "Wilt Thou heal my nose and give me good sight?"

Next morning when he woke up, he found to his great joy that he was healed. That revealed to him that the Lord Jesus Christ was the same yesterday, today and forever. From that time on, he had the privilege of praying for the healing of many and the Lord wonderfully answered his prayers.

(T E Koshy, *Brother Bakht Sing of India*, OM Books)

Great faith also trusts God to pave the way where—humanly speaking—everything seems hopeless.

A missionary told us long ago that he was in a hurry to return to his mission field after a holiday. But a deep stream that had to be crossed was at high water, and there were no boats available or usable for the purpose.

So he and his companions knelt down and prayed. An unbeliever would have laughed out loud. How could God bring them across the river?

But as they were praying, a huge tree that had been struggling with the river for years began to sway and fall. It just fell across the stream. The missionary said, "The Royal Engineers of Heaven have cut a pontoon bridge across the river for the servants of God.

(*Der kniende Christ* [The Kneeling Christian], Herold Verlag)

> **What characterises the great faith of the centurion? What does it mean to have a simple faith? Why does the Lord rejoice when He sees great faith in us?**

Opposites

"Truly, I tell you, with no one in Israel have I found such faith. ... Why are you afraid, O you of little faith?" (Matthew 8:10, 26)

Shortly after the centurion's great faith is shown, we read in Matthew's Gospel that the disciples are in distress at sea. Unlike the Roman centurion, they don't show a humble disposition, but instead their thoughts revolve only around themselves.

They're afraid because of their little faith, so they wake up the Lord and say, "Save us, Lord; we are perishing". Suddenly the voice of the Son of God is heard. With divine authority He commands the wind and the waves, where-upon there is an instant great silence (see Mt. 8:26). The disciples are so impressed by this miracle that they exclaim in amazement: "Who then is this, that even the wind and the sea obey him?" (Mk. 4:41).

How does the different degree of faith in these two incidents come about? The key lies in the realisation of the greatness of the Son of God and the omnipotence of His Word—and these two points are also very important for us.

In order to show great faith, we must realise anew how powerful our Lord actually is: He is the Creator of the universe. One word from Him is enough to call things into existence from nothing. "For he spoke, and it came to be; he commanded, and it stood firm" (Ps. 33:9). But not only that:

every moment He brings all the things He has created into existence by the mighty word of His power (see Heb. 1:3).

When He entered His own creation, He revealed the power of God by breaking the chains of Satan with one word, casting out demons (see Mt. 8:16), commanding the forces of nature and healing every disease that was brought before Him. Can He still do this today? Yes, because "Jesus Christ is the same yesterday and today and forever" (Heb. 13:8).

> **All things are possible to him that believes. Storms are hushed into a perfect calm, rough seas become like glass, lofty mountains are levelled, when faith brings the power of God to bear. The greater the difficulties, the brighter the triumphs of faith.**
> (Charles H Mackintosh)

> *Once when a sudden and terrific hailstorm was pouring down upon the fields, and likely to occasion serious damage, a person rushed into Bengel's[4] room, and exclaimed: "Alas, sir, everything will be destroyed; we shall lose all!"*
>
> *Bengel went composedly to the window, opened it, lifted up his hands to heaven and said, 'Father, restrain it'; and the tempest actually abated from that moment.*
>
> (David McIntyre, *The Hidden Life of Prayer*, Christian Focus Publications)

Such things certainly don't happen every day; but it would also be wrong to say that God could no longer allow such extraordinary things to happen. He is sovereign—and does what pleases Him (see Dan. 4:32)!

By the way, in the course of church history, the Lord has repeatedly answered the prayers of the faithful through

---

4   Johann A Bengel was an 18th century Lutheran theologian

natural events. Sometimes He also allows natural disasters to happen in order to warn people and save them from eternal destruction. Here's an example:

Then in May 1935, Mr. Loughheed again invited [Bakht Singh] to Quetta. He had a burden for the people there because it was like Sodom and Gomorrah. As Bakht Singh had several pressing invitations from different parts of Punjab and South India for gospel meetings, he was reluctant to go to Quetta because he had already been there for nineteen days in the previous year. He thought it would be more profitable to go to some other place. But as he prayed, the Lord kept on saying to him, "You go back to Quetta." The Lord's ways are always higher than our ways; our safety is to be in His will.

The more he prayed, the more peace he had from the Lord to go back to Quetta for gospel meetings. To his surprise, he found that they had arranged special meetings in the military church building. That was the first and the last time they ever had revival meetings in a military building in Quetta. They arranged meetings during the first week for Indians and the second week for the British soldiers. The Lord began to work mightily. People came from different places, and as there were no buses, they had to come on foot or by horse cart. Even though the fare was expensive for some, large numbers came for every meeting. He began the campaign on the 4th of May, 1935. Bakht Singh was greatly burdened by the spiritually lukewarm condition of the people who were complacent and worldly. Quetta truly resembled Sodom and Gomorrah.

Then an earthquake occurred on the 31st of May, 1935 at 3:00 in the morning. An estimated fifty-eight thousand people were killed in eighteen seconds. They had quite a big gathering the night of the earthquake. In his preaching Bakht Singh had urged the people that God wanted them to come to Him, and that those who wished to respond and be saved should remain behind for prayer. Fifty-eight people, one by one, prayed with great conviction, repenting and asking God to forgive them. A little after midnight, Bakht Singh was in his tent feeling worn out, but he could not sleep. The Lord told him to pray for those who went away without finding salvation. Again Bakht Singh knelt down and began to pray, "Lord, wilt Thou wake them and shake them. Shake them until they kneel down. Those still in their sins, wake them and shake them." At about 3:00 in the morning Bakht Singh was assured that God had heard his prayer and he had peace.

The earthquake occurred at 3:00, just as if somebody came and shook the whole place. Bakht Singh thought that it was not an earthquake but God answering his prayer and shaking the people. His friend next door was actually thrown from his bed. Men and women were crying and shouting, but Bakht Singh stayed on his knees.

After half an hour, his friend came into his tent and told him that there had been a terrible earthquake. The walls of the neighbours' houses had cracked and everything had fallen down. However, nothing had happened to the tent where Bakht Singh was staying. He asked his friend to join him in prayer and they continued in prayer until 5:00 in the morning. They told the Lord that they did not know what had happened, but asked Him to save the souls of those who desired to be saved.

(T E Koshy, *Brother Bakht Sing of India*, OM Books)

As the risen victor of Golgotha, the Lord cries out triumphantly: "All authority in heaven and on earth has been given to me" (Mt. 28:18). He is great in power (see Job 37:23) and His greatness is unsearchable (Ps. 145:3). This is the great and mighty Lord we can trust every day!

He is the "God of faithfulness" who cannot lie, but stands rock-solidly by what He promises. "Has he said, and will he not do it? Or has he spoken, and will he not fulfil it?" (Num. 23:19). In view of His mighty unchanging Word, He says: "My word ... that goes out from my mouth; it shall not return to me empty, but it shall accomplish that which I purpose, and shall succeed in the thing for which I sent it" (Isa. 55:11). We can rely on this promise, especially when we proclaim the gospel—for it is God's power for salvation to everyone who believes (see Rom. 1:16).

Unwavering faith founded on the eternal Son of God and His wonderful Word—what joy for our great Lord!

> *How does the faith of the centurion differ from the little faith of the disciples? What do you trust the living Word of God for and how is this expressed in your prayer life? Should we also pray more like the disciples: "Increase our faith!" (Lk. 17:5)? Realise anew who Jesus Christ is and what His living Word can do!*

The Canaanite Woman's Faith

"Then Jesus answered her, 'O woman, great is your faith! Be it done for you as you desire.' And her daughter was healed instantly." (Matthew 15:28)

An unclean spirit takes possession of a little girl. The mother of the child, a Canaanite woman, comes to the Son of God with her despair. Why does she do this? Because she has recognised that Jesus of Nazareth is the promised Messiah of the people of Israel, and because she knows that He is the only One who can help her in this situation. She begs Him and says: "Have mercy on me, O Lord, Son of David; my daughter is severely oppressed by a demon" (Mt. 15:22).

The Lord sees this woman's faith in so boldly turning to Him in her distress, even though she herself doesn't belong to the people of Israel. But at first He doesn't answer her a single word. Why does He do this? To test her faith.

Does she give up now because of the Lord's silence? No! She doesn't let go and continues to cry out after Him. When the disciples ask Him to dismiss her, the Lord says: "I was sent only to the lost sheep of the house of Israel" (Mt. 15:24). This surely wasn't the answer the woman had hoped for, but she had to learn that the Messiah's ministry was primarily directed to Israel and not to the people of the nations.

How does she react to this apparent rejection? Her faith isn't shaken by it. On the contrary, she falls down before the Son of God and asks: "Lord, help me" (Mt. 15:25). She no longer calls Him the Son of David—that is, with the title

He has as Messiah. In this way she acknowledges that she doesn't belong to His people Israel and that she has no right to His help. Instead of becoming despondent or angry, she submits to Him as Lord, the One to whom everything is at His command and who has authority over her life.

Now the Lord goes one step further in testing her faith. He says: "It is not right to take the children's bread and throw it to the dogs" (Mt. 15:26). He compares her to a dog who is totally unworthy of any kind of help from Him. This was a very humiliating statement for the woman. But Jesus knows very well that with these seemingly harsh words He is not overburdening her faith, but that it will shine all the brighter as a result.

> **Our troubles should be steeds upon which we ride to God; rough winds which hurry our bark into the haven of all prayer.**
> (Charles H Spurgeon)

How many would have left at that moment and given up? Not this woman. It's impressive to see the way she responds to these words. She is submissive and says, "Yes, Lord". Thus, she justifies Him and accepts that when it comes to the matter of merit, she is indeed totally unworthy.

But then she adds a remarkable sentence: "Yet even the dogs eat the crumbs that fall from their masters' table" (Mt. 15:27). She still doesn't give up nor does she lose heart because of the apparent rejection of the Lord Jesus.

She's convinced that the Lord is merciful and great in kindness to all who call upon Him (see Ps. 86:5). From where does she get this certainty? Through her faith. In other words, she says: "Yes, I am a dog and can't ask for anything. But just as men are merciful and allow whimpering dogs to snatch up a few crumbs of bread, so I trust that in Your mercy You will give me something, even though I don't deserve anything".

When the Lord hears these words, He says with deep joy: "O woman, great is your faith! Be it done for you as you desire" (Mt. 15:28). Now that her faith has become apparent in its entirety, there is no stopping Him. He meets her need and honours the faith that counts on what is in His heart and clings to His grace and mercy.

> *How does this woman's great faith show itself? What can you learn from it? Why does the Lord sometimes not answer immediately when we bring a need to Him in prayer? What is the connection between the attitude of this woman and her faith?*

Notes:

....

....

....

....

....

....

Faith and Perseverance

"I will not let you go unless you bless me." (Genesis 32:26)

Even if our faith is small, the Lord helps those who trustingly come to Him with their need. But when, in His divine wisdom, He recognises that someone has great faith, He tests them so that their faith becomes evident and comes to the fore. This is exactly what we see with the Canaanite woman. First the Son of God doesn't answer her at all, then He seems to refuse her plea and finally He grants her request after her unfeigned faith has become apparent.

For about 2,000 years God has been inviting us to come with boldness before the throne of grace, where He wants to give us mercy and grace—and always at just the right time (see Heb. 4:16)! Unlike the pagan woman who didn't have the New Testament in her hands and didn't know God as Father, we as children of God have this wonderful promise firmly anchored in His Word. Let's cling to it by praying and saying: "I will not let you go unless you bless me".

Mercy begins where every legal claim ends. We don't ask because we've earned something, but because we're convinced that the God of all grace is rich in mercy (see 1 Pet. 5:10; Eph. 2:4). This knowledge brings us to our knees—and gives us courage to pray!

Let's learn from this woman's perseverance! When we pray, we should fully trust in the Lord's grace and mercy, which He has in His heart! He loves to give! But sometimes He waits with the answer to prayer, so that our faith may become more clearly evident.

A godly mother was for a long time the only Christian in a large family. For years her husband and nine children manifested no concern about their salvation. The mother gave herself to prayer on their behalf, not only in a general way but she felt drawn more especially to pray for them one by one. Soon after she adopted this plan, her earnestness for their salvation became intense; and soon evidences were given that her prayers were being answered. The first to get converted was her eldest daughter, who was followed by her two eldest sons, and successively at intervals after the same manner the whole family were brought to the Saviour.

But up to this time all her tears and prayers and entreaties had not prevailed upon her husband. After much painful reflection upon his lost condition, she resolved to make one final effort and then leave the case with God. She spent a whole night in prayer with such intense earnestness as she had never experienced before. In the morning she approached her husband with her heart well nigh ready to break with a compassionate desire for his salvation, and said to him, "God has given me all my nine children, but you are still without God and without hope. Will you now at this moment seek the salvation of your soul?"

This question, especially when preceded by a night of intensified prayer, came home to his soul with such irresistible force that he appeared to be paralysed and speechless. When able to find utterance he sobbed out under keen conviction of sin, "I will", and there and then resolved to become a Christian. So remarkable was the change wrought in him that it made a great impression upon the whole district in which he lived.

(Thomas Payne & David Dilling, *The Greatest Force on Earth—The Power of Intensified Prayer,* Moody Press)

> **What do you know about God that encourages you to expect much from Him? What role does the fear of disappointment play when you are faced with the challenge of praying with perseverance and urgency for a certain cause? Be specific, courageous and persistent when you come before the throne of grace!**

Notes:

....

....

....

....

....

....

....

....

....

....

....

Little Faith

Twice in the gospels the Lord Jesus speaks of great faith: in connection with the centurion who trusts that He can heal his sick servant from a distance with just a word, and regarding the Canaanite woman who clings to His grace and mercy with her entire heart and doesn't give up until she receives what she asks for.

But unfortunately, the Son of God has to speak more often about the little faith of people. It's very interesting to see what He considers to be little faith. The incidents in which He addresses the disciples as people of little faith show us what kind of trust the Lord would actually like to see in us—for surely we often don't behave any differently than the twelve who accompanied their Master every day for more than three years.

Little Faith Regarding Essential Needs

"And why are you anxious about clothing? Consider the lilies of the field, how they grow: they neither toil nor spin, yet I tell you, even Solomon in all his glory was not arrayed like one of these. But if God so clothes the grass of the field, which today is alive and tomorrow is thrown into the oven, will he not much more clothe you, O you of little faith? Therefore do not be anxious, saying, 'What shall we eat?' or 'What shall we drink?' or 'What shall we wear?' For the Gentiles seek after all these things, and your heavenly Father knows that you need them all. But seek first the kingdom of God and his righteousness, and all these things will be added to you" (Mt. 6:28–33).

It's impressive that the Lord Jesus first speaks of little faith in the disciples with regard to essential needs, such as food and clothing. Isn't it perfectly normal to worry about financial matters in view of the future? Isn't it just "sensible" to secure ourselves as well as possible in order to have everything optimally under control? Hasn't God given us intelligence for this?

If you leave God's promises aside and look at the whole thing purely rationally, then the answer to this question is a clear "Yes". But the Son of God makes it clear in the Sermon on the Mount that all who serve Him have a Father in heaven who knows exactly what they need—and faithfully and lovingly cares for them.

How easily we become restless when we think about the future! Can it be that now and then we're afraid that things will get out of hand or that we might lack the financial means, the health, the strength or the courage we need to live? As a rule, we don't really include God and His promises in these considerations and we forget that He cares for us and is concerned about us (see 1 Pet. 5:7).

Jesus' words from Matthew 6 ultimately lead to the following statement: If we seek first the kingdom of God but at the same time do not count on God being a loving Father who gives us everything we need to live, then this is little faith.

If the Creator takes care that the flowers, which have a very short life span, are so wonderfully "clothed", how much more will He take care of those who know Him as

Father and in whom the future glory shall be revealed (see Rom. 8:18)! The lily blossoms, withers and is no more. We, on the other hand, are destined to be conformed to the image of the Son of God and to radiate His glory for all eternity.

Even the birds aren't afraid, but instead enjoy the wonderful care of their Creator every day. Since we are far more valuable in God's eyes than the flowers of the field and the birds of the air (Mt. 10:31), shouldn't it be natural for us to completely trust our heavenly Father for our daily needs? We have a living God who is the Sustainer of all people—especially believers (see 1 Tim. 4:10)!

Does this mean that we should just sit at home and put our hands in our laps because God will take care of us anyway? No! Paul writes: "If anyone is not willing to work, let him not eat" (2 Thess. 3:10). God wants us to work—whether it is by pursuing a professional occupation or by otherwise being active in His vineyard. You can build His kingdom in different ways!

The question is what tasks the Lord gives each of us and how He leads us individually. The New Testament makes it clear that, as a matter of principle, working for Christ—and seeking His kingdom—should be our governing thought! However, we should be careful not to compare or judge each other in this area. Every servant stands before his Lord and should let himself be personally guided by Him!

However, God has already given us wonderful promises for consistent discipleship and service for the Lord, even for the present time, and we should trust in these promises. Jesus said: "Seek first the kingdom of God and his righteousness, and all these things will be added to you" (Mt. 6:33).

If someone who serves the Son of God gives up financial advantages in his job in order to be more available to his Master, he will experience that God never abandons him. The Father honours those who serve the Lord (see Jn. 12:26). "He who did not spare his own Son but gave him up for us all, how will he not also with him graciously give us all things?" (Rom. 8:32).

> By God's grace, my eyes do not look at the empty pantries and the empty purse, but at the riches of our Lord alone.
> (George Müller)

For example, a Christian may receive spiritual tasks from the Lord that take up so much of his time that he has to reduce his working hours to 80% or 60%—or even give up his earthly profession altogether. If he does this in faith and in dependence on God, the Lord will ensure that the disciple receives everything he needs to live despite the reduced income. But it takes courage of faith to take such steps!

Evangelist Charles Stanley often experienced that God is faithful and stands by what He promises, even when it comes to finances. The following incident from his life makes this clear:

At the time I kept a store of material for the Sheffield trades, I had only small capital, but desired no more than I had. Indeed, I had learnt that the Lord took special care of His little dependent ones.

I was walking about in my shop, having been absent of late about half my time preaching. I had a bill to pay on the following Monday, and I felt a Christian should always pay as payment was due, but in this case I had not the money, and did not know where it was to come from.

I lifted up my heart in prayer to the Lord about this, and immediately thought of a large stock of emery; I had many casks which I could not sell. I told the Lord about this emery. He said, "Cast the net on the right side of the ship." I said, Lord, which is "the right side of the ship"? Immediately the thought came, He must be the right side of the ship. I then asked the Lord to sell for me the emery, for I could not, and the amount would just meet my need.

Whilst I was in prayer, a man walked into my shop, and said, "Have you any emery to sell?" "Yes, I have," I said; and went and took a pinch of the heavy stock I had to sell and placed it in his hands. "Aye," he said, "this is exactly what I want: how much have you?" I told him the number of casks (a twentieth part as much I had never sold at one time in my life); he said, "We will have it all at the price you name, send it down to our firm to-morrow. And we always pay for all we buy casually on Monday morning."

I said, "I will do so; and now tell me how it is you came here, and how is it you can use this kind of emery? I have tried, and could not sell it anywhere; indeed I ought to have returned it, as it was sent in mistake to me." He replied, "Such and such a grinder told me you had a quantity to sell; we wanted it badly, so I came on to see it. You might well not sell it, as we are the only manufacturers who use this particular kind: we use it for scratching saws for the Russian market." I sent it on, and received just the money I needed.

(Charles Stanley, *Incidents of Gospel Work*, Believers Bookshelf USA)

"Those who seek the LORD lack no good thing."

Psalm 34:10

> *Why does the Lord use so many illustrations to show that God cares for those who seek His kingdom first? How would you define little faith in this context? What role does the Lord's individual guidance play in the work of the kingdom?*

Notes:

....

....

....

....

....

....

....

Little Faith despite Great Promises?

In the Old Testament, Elijah said to the poor widow who was about to run out of food: "Do not fear ... But first make me a little cake of it ... and afterward make something for yourself and your son. For thus says the LORD, the God of Israel, 'The jar of flour shall not be spent, and the jug of oil shall not be empty, until the day that the LORD sends rain upon the earth'" (1 Ki. 17:13–14). That's exactly what happened!

In the New Testament the Son of God says: "Truly, I say to you, there is no one who has left house or brothers or sisters or mother or father or children or lands, for my sake and for the gospel, who will not receive a hundredfold now in this time, houses and brothers and sisters and mothers and children and lands, with persecutions, and in the age to come eternal life" (Mk. 10:29–30). Doesn't this promise still apply today? We look after savings accounts and pensions that offer only small interest rates—and often consider them more valuable than the 10,000% interest promised here by the Lord.

Whoever is willing—in dependence on the Lord—to change their place of residence, leave their relatives or give up possessions in order to preach the gospel in the entire creation may cling to this promise and trust that God will provide for them! How God does this exactly is left up to Him. If He prepares food for the ravens (see Job 38:41) and can even use these birds to feed His servants, does not God have all the means at His disposal to give us what we need? He can use a poor widow (1 Ki. 17) or a rich believer (Isa. 53:9), for all things are His servants (Ps. 119:91).

When Albert Winterhoff gave up his job to preach the gospel full time, it sometimes happened that there was nothing to eat at home. But the Lord provided for His servant in an amazing way, as the following incident shows:

Once again Albert had eagerly shared with those in need. It was Sunday. Mother would have liked to cook something nice for the family, but there was nothing in the house. Albert went into the next room with his son Hans, bent his knees and called out to the Lord.

After getting up from his knees and going into the kitchen, the doorbell suddenly rang. "Mimi", said a voice, "we had invited a family today, but they didn't come, so we would like to give you some of our roast pork and red cabbage. We wish you bon appétit." She gratefully accepted the gifts.

Albert just thought: "Before they call I will answer; while they are yet speaking, I will hear" (Isa. 65:24).

Faith concerns not itself about means; it counts upon the promise of God. To the natural man, the believer may seem to lack prudence; nevertheless, from the moment it becomes a question of means which renders the things easy to man, it is no longer God acting; it is no longer His work, where means are looked to.
(John Nelson Darby)

(Andreas Steinmeister, *Das Leben Albert Winterhoffs* [The life of Albert Winterhoff], CSV)

When God gives us a task, He will always give us every-thing that is necessary to fulfil that task. Paul writes about this: "God is able to make all grace abound to you, so that having all sufficiency in all things at all times, you may abound in every good work" (2 Cor. 9:8). In this context, it's also good to remember the words of the apostle when he presents God's thoughts to the Corinthians about the pro-vision for His servants: "The Lord commanded that those who proclaim the gospel should get their living by the gos-pel" (1 Cor. 9:14). The servant expects everything from his Lord, who has said: "The labourer is worthy of his wages" (Lk. 10:7, NKJV).

On the other hand, those who are served have the responsi-bility to support the servant both in prayer and financially, as it is written: "Let him who is taught the word share in all good things with him who teaches" (Gal. 6:6). This also ap-plies to the local ministry of elders, for the apostle writes to Timothy: "Let the elders who rule well be counted worthy of double honour, especially those who labour in the word and doctrine. For the Scripture says, 'You shall not muzzle an ox while it treads out the grain,' and, 'The labourer is worthy of his wages'" (1 Tim. 5:17–18).

This means that if someone is serving as an elder and giv-ing of their time and working for the Lord in this way, one should prayerfully consider supporting them financially. How large and time-consuming are often the tasks and needs in local churches/assemblies—as well as the visits in the homes, which are so often neglected! Could it not be that these needs would be met more if brothers—depending on the Lord—were willing to reduce their professional working hours to devote more time to these tasks?

As disciples who have a living relationship with the Father and know that He is the Giver of every good gift, who cares for us, we should not be of little faith but lean on His promises in faith!

The same apostle who could say: "I have learned in whatever situation I am to be content" (Phil. 4:11), said with the same conviction: "My God will supply every need of yours according to his riches in glory in Christ Jesus" (Phil. 4:19).

> *Why did the Lord command that those who preach the gospel should also live from the gospel? Why could Paul say with firm conviction: "My God will supply every need of yours according to his riches in glory in Christ Jesus" (Phil. 4:19)? How would you express this verse in your own words? To what extent is the concern that your standard of living might change if you seek first the Kingdom of God an obstacle to giving yourself wholly to the Lord?*

Notes:

....

....

....

Little Faith in the Storms of Life

"And when he got into the boat, his disciples followed him. And behold, there arose a great storm on the sea, so that the boat was being swamped by the waves; but he was asleep. And they went and woke him, saying, 'Save us, Lord; we are perishing.' And he said to them, 'Why are you afraid, O you of little faith?' Then he rose and rebuked the winds and the sea, and there was a great calm. And the men marvelled, saying, 'What sort of man is this, that even winds and sea obey him?'" (Matthew 8:23–27)

Thirteen men find themselves in a violent storm on the Sea of Galilee. Some of them are experienced fishermen who have been through a storm or two before. But they have never experienced anything like this. The wind is raging. The waves are hitting the boat, which is slowly filling up with water. The fear of drowning is growing. Twelve of them are panicking. For them it's a matter of life and death. Only one of them lies in the back of the boat and sleeps peacefully.

When the peace of God fills a person, his heart becomes as calm as a mountain lake reflecting the sky—no matter what situation he is in. This is the peace we see here in our Lord and Master. The raging storm and the lashing waves cannot unsettle Him, for He could say with firm confidence: "In peace I will both lie down and sleep; for you alone, O LORD, make me dwell in safety" (Ps. 4:8).

What a Person He is! But the wonderful thing for us is that we can experience this very same peace and serenity in every situation in our lives! That's why Jesus later says to His disciples: "My peace I give to you" (Jn. 14:27). The question is what we can do to ensure that this peace actually fills our hearts. We should trust God!

It is impressive that the Lord expects the disciples—and us as well—to firmly trust Him even in such an apparently life-threatening situation and to remain completely calm. Isn't it understandable that the twelve become weak in the knees and are scared to death? Christ judges differently. He calls it little faith that the disciples in these circumstances think more of themselves and the danger than of Him and His power. To think big of oneself and little of the Lord— that is the mark of little faith! If the Son of God is on board a ship, then this ship can't sink—no matter how strong the wind blows and how high the waves are.

How quickly we criticise the little faith of the disciples in this situation. But we have no reason at all to look down on them, because most of us would probably have feared or behaved just like the twelve—even though we theoretically know that the Lord is all-powerful and able to change situations from one moment to the next.

> We would frequently desire to be allowed to pass on our way without trial, but this would involve serious loss. The Lord's presence is never so sweet as in moments of appalling difficulty.
> (Charles H Mackintosh)

Despite their little faith, He responds to their request. With divine authority He commands the raging forces of nature. Immediately there is a great silence. Normally, after a storm subsides, it takes a while before the waves disappear completely, but here it's entirely different. When the Son of God intervenes, He does so perfectly. He is the Lord of peace (see 2 Thess. 3:16)! Therefore, by His divine power, He can also make our fearful hearts completely calm from one moment to the next.

During the storm, the disciples are afraid because they think that it's a matter of life and death for them. But now, as they witness this mighty miracle, they are suddenly terrified. They are so overwhelmed by the greatness of the Son of God that they say with amazement: "Who then is this, that even the wind and the sea obey him?" (Mk. 4:41).

The example of the so-called Moravian believers, which deeply impressed John Wesley, also shows that it is possible to trust God even in such life-threatening situations and to remain completely calm:

On the evening of Saturday 17 January 1736, John and Charles Wesley were sitting with Colonel Oglethorpe and others in the state cabin of the Simmonds, far out in the Atlantic. The sea had been rough and the clouds thickening all day; now the ship pitched. The storm became more alarming every minute.

Suddenly a huge wave "burst into the cabin where we were, with a noise and shock almost like that of a cannon, and after having steeped one or two of us from head to foot, passed through into the great cabin, from whence we at last emptied it out of the windows".

...

Wesley, as chaplain, had been much impressed by a group of twenty-six German emigrants. They were members of the church of the United Brethren, colloquially known as the Moravian Church.

...

The Germans were always cheerful. They undertook servile tasks which the English emigrants were too proud or lazy to consider, and when crewmen or passengers abused or vilified or even knocked them down, they turned the other cheek. At their service they sang hymns of great beauty; the Church of England's metrical psalms sounded tawdry and stilted in contrast.

...

During the days of storm Wesley tried to keep to his rigorous programme but could not throw off his fear as the ship rocked and jarred "with the utmost violence". The gale died down but another struck a few days later. The captain let the ship drive. On Saturday 24 January, at about one in the afternoon, Wesley stepped outside his cabin. A great wave knocked him over. He was "so stunned that I scarce expected to lift up my head again until the sea should give up her dead". He found that he was unhurt, yet "could but say to myself, 'How is it that thou hast no faith?' being still unwilling to die".

On the Sunday evening, with the ship so rolling that he could hardly walk in the companion-ways, he went to join the twenty-six Moravians. He found them joyfully singing one of their magnificent hymns. As they sang, a great sea struck the ship, split the mainsail and poured in between the decks. "A terrible screaming began among the English. The Germans looked up, and without intermission calmly sang on. I asked one of them afterwards, 'Were you not afraid?' He answered, 'I thank God, no.' I asked,

> **"O LORD God of hosts, who is mighty as you are, O LORD, with your faithfulness all around you? You rule the raging of the sea; when its waves rise, you still them."**
> (Psalm 89:8–9)

'But were not your women and children afraid?' He replied mildly. 'No; our women and children were not afraid to die.'"

(John Pollock, *John Wesley,* Lion Publishing PLC)

What does the story of the disciples on the lake have to say to us? Sometimes in life there are violent storms or situations in which everything "gets out of hand" and we are far too overwhelmed to cope. But just as real as the storm is the One who can calm it!

We may know some things about God in our heads which we have read about Him or heard in sermons. But theoretical knowledge alone is not a good foundation for living faith. What really counts in the end is that we internalise what we know about Him in our hearts and therefore firmly trust in Him. Even if we have been converted for years, we should continue to grow in the grace and knowledge of our Lord and Saviour Jesus Christ (2 Pet. 3:18). The more we truly grasp in faith how great and wonderful He is, the more we will truly enjoy the peace of God and His grace in our daily lives (2 Pet. 1:2).

> *"You came near when I called on you;*
> *you said, 'Do not fear!'"*
>
> ***Lamentations 3:57***

> *What storms has the Lord calmed in your life? When He allows such a storm, it is a special opportunity for you to honour Him by trusting Him. He often uses seemingly hopeless situations to reveal His glory and lead you to admiration and worship. Therefore, take courage and do not be afraid!*

Notes:

....
....
....
....
....
....
....
....
....
....
....
....
....
....
....
....
....

Walking on Water

"And after he had dismissed the crowds, he went up on the mountain by himself to pray. When evening came, he was there alone, but the boat by this time was a long way from the land, beaten by the waves, for the wind was against them. And in the fourth watch of the night he came to them, walking on the sea. But when the disciples saw him walking on the sea, they were terrified, and said, 'It is a ghost!' and they cried out in fear. But immediately Jesus spoke to them, saying, 'Take heart; it is I. Do not be afraid.' And Peter answered him, 'Lord, if it is you, command me to come to you on the water.' He said, 'Come.' So Peter got out of the boat and walked on the water and came to Jesus. But when he saw the wind, he was afraid, and beginning to sink he cried out, 'Lord, save me.' Jesus immediately reached out his hand and took hold of him, saying to him, 'O you of little faith, why did you doubt?'" (Matthew 14:23–31)

Here we have another scene on the lake. This time the disciples are alone in the ship while Jesus is on the mountain praying. For hours the twelve men struggle with the opposing wind and fearsome waves. Then suddenly, in the early hours of the morning, something appears on the water. The disciples think it is a ghost and cry out in fear, but in reality it is the Son of God walking on the violent waters, slowly approaching the boat. The next moment they hear a familiar voice calling out to them: "Take heart; it is I. Do not be afraid."

Peter is deeply impressed by the Lord's appearance and His words. Never has he seen a man walk on water. If Jesus can do this, couldn't He also enable His disciple to do the same?

The desire grows in his heart to draw closer to his Master—even if it means leaving the 'safe' boat. In a loud voice he cries out, "Lord, if it is you, command me to come to you on the water". What is the Lord's answer? "Who do you think you are? Do you want to prove anything to the other disciples?" Nothing of the sort! In the middle of the night, only one word is heard: "Come".

About 2,000 years earlier, the God of glory had called out a divine "Come" to Abraham, the father of faith (Acts 7:3)—"and he went out, not knowing where he was going" (Heb. 11:8). Peter now has a clear goal in mind: the Son of the living God. Now that the Lord has called him, there is no holding back. He sets his foot on the water—and observes how he is carried, step by step.

Humanly speaking, in this situation it was recklessness or even madness to leave the safety of the boat and enter the raging sea. There was no precedent of a man ever walking on water. But when the Lord calls, only one thing counts: obedience of faith! Can there be anything better than coming closer to the "founder and perfecter of faith" (Heb. 12:2) through concrete steps of faith?

Faith means not being dominated by circumstances, but acting on God's Word regardless of circumstances. Christ—our goal—determines the way and the actions of those who trust in Him. If He is the One who calls us to walk a certain path, then we can boldly say: "The Lord is my helper; I will not fear" (Heb. 13:6)!

> **The will of God will never lead you there, Where the grace of God can't keep you, Where the arms of God can't carry you, Where the riches of God can't meet your needs, Where the power of God can't sustain you.**
>
> (Unknown)

In no other disciple do we see the courage of faith that Peter displays in this situation. It is the love for his Master that drives him to give up certainties in order to come closer to Him. Every step he takes on the water shows that the Lord is above the laws of nature and has the power to keep people afloat without human security.

What a powerful testimony for the eleven disciples observing the whole thing from the boat—and for every believer who can read it today in the Word of God! We need the Lord's guidance and His divine "Come" to go where He wants us to go.

Of course, this presupposes that we also experience concretely how He speaks to us and makes His will clear to us. He does this in different ways, but often He repeats Himself to assure us that it is Him who is talking to us.

Walter Mauerhofer has repeatedly allowed himself to be led by the Lord in his evangelistic ministry. After he had some wonderful experiences in Yugoslavia and was on his way to visit friends in Vorarlberg, the following happened:

It was around this time that I stopped at a car park just before the Arlberg Pass and walked into the majestic mountain world under a new moon and a beautiful starry sky. Still filled with the miracle of salvation in Yugoslavia, I sang a hymn to the glory of God:

Oh Lord, my God,
When I, in awesome wonder,
Consider all the worlds Thy hands have made,
I see the stars, I hear the rolling thunder,
Thy power throughout the universe displayed,
Then sings my soul, my Saviour God to Thee,
How great Thou art, how great Thou art.

In the silence of this majestic mountain world—I had heard no footsteps, seen no one approaching me—a clearly audible voice spoke to me out of the darkness: "Walter, come to Vorarlberg and preach the gospel". Overwhelmed and deeply frightened, I hurried back to my car. Trembling had seized me.

In the car I prayed to the Lord: "God, when You call me to the ministry in Austria, I wish that a person from this country where You are calling me would tell me in the same words what You have told me." For the moment, I was unable to understand what was happening.

Since my childhood and even more since my serious illness, it had been my most ardent wish to be able to serve the Lord one day. I saw my own inability, my weakness, my brief time of training in view of such a vocation. Yet I was inspired and filled with love for the Lord Jesus, whom I wanted to serve and belong to with my entire heart.

An hour after the miracle on the Arlberg, I reached my friend's house in Nenzing. I had neglected to inform the family of my arrival in advance. I always had the key to the house with me, and

I knew that I was always welcome there. When I arrived, I went to the kitchen. Here I found some sauerkraut in a pot from the day before. I warmed it and sat down at the kitchen table. I couldn't think about going to bed, I was too agitated.

At the kitchen table, lost in thought, I didn't notice at first that the kitchen door slowly opened. Surprised that Robert was still awake, I asked him if I had been too loud. I noticed that Robert was not particularly surprised by my visit. "Isn't it strange," I asked myself, "that after a hard day's work at the ÖBB[5] signal box, Robert is standing in front of me at one o'clock in the night, dressed and looking lively?"

Quietly, Robert told me that in the evening, when he was about to go to bed, he suddenly had a premonition that I would come to them that night. At first he tried to reject this thought, knowing that I was far away from here at the Bible school. As he was very tired, he kept trying to find sleep. But the thought that I would come this night did not let him fall asleep.

When he asked God for inner peace and a sound sleep, he received a clear order from God. That is why he stayed awake and waited for me. After these words, I got up from the table. "Robert, what do you have to tell me?"

"Walter, you are to come to us in Vorarlberg and preach the gospel."

I told Robert what I had experienced almost an hour before at the Arlberg and how I asked God for a person from this country to tell me the words that were spoken to me there in the silence. We embraced each other and cried tears of joy. Together we prayed to the

---

5   Austrian Railway Services

Lord and gave Him all the glory. Now I was sure: the Lord had called me to His service in Austria.

(Walter Mauerhofer, *Eine Saat geht auf* [A Seed Sprouts], CLV)

> **Was Peter's request appropriate or arrogant? How did he honour the Lord by this step of faith? What can it mean for you today in a figurative sense to put your feet on the water? How does God speak to you?**

Notes:

....
....
....
....
....
....
....
....
....
....
....
....
....
....
....
....

O You of Little Faith, Why Did You Doubt?

"But when he saw the wind, he was afraid, and beginning to sink he cried out, 'Lord, save me.' Jesus immediately reached out his hand and took hold of him, saying to him, 'O you of little faith, why did you doubt?' And when they got into the boat, the wind ceased. And those in the boat worshiped him, saying, 'Truly you are the Son of God.'" (Matthew 14:30–33)

Suddenly Peter begins to doubt. His gaze turns away from the Lord and he becomes caught up in the circumstances. He feels the strong wind whistling around his ears and becomes afraid. At that moment, he loses his footing and slowly begins to sink.

At the word of the Lord he had got out of the boat, but now he has lost the awareness of the presence of the Lord—and that is always fatal. When we lose sight of the Lord and the problems and hardships suddenly stand before us like mountains, it pulls the rug out from under us and we begin to falter in our faith.

This is why in Hebrews we are told to look away from everything and fix our eyes on the "founder and perfecter of our faith" (Heb. 12:2). We stand by faith (2 Cor. 1:24) and it is the power of God that guards us through faith (1 Pet. 1:5). Whenever we are in danger of giving in because of doubt, the Lord is able to make us stand (Rom. 14:4).

Charles H Mackintosh has aptly said about the state of the waters: "Faith can walk on rough water as easily as on smooth. Nature cannot walk on either. It is not a question of the state of the water, but the state of the heart. Circumstances have nothing to do with faith, except, indeed, that when difficult and trying, they develop its power and brightness. ... [Faith] lifts the heart above the winds and waves of this rough world, and keeps it in perfect peace."

Good circumstances are not a security for us. Only the Lord can give true security. He has overcome the world—and we overcome the world through faith in Him (see 1 John 5:4). The Son of God, who enabled Peter to walk on the water, and who even today is high above the circumstances, is the object of our faith and the goal towards which we are heading.

Peter is seized by despair and cries out, "Lord, save me!" In an instant, the mighty hand of Jesus is there to take hold of him and pull him out of the water. Isaiah aptly writes: "Behold, the LORD's hand is not shortened, that it cannot save, or his ear dull, that it cannot hear" (Isa. 59:1). Peter fails; but the Lord never fails! His tender mercies are always there when we call out to Him!

> **"Even to your old age I will be the same, and even to your greying years I will bear you! I have done it, and I will carry you; and I will bear you and I will deliver you."**
> (Isaiah 46:4, NASB)

The psalmist says: "When I thought, 'My foot slips,' your steadfast love, O LORD, held me up" (Ps. 94:18). David also experienced this and wrote it down in a song: "He sent from on high, he took me; he drew me out of many waters" (Ps. 18:16).

God will exalt us in due time if we humble ourselves before Him in our affliction, casting all our cares upon Him—for He cares for us (see 1 Pet. 5:6–7)!

Then Peter again hears the voice of his Master saying to him, "O you of little faith, why did you doubt?" Why does Jesus call His disciple of little faith here? Because Peter turns his gaze away from Him and lets the circumstances strike fear into his heart. So the Lord expects Peter—despite the fact that he is walking on the water in the middle of the night with a raging wind and lashing waves—not to be overcome by the circumstances but to keep his gaze fixed on Him alone with firm confidence.

This is what God wants from us too. No matter whether we are going through highs or lows, we should recognise God in all circumstances and trust that He has good intentions for us. Especially when we encounter disappointments, we are in danger of losing sight of the Lord. He wants to draw us closer to Himself especially through problems and trials, just as Peter came ever closer to the Lord through the waves.

Jim Elliot experienced some devastating disappointments in his ministry in South America. The following story shows how he dealt with it—and it is certainly also an appeal to us:

In May Jim went out to Quito to attend the Inter-Mission Fellowship conference and to see me again. We spent a happy two weeks shopping for materials for the buildings in Shandia, and visiting friends, and finally went down to the station in the west jungle where I was working. Of his trip back to Quito on a banana truck Jim wrote to me:

"Of all trips I have made, it was the most difficult, and, for its length, way and above the most expensive. We hadn't gotten much past town when the gas-pump was full of water. At kilometre 106 we

had a flat that held us up in repair until three o'clock. From there to Chiriboga the thing averaged the aching pace of five miles an hour. We arrived at the chain at nine pm and the guard refused to let us pass. Finally after a miserable snooze in the cab I persuaded him to lower the chain at five am. The chofer then encouraged me to take another truck because he was not sure his could make it to Quito.

So I went to get my bag and discovered that it had been stolen. In the long, slow grind up to Chiriboga the conductor had come into the cab because of the rain. Evidently someone had hopped on the cargo bed and thrown off my bag with other baskets belonging to passengers, while we were all huddled thoughtlessly in the front. Keep your eyes open for a green carp, a seventy-dollar camera, light-meter, harmonica, all my coloured slides, boots, nylon shirts and wool slacks. Tell all the señoritas in San Miguel that their letters will have to be re-written and posted by someone more reliable than I am. ...

The Lord gave me victory in the loss, reminding me to be thankful for the abundance of possessions I have had. God knows, and I believe He sent this that I might be weaned more and more from things material—even good, legitimate things—and have my affections set more firmly on Him who to possess is to have everything. Who could ask for more?"

(Elisabeth Elliot, *The Shadow of the Almighty*, Authentic Media)

Back to Peter. It's easy to criticise him from our 'boats' or to shout cleverly after him: "You should just look to the Lord and you won't sink". But you can ask yourself the question: Would you have looked to the Lord with uninterrupted trust when you first walked on the water, in the strong wind and waves, without letting your gaze wander to the raging forces

[Faith] lifts the heart above the winds and waves of this rough world, and keeps it in perfect peace.
(Charles H Mackintosh)

of nature? Would you have ventured out of the boat in the first place?

Circumstances change—the wind and the waves come and go—but "Jesus Christ is the same yesterday and to-day and forever" (Heb. 13:8). If He calls out to us to "Come" and encourages us to take a step in faith, then He will surely bring us to our destination. Those who hope in Him will not be put to shame!

> *Why does the Lord Jesus call Peter "of little faith" in this situation? What would He have expected of him? What is typically the core problem that causes you to falter in your faith from time to time? How do you deal with disappointment?*

Notes:

....

....

....

....

....

....

....

....

....

Little Faith despite Wonderful Experiences with the Lord

"When the disciples reached the other side, they had forgotten to bring any bread. Jesus said to them, 'Watch and beware of the leaven of the Pharisees and Sadducees.' And they began discussing it among themselves, saying, 'We brought no bread.' But Jesus, aware of this, said, 'O you of little faith, why are you discussing among yourselves the fact that you have no bread? Do you not yet perceive? Do you not remember the five loaves for the five thousand, and how many baskets you gathered? Or the seven loaves for the four thousand, and how many baskets you gathered?'" (Matthew 16:5–10)

This is the last incident in the Gospel of Matthew in which the Lord calls the disciples of little faith. He gets into the ship with them and together they sail to the other shore. On the way, the disciples notice that they have forgotten to take bread for the journey or have only one loaf with them (see Mk. 8:14) and begin to reproach themselves.

When they reach the other shore, Jesus warns them against the bad spiritual influences of the Pharisees and Sadducees. But they do not understand what He wants to tell them. Why not? Their worries about material things and their preoccupation with their own failures obscure their understanding of His words. They think only of the food that perishes (see Jn. 6:27), while the Lord thinks of something much more important than the needs of their bodies: protection from false teaching.

Does this sound familiar to you? Can it be that the Lord also wants to say something to us sometimes and we don't understand Him because our inner orientation simply isn't right? How often are we preoccupied with superficial things or material needs instead of concentrating on the much more essential—the spiritual?

> **"I will remember your wonders of old. I will ponder all your work, and meditate on your mighty deeds. Your way, O God, is holy. What god is great like our God? You are the God who works wonders."**
> (Psalm 77:11–14)

When Jesus discerns their thoughts, He asks them some searching questions that speak to our hearts as well:

"O you of little faith, why are you discussing among yourselves the fact that you have no bread?"—In other words: Why do your thoughts revolve around your human failings?

"Do you not yet perceive?"—Have you still not realised that I am the Son of God in whom you can trust without reservation?

"Do you not remember?"—Why don't you think of the miracles I have already done right before your eyes?

"Do you not yet understand?"—Don't you understand what I am able to do? You have seen with your own eyes what I can do. Don't you believe that if I can feed 5,000 men with five loaves, or a crowd of 4,000 with seven loaves, it is no problem at all for me to feed 13 people with one loaf?

"Are your hearts hardened?"—Aren't you willing to learn through the faith experiences you have already had with

me? Mark 6:52 says: "They did not understand about the loaves, but their hearts were hardened".

The Lord's questions make it clear how important it is that we keep reminding ourselves of the wonderful things God has already done in our lives. It can be very useful to write down experiences of faith and recall them from time to time. The psalmist writes: "Bless the LORD, O my soul, and forget not all his benefits" and "Remember the wondrous works that he has done, his miracles" (Ps. 103:2; 105:5).

God challenged the people of Israel at the end of the wilderness journey to remember the things they had experienced with God (see Deut. 8:2). He had given them daily manna from heaven and demonstrated His faithful care on many occasions (see Ex. 16). Nevertheless, they questioned whether God could give the people in the wilderness meat to eat for a whole month (see Num. 11:22).

> **I regret one thing in my life: that I have not kept a diary of God's miraculous answers to prayer in my life and of His miraculous leading.**
> (William MacDonald)

Even Moses shows little faith on the occasion when he says to God: "The people among whom I am number six hundred thousand on foot, and you have said, 'I will give them meat, that they may eat a whole month!' Shall flocks and herds be slaughtered for them, and be enough for them? Or shall all the fish of the sea be gathered together for them, and be enough for them?" (Num. 11:21–22). If Moses had remembered the miracles the LORD had already performed, these questions would not have been necessary. God responds to his little faith with an apt rhetorical question: "Is the LORD's hand shortened?" (Num. 11:23).

He had carried them up to this point as a man carries his son (see Deut. 1:31). For 40 years their clothes had not worn out and their sandals had not worn off their feet (see Deut. 29:5). They hadn't lacked anything (see Deut. 2:7). Just as the Lord had helped them to leave Egypt, He would help them to conquer the land (see Deut. 1:30). They should look back and take courage for the future because of the wonderful experiences they had had with God! "Remember the wondrous works that he has done" (1 Chron. 16:12). This is also true for us!

How often have we ourselves experienced the mighty hand of our Lord and learned that He is kind! But only a short time later we seem to have forgotten everything again. The preoccupation with the worries of life or our own failures often robs us of our view of the invisible—and weakens our trust in the Lord, who always has everything under control.

Instead of making everything revolve around ourselves, let us learn from the past and trust the Lord for great things even today!

> *"He delivered us from such a deadly peril,*
> *and he will deliver us.*
> *On him we have set our hope*
> *that he will deliver us again."*

> **2 Corinthians 1:10**

> *What can obscure your understanding of what God is trying to say to you right now? How often do you think about the miracles of God in your life? What can you learn for the future from the things you have already experienced with the Lord?*

Notes:

....

....

....

....

....

....

....

....

....

....

....

....

....

....

....

....

....

....

....

Disbelief

Loss of Joy Due to Doubt

"Behold, you will be silent and unable to speak until the day that these things take place, because you did not believe my words, which will be fulfilled in their time." (Luke 1:20)

A godly couple asks God to give them a child. But their prayer isn't answered for a long time. One day, as the husband, Zechariah, is ministering in the temple, the angel Gabriel suddenly appears to him.

Gabriel tells Zechariah that God has answered his plea and will give him a son. This son would be the forerunner of the Messiah. He would prepare the people for the coming of the King, as had already been foretold in the prophet Malachi. What a great message! The Lord was going to use Zechariah and his wife to make His plans a reality.

How does Zechariah react to this announcement? Instead of taking God at His word, he doubts the promise. He sees his own inability and therefore doesn't trust God to fulfil His plan through him. In his unbelief, the priest demands a sign to confirm the angel's words—although Gabriel's appearance was already a clear sign.

His unbelief has sad consequences: he becomes instantly mute and remains so until the angel's words are fulfilled. This was a sign from God, but a painful and humiliating one. Through his unbelief he deprives himself of the possibility of thanking God for His wonderful grace and mercy and to praise Him for it.

Abraham behaved quite differently. When God told him that He would make his descendants like the number of stars, the patriarch believed the words of the LORD. Sarah also gave God the glory, because "she considered him faithful who had promised" (Heb. 11:11)—even though it was actually biologically impossible in their case.

If we mistrust God's promises, this has consequences for our lives. On the one hand, the thanks we ought to give God for His promises and faithfulness is diminished, and on the other hand, we are deprived of the valuable experiences we could have had if we had really taken God at His word.

It is impressive in this respect to see the contrast between the beginning and the end of Luke's Gospel. At the beginning we see a priest who is mute because he doubts God's promise. At the end we see spiritual priests praising God with joy in the temple because they have taken the Son of God at His word and are waiting in faith for the promise of the Holy Spirit.

When a gospel campaign is planned, it is perfectly normal to pray that many people will come and, above all, that God will also grant conversions! But what if suddenly almost no one comes and everything turns out differently than we had hoped? Do we give up, or do we continue to fight for the salvation of souls? Walter Mauerhofer reports about such an outreach where the following happened:

> **Trials are only blessings in disguise.** (John Wesley)

The people of Kufstein [Austria] had been close to my heart for a long time. So I planned a gospel campaign and rented a hall which could have accommodated a good 200 people. Motivated, I went from house to house to draw attention to the evangelistic lectures. My anticipation was great when many people promised to come. Soon I was worried about whether the size of the hall would be enough.

The first lecture evening came, and I stood at the entrance an hour before the start in the hope of soon being able to receive the first visitors. It was 7:30 pm. The lecture would begin in half an hour. Soon they would all come. 7:45 pm, still no one there. Tense and excited, I slowly began to understand that the many promises were probably not meant seriously. When 7:55 p.m. came, I stood at the front door, disappointed and downhearted. At such moments, one feels that one has no hope or strength for further undertakings.

It was 8 pm when a woman entered the room. I told her that the evening's event had been cancelled due to lack of visitors. But the woman with her dog on a leash didn't think of going home right away. She had been looking forward to the lecture and asked me to give it. I replied that I couldn't possibly give my talk in my present condition. But the woman insisted, and the dog did not seem to want to leave immediately either.

So I took one of the chairs, sat down opposite this woman and preached my sermon. The listener was visibly moved by my words and wanted to know more about Jesus. She understood the gospel, how Jesus died for the guilt of humanity and how he in His love wants to absolve of guilt and set free those who believe in Him.

When this woman claimed forgiveness of sins, the initial sadness because of the lack of visitors turned into great joy over the one person who had accepted Jesus into her life.

(Walter Mauerhofer, *Eine Saat geht auf* [A Seed Sprouts], CLV)

How do you react when you realise that God is speaking directly to you through His Word? Ephesians 3:20 says that God is "able to do far more abundantly than all that we ask or think, according to the power at work within us". What does this statement mean for your life of faith?

Notes:

....

....

....

....

....

....

....

....

....

....

....

....

....

....

....

....

....

....

Doubting Disciples

"But when they heard that he was alive and had been seen by her, they would not believe it. After these things he appeared in another form to two of them, as they were walking into the country. And they went back and told the rest, but they did not believe them." (Mark 16:11–13)

Over and over again the Lord Jesus announced to His disciples that He would die and rise again, as had already been proclaimed in the Old Testament (see Mk. 8:31; 9:31; 10:34). Then the first part of His words came true: He was crucified and died. At that point, they should have remembered and waited for His words concerning His resurrection to be fulfilled. However, the opposite was the case.

When Mary Magdalene tells the disciples that she has seen the Lord, they do not believe her. The same happens to the two disciples on the road to Emmaus after they tell the eleven about their encounter with the risen Lord. The disciples have such unbelieving hearts that they do not want to accept a twofold testimony, even though it had been announced to them beforehand.

Shortly thereafter, the Lord appears to them when they are all together. What message does He have for them? He rebukes them for their unbelief and hardness of heart because they did not believe those who had seen Him risen.

When Peter and John came to the empty tomb after three days, the Bible says: "For as yet they did not understand the Scripture, that he must rise from the dead" (Jn. 20:9)—and this was the case even though the Lord had told them that it was written in the Old Testament (see Lk. 18:31–33). Finally, He must tell His disciples, "He said to them, 'O foolish ones, and slow of heart to believe all that the prophets have spoken!'" (Lk. 24:25).

What can we learn from these incidents? It may be that we have heard a truth many times but still do not really believe it in our hearts! This, in turn, has definite repercussions on our life of faith.

The disciples on the road to Emmaus were downcast and disappointed because they had not taken the Lord's words about His resurrection in faith. As such, they themselves were responsible for being so discouraged. Had they clung to the Lord's promises, their mood would surely have been quite different.

This is often the case with us as well. When we lose sight of God's promises and focus only on the negative things that surround us, it will drag us down so that we become discouraged. However, it is God's will that we

> **If I take God at God's word, then the fulfilment of His promise is not mine, but His business, since He gave it.**
> (Charles H Spurgeon)

be filled with peace and joy if we take Him at His word and rely on His promises in faith (see Rom. 15:13).

The longsuffering and grace of the Lord are incomprehensibly great! Directly after He reprimanded the disciples for their unbelief, He sends these exact same men out to preach the gospel throughout the world. Wonderful Lord!

This should encourage us not to give up, even though we may have shown a lack of faith in one situation or another!

Speaking of the Great Commission: there are still many people who to this day are waiting for the good news to finally be brought to them. The following story makes this clear:

Hudson Taylor was discouraged. He had been preaching in the city of Ningpo for a year. The Chinese were polite and enjoyed gathering to hear Taylor speak. Discussing new ideas was fun to them. But no one seemed to take the gospel seriously. No one believed it.

And then, after one message, when Taylor felt most like giving up, a respected man stood up and turned to his Chinese countrymen.

"I have been searching for the truth a long time," he said earnestly. "My father and my grandfathers before me searched for the truth, but they never found it. I have travelled far and wide looking for it. I have tried Confucianism, Taoism, and Buddhism, but have found no rest."

Taylor looked at the man with new interest. He knew that this man was a leading officer among the Ningpo Buddhists. What was he saying? Was he saying that this religion gave him no peace?

"But tonight," said the man honestly, "tonight I have found rest. I have heard the truth, and from now on I am a believer in Jesus."

Hudson Taylor could hardly believe his ears. Could it be true? A short time later, the man proved his sincerity by taking Hudson with him to the Buddhist meeting and giving his testimony.

Soon one of the man's friends also became a Christian and was baptised. However, a few nights after the man accepted Jesus as his Saviour, he asked Hudson Taylor a very hard question.

"How long have the people in your land known about Jesus?"

"Oh hundreds of years," answered Hudson Taylor.

"What?" said the man in amazement. "You knew the truth for hundreds of years and didn't come to tell us? My father searched for the truth all his life and died without finding it. Why didn't you come sooner?"

It was a hard question. Jesus had told His followers to go into the world and preach the gospel to everyone, but too often Christians didn't obey Him.

This man knew the result. He knew people who wanted to know the truth and were just waiting for someone to come and tell them. Wanting to obey his newfound Saviour, the former Buddhist leader spent the rest of his life telling others about Jesus.

(Dave & Neta Jackson, *Heroes of Faith*, Bethany House)

**"For so the Lord has commanded us, saying,
"'I have made you a light for the Gentiles,
that you may bring salvation to the ends of the earth.'"**

Acts 13:47

> *What promises of God do you have in your head, but not in your heart? Pose yourself the question: How often do you feel down in the dumps only because you no longer have the promises of God before your eyes?*

Notes:

....

....

....

....

....

....

....

....

....

....

....

....

....

....

....

....

....

....

....

....

Loss of Blessing through Unbelief

"Then they despised the pleasant land, having no faith in his promise." (Psalm 106:24)

The LORD repeatedly promised Israel that He would bring them into the land of Canaan and drive out their enemies before them. For this reason He had delivered them from slavery in Egypt and brought them out of the iron furnace.

During the wilderness journey, Moses said to them, "See, the LORD your God has set the land before you. Go up, take possession, as the LORD, the God of your fathers, has told you. Do not fear or be dismayed" (Deut. 1:21). Now it was up to them to simply trust God and to go forward courageously in faith.

However, the closer they got to the land, the more worried they became. Finally, they came before Moses and said, "Let us send men before us, that they may explore the land for us and bring us word again of the way by which we must go up and the cities into which we shall come" (Deut. 1:22).

It was concern coupled with a lack of faith that led them to send scouts into the land to spy out the power of the enemy. And so disaster began its course. Twelve men were chosen to scout out the land for 40 days and then return to the people to report back to them. They all had one thing in common: they were impressed by the beauty of Canaan.

Two of them, Joshua and Caleb, were full of courage of faith because they had God before their eyes. Therefore they said, "Let us go up at once and occupy it, for we are well able to overcome it. ... Only do not rebel against the LORD. And do not fear the people of the land, for they are bread for us. Their protection is removed from them, and the LORD is with us; do not fear them" (Num. 13:30; 14:9). This was the language of faith that counts on God despite great opposition!

The words of the ten other men were quite different. They said, "'We are not able to go up against the people, for they are stronger than we are.' So they brought to the people of Israel a bad report of the land that they had spied out, saying, 'The land, through which we have gone to spy it out, is a land that devours its inhabitants, and all the people that we saw in it are of great height. And there we saw the Nephilim (the sons of Anak, who come from the Nephilim), and we seemed to ourselves like grasshoppers, and so we seemed to them.'" (Num. 13:31–33)

Now it was up to the people to make a decision: Would they trust the words of Joshua and Caleb, or would they allow themselves to be carried away by the fear and unbelief of the other ten scouts? They chose unbelief and even considered stoning those who clung to the promises of God. What a picture: two men trusting God versus 600,000 men who, by their unbelief, drag the glory of God through the dirt.

What happens? God intervenes! He honours the faith of Joshua and Caleb in front of all the people and exercises judgment on the ten men who pulled the people behind them in unbelief. The people who chose unbelief are also held accountable. None of them is able to enjoy the blessings of the land, for they all die in the wilderness over the course of the next forty years. Due to their lack of faith, they deprive themselves of the blessings God had intended for them.

We often see this principle of being able to lose blessings due to unbelief in the Word of God. On one occasion, during a severe famine, Elisha received a wonderful promise from God, which he proclaimed to the people: "'Hear the word of the LORD: thus says the LORD, Tomorrow about this time a seah of fine flour shall be sold for a shekel, and two seahs of barley for a shekel, at the gate of Samaria.' Then the captain on whose hand the king leaned said to the man of God, 'If the LORD himself should make windows in heaven, could this thing be?' But he said, 'You shall see it with your own eyes, but you shall not eat of it'" (2 Ki. 7:1–2).

> **Christians are either overcome because of their unbelief or [are] overcomers because of their faith.**
> (Warren Wiersbe)

This is exactly how it happened. Shortly after, when the people plundered the camp of the Syrians and returned to Samaria, the captain was trampled in the gate so that he died and could not enjoy any of the spoils (see 2 Ki. 7:16–17).

In the New Testament, when some people laughed at the Son of God because He said that the daughter of Jairus had not died but was only asleep, the Lord made sure that none of them was present when the girl was raised from the dead (see Mk. 5:40–41).

"He who worries thinks he has to do everything himself, but he who trusts knows that God does everything."

Ernst Modersohn

Have there been situations in your life where you realised in retrospect that you had missed out on blessings because you lacked faith? What can you learn from this? Is the word of the Lord enough for you, without knowing exactly what is coming when you take a step of faith? Childlike faith is walking forward simply by taking the hand of God and not running on ahead of Him to explore the path when He wants to lead us!

Notes:

....

....

....

....

....

....

....

....

....

Discontentment Due to Unbelief

"We remember the fish we ate in Egypt that cost nothing, the cucumbers, the melons, the leeks, the onions, and the garlic. But now our strength is dried up, and there is nothing at all but this manna to look at." (Numbers 11:5–6)

At least ten times the people of Israel grumbled during the wilderness journey. Why? Because they didn't trust God and were discontented with what He gave them. The LORD had often performed miracles before their eyes: He had made bitter water sweet, rained bread from heaven, given them meat, and turned a rock into a spring of water. He repeatedly tested their faith so that it would be evident whether they trusted Him or not.

Looking back, both Moses and Nehemiah could say, "He knows your going through this great wilderness. These forty years the LORD your God has been with you. You have lacked nothing" (Deut. 2:7); as well as "Forty years you sustained them in the wilderness, and they lacked nothing" (Neh. 9:21). God had faithfully provided for them!

Nevertheless, their discontentment kept breaking through. For example, they didn't want just bread but also coveted meat. Therefore, they began to grumble again, speaking against God and saying, "Can God spread a table in the wilderness? He struck the rock so that water gushed out

Thou shalt not wander in the wilderness of murmuring and complaining, but shalt dwell in the promised land of contentment and rest.
(Charles H Spurgeon)

and streams overflowed. Can he also give bread or provide meat for his people?" (Ps. 78:19–20).

How ungrateful and brazen these people were! It's terrible, isn't it? But wait a minute: What about us? Are we any better? How often are we dissatisfied with what God gives us! We may not reproach God as directly as Israel did here, but in the end, the reason for our discontentment is often a hidden distrust or an accusation against God. When we are discontent, we are actually expressing that we would like to have something that God appears to be withholding from us. Where does this discontentment come from? It comes through unbelief! In the end, we often don't believe that God means the best for us and that He gives us exactly what we need at exactly the right time.

There is a different option. Paul could say, "Not that I am speaking of being in need, for I have learned in whatever situation I am to be content. I know how to be brought low, and I know how to abound. In any and every circumstance, I have learned the secret of facing plenty and hunger, abundance and need. I can do all things through him who strengthens me" (Phil. 4:11–13). This is living faith! Because of his faith, he could also say: "Rejoice in the Lord always; again I will say, rejoice" (Phil. 4:4).

How God can sometimes put unbelief to shame and turn discontentment into joy is shown by the following incident:

Emil often came to his mother and sat many an hour at her sickbed. He gladly let her tell him about her rich experiences in life. They were so varied. Once she spoke of how, as a widow, she had often sat alone in her parlour while her grown children were scattered to the four winds.

Necessity knocked heavily at her door. The food had been used up except for a little salt and a piece of bread. Discontentment was about to come upon her. Sighing, she thought, "My children will all live better, but their mother, who has laboriously brought them up, must starve."

With that thought, she pushed the bread away and didn't want to eat anymore. At the same moment, she remembered the Bible verse, "the Son of Man has nowhere to lay his head" (Matt. 8:20). "Oh, and I still have a warm bed," she thought, ashamed. "Forgive me, my Saviour!"

Quickly she pulled the bread back and was about to sprinkle a little salt on it when there was a knock at the door. At her "Come in!" a sister in faith entered her room. She brought the sick woman a whole basket of food: butter, sausage, coffee, sugar, flour and other good things. "I felt as if you could use it," she said kindly. With that, she put everything on the table in front of her. The other could hardly believe her eyes. "Thank you, my Lord Jesus!" she could only stammer, and with tears she squeezed the sister's hand.

> **The enjoyment of God is the only happiness with which our souls can be satisfied.**
> (Jonathan Edwards)

(H W Räder, *Der Kunstglaser aus dem Vogtland* [The Art Glazier from Vogtland], CSV)

> *In which areas of your life do you struggle with discontentment? What role does unbelief play in this? What was the key to a fulfilled life for Paul? What can help you become more grateful and content?*

Notes:

....

....

....

....

....

....

....

....

....

....

....

....

....

....

....

....

....

....

....

....

Praying in Unbelief

"But let him ask in faith, with no doubting, for the one who doubts is like a wave of the sea that is driven and tossed by the wind. For that person must not suppose that he will receive anything from the Lord." (James 1:6–7)

True faith takes a letter to the mailbox and then lets it go. Unbelief, on the other hand, holds on to a corner of the letter and then wonders why there is no response.

It is not enough for us to write beautiful letters if we never bring them to the post office. We must release them from our hands and let them go. Faith means giving a matter to God in prayer and then trusting that He will take care of it. In Psalm 37:5 it is written, "Commit your way to the LORD; trust in him, and he will act".

God calls us to cast our cares and burdens upon Him (see 1 Pet. 5:7). We are to completely give them over to Him. Luther describes it simply as "throwing the bag at God's feet". If we cast our burden upon Him and unload it at the throne of grace, can it still weigh us down? No—unless we take it back from there again.

Someone once said, "As for me, I test my prayers as follows: If I have given a thing to God and then, like Hannah, can go away with a glad, relieved heart, I take that as proof that I have prayed in faith. However, if I take my burden away with me again, I conclude that my faith was not active."

If one prays for a cause for a long time and the answer still fails to come, there is a danger that at some point unbelief will take over and force us to stop praying. Yet, in precisely such moments faith should dominate and unbelief should be silenced through intensified prayer.

Praying without faith is like cutting bread with a dull knife.
(James O Fraser)

Jonathan Goforth, working in China at the time of revival in 1908, wrote of the great impression that the prayer life of missionaries in Korea made upon him:

"Mr. (William) Swallen of Pyongyang told me how that the missionaries of his station, both Methodists and Presbyterians, upon hearing of the great Revival in the Khassia Hills of India, had decided to pray every day at the noon hour until a similar blessing was poured out upon them.

'After we had prayed for about a month,' said Mr. Swallen, 'a brother proposed that we stop the prayer meeting, saying, "We have been praying for a month, and nothing unusual has come of it. We are spending a lot of time. I don't think we are justified. Let us go on with our work as usual, and each pray at home as he finds it convenient."'

'The proposal seemed plausible. The majority of us, however, decided that, instead of discontinuing the prayer meeting, we would give more time to prayer, not less. With that in view, we changed the hour from noon to four o'clock; we were then free to pray until supper time, if we wished. We kept to it, until at last, after months of waiting the answer came.'"

(Brain H Edwards, *Revival—A people saturated with God*, Day One Publications)

Can one get to the point of living without worry? How often do you really keep a lookout for answers to prayer, like Elijah did in 1 Kings 18 for example? What does that tell you about your prayer life? Take God seriously when you talk to Him!

Notes:

....

....

....

....

....

....

....

....

....

....

....

....

....

....

....

....

....

....

....

....

When Unbelief Dominates

"And he did not do many mighty works there, because of their unbelief." (Matthew 13:58)

People were often impressed by the miracles the Lord did in certain places. However, because they themselves did not have a living faith, this hindered His work in their own area. It is distressing when unbelief hinders the work of God! Yet it is exactly this that probably happens more often than we think.

Back when the Lord was here on earth, He preached the gospel and directly addressed the needs of the people. Now He is in glory—and He has sent us out into this world as His ambassadors.

Faith neither reasons nor reckons, but it obeys.
(Unknown)

God wants to use each of us to bring the gospel to people. However, we must also make ourselves available to Him and allow Him to guide us. How often does it happen, for example, that the Lord gives us the task of sharing the gospel with someone, and then we doubt and hesitate so long until the opportunity eventually passes?

Georg von Viebahn relates a heartfelt example of this:

In the records of a blessed servant of God is found the following: He came to the funeral of a young girl who had died quite unexpectedly. Upon entering the funeral home, he met with the faithful pastor who had close ties with this family.

He asked him, "Was Mary a true Christian?" To his astonishment, he saw a pained look on the face of the person he had addressed, who replied, "Three weeks ago I felt a strong impulse to talk to her; but I did not, and now I do not know how to answer you."

A moment later the schoolmistress of the deceased arrived; the questioner turned to her with the same words, "Was Mary a true Christian?" Tears welled up in the eyes of the one addressed, and she replied, "Two weeks ago it was as if voice said to me, 'Speak to Mary,' and I knew what it meant. I wanted to speak too, but I didn't, and now I don't know what her position was."

Deeply moved, the servant of God approached the mother of the deceased and quietly asked, "Wasn't Mary a believing girl?" Tears streamed from the mother's eyes, and she sobbed, "A week ago an inner voice admonished me, 'Talk to Mary!' I always thought of it, but I missed the right time, and you know how unexpectedly quickly she was called away— now I don't know!"

How poignant this account is! The Holy Spirit wanted to use the lips of three people to say a word to this young girl who stood close to the gates of eternity—but He could not, because these children of God were not ready to obey instantly. One could undoubtedly easily fill a volume with real events of this kind, in which the guidance of the Holy Spirit is tangible before our eyes.

(Georg von Viebahn, *Geleitet durch den Heiligen Geist* [Led by the Holy Spirit], Schwert & Schild)

"We shall have all eternity to celebrate the victories, but we have only the few hours before sunset in which to win them."

Amy Carmichael

> *Where do the inhibitions come from that prevent you from being immediately obedient when the Lord gives you a task? What is the connection between unbelief and the fear of man? In what areas of your life does your unbelief hinder God's work?*

Notes:

....

....

....

....

....

....

....

....

....

....

....

....

....

Impact of Faith on Our Daily Lives

Living faith is not a theoretical thing. If it is present, it will always show itself in our lives. This happens in very different ways. Sometimes we need faith to patiently wait for God's timing. At other times, the Lord wants us to become active and act out of faith. Whatever we do, it should be done by faith. This means that we do things in fellowship with God and for Him. As Paul writes to the Colossians, "Whatever you do, in word or deed, do everything in the name of the Lord Jesus, giving thanks to God the Father through him" (Col. 3:17).

Faith and Works

God wants our faith to be visible to others. This is what the Epistle of James is all about. But exactly how does this happen? Through works of faith. Living faith will always show itself in our actions. In this way, we demonstrate the authenticity of our faith to others. It is not enough, therefore, to only have a pious confession, because without works faith is dead (see Jas. 2:17).

On the other hand, there is also the danger that works are present but faith is absent. The Thessalonians had works of faith; that is, they acted by faith while serving the Lord (see 1 Thess. 1:3). In contrast, with the church at Ephesus only works are spoken of (see Rev. 2:2). In a similar way it can happen that a Christian may, at some point, only be active in service without that service really being done by faith and in dependence on the Lord!

Let's go back to the first point: How does living faith become visible? The Epistle of James gives us the answer. It is through love for God and for His people. To illustrate this, James uses two extraordinary examples out of the Old Testament: Abraham, who is willing to sacrifice his son for God through obedience that is born out of faith; and Rahab, who sides with God's people and thereby betrays her fellow countrymen. Abraham shows by his act of faith that he loves God above all else, while Rahab becomes one with those who belong to God. In order to hide the Israelite scouts, she even risks her own life.

Good works are the seals and proofs of faith; for even as a letter must have a seal to strengthen the same, even so faith must have good works (Martin Luther)

Through deeds of faith we show the world—and also our brothers and sisters in faith—that our faith is genuine and alive. At the same time, works of faith done in dependence on God can also be a visible testimony that God has not changed and still stands firmly by His promises. The life of George Müller makes this very clear.

This man is a wonderful example of someone who glorified God through works of faith. Through his example, thousands of believers were encouraged to trust God more—and this is still the case today. Müller had experienced God's faithfulness in his own life and wished for others to have the same, blessed experience.

"I therefore judged myself bound," he wrote, "to be the servant of the church of Christ in the particular point on which I had ob-

tained mercy; namely, in being able to take God by his word, and to rely upon it."

More and more there grew in his heart a desire to present to the church and to the world a proof that God had not changed at all. It seemed to him that the best way to do that would be to establish an orphanage. It would have to be something that could be seen with the naked eye.

"Now, if I, a poor man, simply by prayer and faith, obtained, without asking any individual, the means for establishing and carrying on an orphan house, there would be something which, with the Lord's blessing, might be instrumental in strengthening the faith of the children of God, besides being a testimony to the consciences of the unconverted of the reality of the things of God ... whereby it may be seen that God is faithful still, and hears prayer still."

God made a miraculous commitment to this faith. When Müller finally died at the ripe old age of 93, he had:

- *taken in and cared for 10,024 orphans,*
- *educated 81,501 children in schools,*
- *given away 1,989,266 Bibles and Bible portions,*
- *supported 115 missionaries on a regular basis, and*
- *experienced about 50,000 concrete answers to prayer.*

According to today's value, the equivalent of at least 70 million euros passed through the hands of this man, but the value of his personal property at his death was only about 4,000 euros.

(W Bühne, *Fest & Treu* [Firm & Faithful], 2005, CLV)

This man made himself available to God without reserve and honoured Him by faith—and the Lord was able to use him wonderfully. This happened about 200 years ago. Should it be any different today?

The Bible gives the answer: "Jesus Christ is the same yesterday and today and forever" (Heb. 13:8). This also applies to God's promises, which He can fulfil in our lives. He is looking for people who take Him at His word and dare to take steps of faith at His word. He will certainly stand by His promises! "For all the promises of God find their Yes in him. That is why it is through him that we utter our Amen to God for his glory" (2 Cor. 1:20).

> *In what manner do works of faith appear in your life that make it clear to people that you not only have a Christian confession, but you also really trust God? Why, out of all things, does God use Abraham's willingness to sacrifice Isaac and Rahab's willingness to side with Israel to present works of faith to us? What is the difference between doing service in dependence on God or, on the other hand, simply being active in service?*

Notes:

....

....

....

....

Obeying by Faith

"By faith Abraham obeyed when he was called to go out to a place that he was to receive as an inheritance. And he went out, not knowing where he was going." (Hebrews 11:8)

Faith lets us act without ifs, ands or buts in obedience to God's Word. We may leave the consequences of this to God. Abraham went out in obedience through faith, not knowing where the journey would lead. It's easy to just say that, but let's imagine what this meant for him, practically speaking: What should he have answered if someone had asked him along the way where he was going?

Many of the people at that time certainly had no understanding of this step of faith and could only shake their heads at it. Unfortunately, this is often still the case: when we carry out a mission for God that is perhaps somewhat unusual, we have to expect sceptical looks and critical voices. It is exactly then that we, by trusting in the Lord, have to do what He wants us to do—even without being able to fully foresee the consequences of our obedience of faith. God will give enough light for the first step, even if we cannot yet foresee what the next one will look like. Faith, after all, also involves driving as far as the eye can see, just until the first turn.

This is particularly clear in the case of Philip. Although many had come to faith through him in the city where he was staying, and there were certainly many tasks still to do there, the Lord suddenly sends him to a remote road where usually only very rarely you encounter others. The evangelist doesn't know what the Lord has in mind, but he obeys Him without objection.

What should he have answered if someone had suddenly asked him the question, "Why are you leaving this city at this time, when there is so much work to be done amongst the new converts?" He must accept the possible lack of understanding on the part of the people and simply go ahead in obedience by faith. Because he does this, the Lord gives him directions for the second step through the guidance of the Holy Spirit: when an Ethiopian eunuch comes along the road, the Spirit says to Philip, "Join this chariot" (Acts 8:29).

We prefer to know in advance what the entire path God is leading us on will look like. But the Lord wants to keep us dependent on Him—and that's why He leads us step by step! For this very reason it's so important that we're always willing to let go and let God take the wheel. When we do that and let God lead us, He can use us to bless others.

> **I do not need to know the way, I only need to trust the Guide.**
> (Elisabeth Elliot)

The Indian evangelist Bakht Singh often experienced the blessings associated with obedience by faith:

Early one morning at about 1:00 Bakht Singh was feeling very tired. As he went to bed, he heard a Voice saying to him, "Rise and go out." Bakht Singh answered that he was tired and his legs were aching and he was feeling sleepy. But the Voice came again. "Arise and go out." With much grumbling, Bakht Singh put on his coat. In the pocket of his coat there were always tracts in various languages for the cosmopolitan peoples of Karachi.

He went out and as soon as he did, he found two young men walking in front of him. He called them and said, "Please stop. I have something to tell you." When they came near, Bakht Singh told them how he was going to lie down, but the voice of God told him to go out, and that he felt that God had sent him out. They said that it must be God's voice because it was such an unusual hour to go out. They then asked Bakht Singh to open the Bible and read some verses. Then he told them of his conversion.

One of the men, by the name of Kulkarni, said, "I know God has sent you for my sake. I was unhappy and have longed for a Bible. Could you give me a Bible?" He bought a Bible and received the Lord Jesus Christ. What a joy for Bakht Singh to find these people with spiritual hunger in India!

(T E Koshy, *Brother Bakht Singh of India*, OM Books)

Press onward, press onward, and trusting the Lord,

**"Remember the promise proclaimed in His Word;
He guideth the footsteps, directeth the way
Of all who confess Him, believe, and obey."**

Fanny Crosby

> *Are you willing to accept assignments from God that require you to let go in faith because you cannot foresee the consequences? Will you let the Lord use you when, for example, He puts it on your heart today to spontaneously visit someone who is not doing well spiritually? Maybe He also wants you to ring your neighbour's doorbell and present the gospel to him without knowing how he will react.*

Notes:

....

....

....

....

....

....

....

....

....

....

....

....

....

....

....

Persevere through Trusting by Faith—and Keep Going!

"For you have need of endurance, so that when you have done the will of God you may receive what is promised." (Hebrews 10:36)

What does perseverance actually mean? The word can also be translated as "staying under", in the sense of "withstanding, enduring". It's about continuing to trust in the Lord, no matter what opposition we may face. Perseverance is one of the most important things in the life of faith. Therein lies a key to spiritual growth!

The apostles were characterised by perseverance (see 2 Cor. 12:12)—and this should also be the case for everyone who wants to serve the Lord (see 2 Cor. 6:4)! We must press on in the face of difficulties rather than give up. The Hebrews, who were persecuted by their own countrymen and were in danger of becoming discouraged, are told: "Therefore do not throw away your confidence, which has a great reward. For you have need of endurance" (Heb. 10:35–36).

Especially in this day and age, when we are used to always getting everything immediately with just a few clicks or text messages, it's often difficult for us to wait. In addition, we have the tendency, while facing a trial, to distract ourselves with something else or to even avoid it altogether, instead of facing the facts and enduring difficulties.

There is, however, another way. When faith becomes active, we trust God and always involve Him in the present circumstances. This is exactly what will change our outlook and inner attitude. We will then be able to overcome trials and waiting periods in our fellowship with the Lord, without acting in self-will to break out of them or give up.

Often it is even the case that God sends trials to instruct us and to teach us perseverance. That is why Paul writes, "Not only that, but we rejoice in our sufferings, knowing that suffering produces endurance" (Rom. 5:3).

The question is, how long should we persevere? Until God ends the trial! That is, we are to trust Him until His time comes and He lifts the burden from our shoulders. This is what James means when he writes, "Let steadfastness have its full effect, that you may be perfect and complete, lacking in nothing" (Jas. 1:4).

> **It is not enough to begin to pray, nor to pray aright; nor is it enough to continue for a time to pray; but we must patiently, believingly, continue in prayer until we obtain an answer.**
> (George Müller)

God always has our good in mind when He allows hardships and difficulties in our lives—even if they sometimes drag on for many years. We honour Him when we trust in Him during these times, bring everything to Him in prayer, and lean on His promises.

Caleb persevered in the wilderness for 45 years, patiently waiting in faith for God's promise to be fulfilled—and he was richly rewarded! At the age of 85, he looks back and says, "I am still as strong today as I was in the day that Moses sent me; my strength now is as my strength was then, for war and for going and coming" (Josh. 14:11). This corresponds exactly to what Isaiah writes on this subject: "They who wait for the Lord shall renew their strength; they shall mount up with wings like eagles; they shall run and not be weary; they shall walk and not faint" (Isa. 40:31). God is both the God of perseverance and of encouragement (cf. Rom 15:5)!

In a sermon on the subject of prayer, George Müller once told of the way God responds to persistent or persevering prayer and how important it is that we do not give up, but continue to pray, even if the answer has still failed to materialise:

During the first six weeks of the year 1866 I heard of the conversion of six persons for whom I had been praying for a long time. For one I had been praying between two and three years; for another between three and four years; for the fifth about fifteen years; and for the sixth above twenty years. I asked once a thing of God, which I knew to be according to His mind, and though I brought it day by day and generally many times a day before Him, in such assurance as to be able to thank Him hundreds of times for the answer before it was received, yet I had to wait three years and ten months before the blessing was given to me.

At another time I had to wait six years; and at another time eleven and a half years. In the last case I brought the matter about twenty thousand times before God, and invariably in the fullest assurance of faith, and yet eleven and a half years passed before the answer was given.

In one instance my faith has been tried even more than this. In November 1844, I began to pray for the conversion of five individuals. I prayed every day without one single intermission, whether sick or in health, on the land or on the sea, and whatever the pressure of my engagements might be.

Eighteen months elapsed before the first of the five was converted. I thanked God, and prayed on for the others. Five years elapsed, and then the second one was converted. I thanked God for the second, and prayed on for the other three. Day by day I continued to pray for them and six years more passed before the third was converted. I thanks God for the three, and went on praying for the other two. These two remain unconverted.

The man to whom God in the riches of His grace has given tens of thousands of answers to prayer, in the self-same hour or day on which they were offered, has been praying day by day for nearly thirty-six years for the conversion of these two individuals, and yet they remain unconverted; for next November it will be thirty-six years since I began to pray for their conversion. But I hope in God, I pray on, and look yet for the answer.[6]

Therefore, beloved brethren and sisters, go on waiting upon God, go on praying; only be sure you ask for things which are according to the mind of God. The conversion of sinners is according to the mind of God, for He does not desire the death of the sinner. This is the revelation God has made of Himself — "Not willing that any should perish, but that all should come to repentance." Go on, therefore, praying; expect an answer, look for it, and in the end you will have to praise God for it.

(George Müller, *The Prayer-Hearing God*)

---

6   One of these persons was converted before Mr Müller's death, and the other only gave clear evidence of conversion after Mr Müller had passed away.

"Continue steadfastly in prayer."

Colossians 4:2

> *Why is it so fundamentally important to your life of faith that you persevere in trials and suffering and don't give up? What can help you to pray with more perseverance and not give up when you go through difficulties (see, e.g., Luke 18:1–7; Heb. 12:3)? What biblical examples can you think of where role models of faith waited a long time for God to intervene?*

Notes:

....

....

....

....

....

....

....

....

....

....

....

....

Faith and Hope

"May the God of hope fill you with all joy and peace in believing, so that by the power of the Holy Spirit you may abound in hope." (Romans 15:13)

Through faith we gain hope. Because we trust God and rely on His promises, we gain confidence for the future. Why? Because we know that God means well for us and that indescribably beautiful things are waiting for us in heaven.

The Thessalonians were severely persecuted. However, they didn't give up in these difficult circumstances but patiently endured hardship. Not only that: Paul writes that in this difficult time their endurance was connected to their hope (see 1 Thess. 1:3).

How did they get this hope? By keeping their eyes fixed on the goal: they had a living expectation that the Son of God would soon return to take them to Himself in heaven. The hope of being with Him soon helped them to endure the present persecutions and not give up. We see the same principle in the life of Jesus: He endured the cross for the joy that was set before Him (see Heb. 12:2).

> **I have felt like working three times as hard since I came to understand that my Lord was coming back again.**
> (Dwight L Moody)

If we take seriously what the Bible tells us about the Christian hope, occupy ourselves with it and in faith expect it daily, then something wonderful will happen that will shape our lives: we will be filled with joy and peace (see Rom. 15:13). Of course, though, we must sincerely ask ourselves whether we're really looking forward to the coming of the Lord and truly expecting it every day!

Evangelist Charles Stanley once told the following story, which shows how fulfilling a life of waiting on the Lord can be:

I will here give a case for the encouragement of the young evangelists, who may not, at the time, see any fruit of their labours in the gospel. An aged woman, of the name of Hannah F., had come some eight miles to hear a lecture, on the Lord's coming, in the Mechanics' Hall, Rotherham. She was nearly blind, but God was pleased to open her spiritual eyesight, and two things were made known to her in the power of the Holy Ghost. God gave her the certainty of eternal salvation, and also made known to her the blessed hope of the coming again of the Lord to take His saints. These two things were entirely new to her; she had never heard them before.

She returned to her home at Anston, filled with "the peace of God which passes all understanding." She told her aged husband, about one year older than herself, the blessed news she had learned. The Lord opened his heart also to receive the glad tidings, and much of their time was spent in thanksgiving and worship.

They had an aged neighbour, a farmer, about the same age as themselves. One day they had knelt down, giving thanks together that they were both washed in the blood of the Lamb from all sin and were waiting and longing for the coming of the Lord in the air to take them to Himself. The aged farmer came in to see them, as had been his custom; and as both of them were rather deaf, and so entirely absorbed in thanksgiving, they did not hear him come in.

He listened with amazement, such joy he had never witnessed, such words he had never heard. It was not prayer, but they were giving thanks to Him who had saved them with an everlasting salvation, who had made them fit for His holy presence, in purity and glory. They were in spirit in heaven, not at Anston; and they were talking to One they knew so well, and never seemed tired of talking to Him. They talked to Him about His coming, to take them to Himself.

The old farmer was fairly lost in amazement. At last the dear aged couple rose from their knees. Their visitor said, "Whatever does all this mean? I have been going to church these seventy years, and saying my prayers; but I cannot say that I am even saved, much more saved for ever, and saved perfectly. No, indeed, I cannot. And you are speaking to God as if you knew Him. And what can you mean about the coming of Christ to take you?"

Then aged Hannah told the gospel she had heard: how God loved; how He had sent His Son; how He had offered Himself the infinite sacrifice for sins; how God declared that all who believed were justified from all things, and their sins and iniquities God would remember no more. Yea, how that, by one offering, all who believed were perfected for ever. And Jesus assured all who heard His words, and believed God that sent Him, that they had eternal life, and should never come into judgment, but were passed from death to life. And that Jesus told them not to be afraid; He was gone to prepare a place for them, and would come again to receive them to Himself.

She spoke from the deep enjoyment of Christ in her own soul. God blessed her words to their aged farmer friend. Though over 80, he, too, was brought into the enjoyment of peace with God. As a little child did he receive the truth from the lips of Hannah. Heavenly was the communion of these three aged pilgrims, when a friend of mine found them some months afterwards. Much of their time was spent together in worship and communion, waiting for Jesus from heaven.

(Charles Stanley, *Incidents of Gospel Work*, Believers Bookshelf USA)

> *How does trust produce hope? If God wants to fill you with all joy and peace (see Rom. 15:13), what is the reason why these things may often not come to fruition in your life? How often do you think about the Lord's coming, and are there any ways that you can measure whether you are really expecting Him?*

Notes:

....

....

....

....

....

....

....

....

....

Faith and Love

"Faith working through love." (Galatians 5:6)

We love the Son of God even though we have never seen Him with our natural eyes (see 1 Pet. 1:8). How is this possible? By faith alone. We believe what the Word of God says about Him: that He loved us and gave Himself for us. Faith in this love causes an echo in us: "We love because he first loved us" (1 Jn. 4:19).

This is also true about love for our brothers and sisters in the faith. If we grasp by faith that we belong to the family of God because we are born of God, then it should be perfectly normal to love all of God's children—and not only those whom we find to be likeable or those who think the same way as we do. John writes: "Everyone who believes that Jesus is the Christ has been born of God, and everyone who loves the Father loves whoever has been born of him" (1 Jn. 5:1). By faith, we can see our brother or sister in faith as someone for whom Christ died (see Rom. 14:15; 1 Cor. 8:11). Isn't that by itself a great motive for loving one another?

Now, of course, the question arises as to how love becomes visible or how it expresses itself. Love shows itself through sacrifice and responding to the needs of our fellow human beings. That is why it is said, "Through love serve one another" (Gal. 5:13). John also speaks of this when he says, "If anyone has the world's goods and sees his brother in need, yet closes his heart against him, how does God's love abide in him? Little children, let us not love in word or talk but in deed and in truth" (1 Jn. 3:17–18).

The Son of God told His disciples to love one another as He loved them (see John 15:12). Thus, He Himself is the standard for the love we are to have for one another—and that goes a long way. John, in a sense, picks up on this idea when he says, "By this we know love, that he laid down his life for us, and we ought to lay down our lives for the brothers" (1 Jn. 3:16).

The first Christians lived this way and were thereby a wonderful witness to the glory of God. They had open eyes to the needs of their brothers and sisters in faith, which is why they were selflessly willing to give up material possessions for one another. The Lord said, "By this all people will know that you are my disciples, if you have love for one another" (Jn. 13:35). That was indeed the case then. What is it like today?

> **It is the very nature of love to give up and forget itself for the sake of others. It takes their needs and makes them its own, it finds its real joy in living and dying for others as Christ did.**
> (Andrew Murray)

Faith works through love (see Gal. 5:6). This means that faith becomes evident through practical love. Thus, faith is not an intellectual conviction, but rather it is something that is alive and can be experienced.

The life of Robert Chapman is an impressive example of how love can show itself in the life of a Christian. He once said, "There are many who preach Christ, but not so many who live Christ. My great aim will be to live Christ." John Nelson Darby said of him years later, "He lives what I preach".

A biography about him states:

Once given a new coat by a friend, he soon gave it to a poor man living nearby. After a while the friend remarked on the absence of the coat and Chapman confessed that he had given it away. He always preached that such behaviour should not be considered extraordinary for a Christian. He frequently quoted from Luke 3:11, "He that hath two coats, let him impart to him that hath none".

Of course not everyone liked Chapman. Some people were greatly offended by his plain preaching on sin and the need for repentance. A touching story is told of his love and concern for one of those critics. A grocer in Barnstaple became so upset when Chapman was preaching in the open air that he strode up to where Chapman was standing and spit on him.

Later one of Robert's wealthy relatives came to Barnstaple to visit him and to try to understand his activities. Arriving by horse-drawn cab at the address given to him, the relative at first would not believe that Chapman lived in such a simple abode in such a poor neighbourhood.

Chapman ushered him into the clean but simple interior and explained what living in dependence on the Lord meant and how the Lord had provided for all his needs. The relative asked if he could purchase groceries for him. Chapman gladly assented, but stipulated that he must buy the food from a certain grocer. The relative went there, made a large purchase, and paid the bill.

When the grocer learned that the food was to be delivered to R. C. Chapman, he said that the visitor must have come to the wrong shop. Chapman's relative, however, replied that Chapman himself had specifically directed him to that shop. The grocer, who had viciously attacked and castigated Chapman for years, broke down in tears. Soon he came to Chapman's house asked forgiveness, and yielded his life to Christ.

On one occasion an excluded man became bitter and vowed never to speak a word to Chapman again. Sometime later they found themselves approaching each other on a street. Knowing all that the man had been saying about him, Chapman embraced him and said, "Dear brother, God loves you, Christ loves you, and I love you." This action broke the man's animosity; he repented and was soon breaking bread at Bear Street Chapel.

> **"Beloved, let us love one another, for love is from God ... because God is love."**
> (1 John 4:7–8)

(Robert L Peterson, *Robert Chapman: A Biography*, Lewis & Roth Publishers)

*"For the love of Christ controls us...
Therefore, we are ambassadors for Christ."*

2 Corinthians 5:14, 20

> *The Colossians were issued the wonderful testimony that they had faith in Christ and love for all the saints (see Col. 1:4). How often is your love limited to those Christians whom you find to be likeable and who have the same convictions as you? What can help you change that? How does your love for your fellow human beings become visible in a practical manner in your life? What can we learn from the exemplary love of Priscilla and Aquila in Romans 16:4?*

Notes:

....

....

....

....

....

....

....

....

....

....

....

....

....

....

Peace through Trusting

How often does it happen that worries get to us and rob us of our joy? Yet, God wants to actually free us from them. It is His will that we do not torment ourselves with worries but rather give them to Him in prayer—and then leave them there. Peter says, "casting all your anxieties on him, because he cares for you" (1 Pet. 5:7).

Paul shows us what happens when we really do that and in faith unload our cares on God: "The peace of God, which surpasses all understanding, will guard your hearts and your minds in Christ Jesus" (Phil. 4:7). A living trust in God fills us with unshakable peace!

This is exactly what we see in the life of Jesus. While the storm rages so that the boat fills with water, He sleeps soundly on a pillow in the back of the boat. Because He trusts God in all circumstances without reserve, He can say with conviction: "In peace I will both lie down and sleep; for you alone, O LORD, make me dwell in safety" (Ps. 4:8).

The story of Peter when he is in prison is also impressive. Even though James has just been killed by the sword and Peter is probably next in line, he is still able to sleep peacefully the night before his potential execution. How is this possible? His former self-confidence, which led him to deny His Lord three times out of fear, has been replaced by a deep trust in God: a beautiful illustration of

> I have no idea why I have had to suffer so much. But what I do know is that God is determined to make you and me into masterpieces.
>
> (Richard Wurmbrand)

what Isaiah writes: "You keep him in perfect peace whose mind is stayed on you, because he trusts in you" (Isa. 26:3).

In church history there are several examples of Christians who had deep peace in their hearts even at the moment when they were led to execution. Jerome of Prague, like Peter, had for fear of torture denied things of which he was actually convicted. Nevertheless, God strengthened the faith of his servant again. The latter recanted his statement and was therefore condemned by the clergy of the Catholic Church to death at the stake—at the place where Jan Hus had been executed a year earlier.

Jerome was led out of the cathedral and began to sing at the door. He sang the entire long march through the city until he finally arrived at the place of execution. As they prepared to light the pyre behind his back, he said: "Come forward and light the fire where I can see it; if I feared it, I would not be here". He sang again and prayed in the flames until his voice finally faded away.

This steadfastness made a strong impression on even his bitter enemies. The papal secretary Poggio wrote, "Fearless he stood, unbroken, not only despising death, but welcoming it".

David writes in one of the most famous psalms, "Even though I walk through the valley of the shadow of death, I will fear no evil, for you are with me" (Ps. 23:4). This is possible only through living faith—and through the peace of God that surpasses all understanding!

"Be faithful unto death,
and I will give you the crown of life."

Revelation 2:10

Why does the peace of God transcend human
understanding? What does it mean that
God keeps the mind that is stayed on Him in
peace? Don't just say a prayer but take God
seriously and trust that the Lord will take
care of the worries you cast onto Him!

Notes:

....
....
....
....
....
....
....
....
....
....
....
....
....
....

Fellowship and Godliness

Faith enables us to have and also to enjoy fellowship with God. This happens when we come to Him in prayer or when we let Him speak to us through His Word.

The faith-filled gaze toward heaven that we can have in prayer keeps us in living fellowship with God our Father. He tells us that His eyes are upon the righteous and that His ears are attuned to their crying (see 1 Pet. 3:12).

Daniel prayed three times a day and consciously sought fellowship with God. In this he is a very good example for us. Yet, we may know God in a much deeper way than Daniel or other men of faith in the Old Testament because the Son of God came to give us eternal life. This life of abundance is a whole new quality of life that enables us to know the Father and the Son and to have fellowship with them.

However, in order for this fellowship to really come about and be enjoyed, we must also practically take hold of eternal life in faith. How does this work? It works by reaching out to have fellowship with these divine Persons and by consciously living in the relationship which we have with them.

This is a process of growth. At first, like the bride in the Song of Songs, we might say, "My beloved is mine, and I am his" (Song 2:16). Yet God wants to lead us on further in the consciousness of His love, so that at some point we can say, "I am my beloved's, and his desire is for me" (Song 7:10). Someone once said, "The Lord longs for us much more than we long for Him". Grasping this in faith draws us near to

His heart and gives us joy in the relationship that we have with Him!

Our heavenly Father not only wants to give us joy, but He also wants our joy to be overflowing and complete. But how does such joy come to be? It is through the enjoyment of the relationship we have with Him, through a living fellowship with the Father and the Son. As John writes: "Our fellowship is with the Father and with his Son Jesus Christ. And we are writing these things so that our joy may be complete" (1 Jn. 1:3–4).

Godliness means involving God in everything and finding our full satisfaction in Him. As Jesus Himself says, "I have set the LORD always before me ... in your presence there is fullness of joy" (Ps. 16:8, 11). When we live this way, we also better understand why Paul himself could say in prison, "Rejoice in the Lord always; again I will say, rejoice" (Phil. 4:4). Christ was his everything. If it is the same with us, we will learn to be content with what God has provided for us (see Phil. 4:11).

> **God is most glorified in us when we are most satisfied in Him.**
> (John Piper)

Here is an example from church history:

One of the most powerful paragraphs in his [John Paton's] autobiography describes his experience of hiding in a tree, at the mercy of an unreliable chief, as hundreds of angry natives hunted him for his joy and courage. In fact, I would dare to say that to share this experience and call others to enjoy it was the reason that he wrote the story of his life.

He began his autobiography with the words, "What I write here is for the glory of God." That is true. But God gets glory when his Son is exalted. And his Son is exalted when we cherish him above all things, especially when "all things" are about to be snatched from us, including our life on earth. That is what this story is about. Here is the story of Paton in the tree.

"Being entirely at the mercy of such doubtful and vacillating friends, I, though perplexed, felt it best to obey. I climbed into the tree and was left there alone in the bush. The hours I spent there live all before me as if it were but yesterday. I heard the frequent discharging of muskets, and the yells of the Savages. Yet I sat there among the branches, as safe as in the arms of Jesus.

Never, in all my sorrows, did my Lord draw nearer to me, and speak more soothingly in my soul, than when the moonlight flickered among those chestnut leaves, and the night air played on my throbbing brow, as I told all my heart to Jesus. Alone, yet not alone!

If it be to glorify God, I will not grudge to spend many nights alone in such a tree, to feel again my Saviour's spiritual presence, to enjoy His consoling fellowship. If thus thrown back upon your own soul, alone, in the midnight, in the bush, in the very embrace of death itself, have you a Friend that will not fail you then."

(John Piper, Filling up the Afflictions of Christ, Crossway Books)

> *What gives you true satisfaction in life?*
> *What does it mean to you to have fellow-*
> *ship with the Father and the Son? Why is*
> *God glorified in your life when you find all*
> *your satisfaction in Him?*

Notes:

....

....

....

....

....

....

....

....

....

....

....

....

....

....

....

....

....

....

....

Trusting God and Fearing God

"The fear of the LORD is the beginning of knowledge."
(Proverbs 1:7)

If we want to grow in the knowledge of God, then we must begin to fear Him. What does that actually involve? It means living before His eyes and having the awareness that our God is also a consuming fire (see Heb. 12:29). When we realise this, we will shrink from doing anything that goes against His will. God is not the "dear God in heaven", but He is light and love—full of goodness and grace, but also terrible, just and hating evil!

God is holy, pure, matchless and exalted. If we live in faith before His face and involve Him in all circumstances of life, it will then promote our practical holiness. Joseph lived this way and fled for that exact reason when temptation came. Solomon explains to us what the fear of God consists in: "The fear of the LORD is hatred of evil" (Prov. 8:13).

The Lord was the Holy One of God here on earth. His delight was in the fear of the LORD (see Isa. 11:3) and He lived at all times before the holy eyes of God. He knew the holiness and greatness of God and said: "The sorrows of those who run after another god shall multiply; their drink offerings of blood I will not pour out or take their names on my lips" (Ps. 16:4). The more God stands before us in His holiness and greatness, the more we will also live in true fear of God!

Solomon goes on to write, "In the fear of the LORD one has strong confidence, and his children will have a refuge" (Prov. 14:26). How can we understand this? True fear of God leads us to feel holy awe before the greatness and omnipotence of God—and to realise that we are nothing compared to Him.

When we have this fear, we will also believe that there is nothing that God is not able to do. We will then trust that He can solve all our problems and give us the strength and grace to deal with them. This fear thus becomes a refuge for us and gives us a strong faith. As beloved children, we may trust in the unlimited power and goodness of heart of our heavenly Father. He who lives in awe of God and hates evil need not fear man, for "the fear of man lays a snare, but whoever trusts in the LORD is safe" (Prov. 29:25).

God gives wonderful promises in His Word for those who fear Him. David, for example, writes in Psalm 34:9: "Oh, fear the LORD, you his saints, for those who fear him have no lack!" George Müller also set his foot on this promise of God and thereby had wonderful experiences of faith.

However, this does not only apply to the orphan father of Bristol. The following incident, which happened in China many years ago, shows very beautifully how God sometimes shows His commitment to believers when they do not go with the flow, but act in true fear of God and with trust in Him:

Li-ming, a warm hearted, earnest evangelist, owned land some miles north of Chang Te Fu. On one occasion, when visiting the place, he found the neighbours all busy, placing little sticks with tiny flags around their fields. They believed this would keep the locust from eating their grain.

All of them urged Li-ming to do the same, and to worship the locust god, or, they warned, his grain would be destroyed. Li-ming replied, "I worship the one only true God, and I will pray Him to keep my grain, that you may know that He alone is God." The locust came and ate on all sides of Li-ming's grain but did not touch his own.

There is no cure for the fear of man like the fear of God.
(Charles H Spurgeon)

When Mr. Goforth heard this story, he determined to get further proof, so he visited the place for himself and inquired of Li-ming's heathen neighbours and what they knew of the matter. One and all testified that, when the locust had come, they had eaten their grain but not Li-ming's.

(Rosalind Goforth, *Proof to God's Power and Loving Faithfulness,* Whitaker House)

> **How can you tell that a person is living in true fear of God? What is the difference between godliness and legalism? Try to describe the connection between fearing God and trusting God in your own words.**

Overcoming Sin through Faith

"For I am not ashamed of the gospel, for it is the power of God for salvation to everyone who believes, to the Jew first and also to the Greek." (Romans 1:16)

The gospel includes not only the eternal salvation of our souls, but also the present salvation from the power of sin. Just as we believe that Jesus died at Calvary for our sins and we will thus never go to hell, we are also to believe that our old man was crucified with Christ, we have now received new life, and the Holy Spirit gives us the power to practically live out that life now (see Rom 6:4, 6; 8:2). Why should we believe this and live accordingly? Because God tells us—and what He says is true!

The Son of God Himself said, "The truth will set you free" (Jn. 8:32). That's why it's so important that we know the truth and thereby better understand what God has made us to be. You need to know who you are in the eyes of God, or what position He has given you, so that you can live accordingly. Before your conversion, you were a slave to sin. It ruled you and you had to obey it. But that is over now. Why? Because you died with Christ. God tells you that because of this you have been freed from the dominion of sin—and this is what you are to practically put into effect through a living faith.

That is why Paul writes, "So you also must consider yourselves dead to sin and alive to God in Christ Jesus" (Rom. 6:11). We are not to simply desire to be dead to sin, but we are to accept it as a God-given truth and accordingly simply stop responding to the temptations of sin. God Himself gives you the right to do so. In other words, live out the position God has given you! Be what you are! You are crucified with Christ—that is to say, your old life is over—and now Christ lives in you because you have received His life. The identity of a Christian can be described in two simple words: "in Christ" (see Rom. 8:1).

A young believing girl was once asked by an adult what she does when the devil knocks on her heart's door. Her answer was, "I don't do anything, I just send Jesus to the door". This hits the nail on the head: we are not to fight against sin but look to the Lord, ask Him for help and leave the fight to Him—victory is then certain!

If we keep the Son of God vividly before our eyes and trust in Him, then we will victoriously overcome the sinful world that surrounds us. The challenging words of John are also impressive: "For everyone who has been born of God overcomes the world. And this is the victory that has overcome the world—our faith. Who is it that overcomes the world except the one who believes that Jesus is the Son of God?" (1 Jn. 5:4–5).

> **"For the righteous falls seven times and rises again."**
> (Proverbs 24:16)

Christian Briem writes: "To the extent that our faith is occupied with Him, we will overcome the world as an enemy. What power, what mystery lies in the knowledge of the person of Jesus our Lord! That we would reach out for it more! What could the world do even with one for whom the Son of God is everything?" (*Dies ist das ewige Leben* [This is the Eternal Life], CSV)

You may find that your practical experience (of yielding to temptation) often does not match the position God has given you (of being dead to sin). Then there is the danger of thinking, because of the failure, that God's Word here does not apply to you. But this is not true. It is not your experience but God's truth that is the basis for your faith! A short allegorical story may help you understand this point a little better:

Fact, Faith and Experience balance on a high wall. Fact walks ahead of the other two with a firm and sure step, while looking neither to the right nor to the left, or behind him. Faith follows Fact—and everything goes well as long as he keeps his eyes on Fact. But the moment Faith looks behind him to see how Experience is doing, he loses his balance and falls off the wall—and poor old Experience, dependent on Faith, falls right after him.

What do we learn from this? That faith must be focused on God and the facts of His Word, and not on our experiences, feelings, or failures!

> **The charm of sin is gone the moment it is perpetrated.**
> (John G Bellett)

A Jew who used to live under the law and then came to know Jesus Christ as his Saviour tells what struggles he had in living a holy life as a Christian. After coming to Germany from Russia and meeting believers there, the following happened:

I found among these Christians a striving and struggling for a sanctification of the flesh. The glorious, precious position which the believer possesses in Christ and which God had shown me in

His Word during my loneliness in Russia, especially in the Epistles of the Apostle Paul, became clouded and obscured to me under their teachings. I also began to want to make my own self, i.e. my old corrupt nature, holy in itself, and thus to place myself under the law again...

Since this work is in vain and, of course, I failed at it and did not discover any progress of sanctification of the flesh in me, I became unhappy and miserable and went through hard times. I found myself in the state of Galatians and Colossians, so condemned by the Apostle Paul, and I no longer represented pure biblical Christianity, but rather Judaised Christianity.

My gaze had been turned away from the perfect position of a Christian in Christ and had been turned away from the risen Christ Himself, who is enthroned at the right hand of God in glory. In exchange, my eye had now been turned toward myself, in order to be able to deal with my naturally depraved heart; my poor, wretched me; the "old self," of whom it must be true what the Apostle Paul testified from his own experience: "I know that nothing good dwells in me, that is, in my flesh" (Rom. 7:18).

Like all those Christians, I was only concerned with Christ to the extent that I called on Him almost day and night to have Him make me holy in my inner being and to free me from the sinful nature that dwells in me. But could He answer these pleas, since His death had already freed me (and all believers) on the cross from the old nature? (Read Romans 6:6–7.) Certainly not! "Our old self is crucified with us." This is not the goal that the believer needs to first reach, but it is a fact that has already been accomplished in God's eyes for every believer, from which the insightful believer proceeds and which, according to God's Word, he grasps in faith.

That is why the Apostle says, "So you also must consider yourselves dead to sin and alive to God in Christ Jesus" (Rom. 6:11). We, therefore, who are the Lord's own, through the indwelling Holy Spirit and in faithfully looking up to Himself, our Lord, enthroned at the right hand of God, can not only keep the "old self" (the corrupt nature), which was co-crucified in the death of Christ, in death, but can also always walk in newness of life (Rom. 6:11, 14; 8:1–16). But never does the Christian's "old self" become holy!

...

I had become so poor and miserable that I hardly knew whether I was a Jew or a Christian; at any rate, the Christianity I now saw and had was almost nothing better than Judaism. My heart had gained nothing.

But God had mercy on me and, through the power and clarity of His Word and Spirit, led me back to "sincere and pure devotion to Christ" (2 Cor. 11:3). He showed me that my place and part before Him is "in Christ", that in Him I am already "holy" and "fit" for "the inheritance of the saints in light" (Col. 1:12) and am already now "a new creation" (2 Cor. 5:17), His "child and heir" (Rom. 8:14–16, etc.).

I was also enabled to see that I am a member of Jesus Christ, eternally one with Him, so that nothing can separate me from Him and no one can snatch me out of His hands (Rom 8:36–38; Jn. 10:27–28).

In this blessed certainty of my glorious position in Christ and my intimate and eternal belonging to Him lies the strength and motivation to please the Lord and pursue His holiness, which I do suc-

cessfully only when He is my delight and when my eye remains faithfully fixed on Him in faith (2 Cor. 3:18).

Since then, my heart is again happy and able to exalt and worship God my Father in spirit and truth.

(*Friede über Israel* [Peace upon Israel], Ernst Paulus Verlag)

**"And you will know the truth,
and the truth will set you free."**

John 8:32

> *What is the key to living a victorious life over sin? What role does faith play in this? Take God at His word and act in the manner in which He sees you and in accordance with what He has made you!*

Notes:

....

....

....

....

....

....

....

....

....

Spiritual Guidance and Trust

God promises us in His Word that everyone who believes the gospel of salvation will receive the Holy Spirit (see Eph. 1:14). This is a divine fact that we must believe simply because God tells us: "Or do you not know that your body is a temple of the Holy Spirit within you, whom you have from God?" (1 Cor. 6:19). If we grasp this truth in faith, it will have a tremendous impact on our lives!

Thus in every born-again Christian there dwells a divine Person who has a will and wants to fulfil and guide us daily. Unfortunately, we often forget this or have trouble truly trusting in His guidance. For us, who are children and sons of God, it should actually be characteristic and normal for us that we are guided by the Holy Spirit. That is why Paul writes in Romans 8:14: "For all who are led by the Spirit of God are sons of God".

The Spirit not only dwells in the believer, but He also desires to fill him completely, that is to say, to exert His influence in all areas of his life. It is impressive to read of both Stephen and Barnabas that they were full of faith and the Holy Spirit (Acts 6:5; 11:24). Obviously, practical faith is related to being filled with the Holy Spirit. The more we trust the leading of the Spirit and are willing to obey His quiet voice, the more we will experience that He leads and guides us wonderfully in our daily lives and in our gatherings as Christians!

The evangelist Charles Stanley often experienced the way the Holy Spirit led Him to make the right decisions. He writes about this:

> It is written, "All things are possible for one who believes" (Mk. 9:23). We read the words, we don't doubt them, and yet we very seldom think about the possibility that they might come true in our own experience.
> (Edward Dennett)

It is important to look to the Lord every day, for the guidance of the Holy Spirit, as we never know when or where He may use us in sovereign grace. I was crossing the country, one day from Bristol, where I had been preaching, to Tetbury. I had never been in this part of the country before.

On arriving at Wootton-under-Edge, I had some time to spare before going on. It was about five o'clock on a hot day in the midst of harvest. There was scarcely a person to be seen in the little town. I was very distinctly impressed from the Lord, that I must preach the gospel there that afternoon, yet there appeared to be no people to preach to. Nearly all seemed to be out in the harvest field. Yet the conviction deepened, that I must preach. I took a few tracts, and gave them where I could find anyone.

I was standing in a little shop, speaking to a woman about her soul, when a man came running up the road, the perspiration streaming off his face. He turned into the shop, and said, "Please, sir, are you a preacher of the gospel?"

"Yes," I said, "I am, through the Lord's mercy, but why do you ask?"

He replied, "I am the bellman, and if you will preach today I will cry it."

"Well," I said, "it was very much laid on my heart to preach the gospel here today, but I do not see any to preach to. Tell me, how is it you came in such haste, and asked me the question?"

He replied, "I was working in the field, and a woman came past and told me someone was distributing tracts in Wootton, and it was just as if a voice had said to me, 'You must run, and there must be preaching in Wootton today.' That is why I left my work, and came immediately."

As he was the bellman, I involuntarily put my hand in my pocket to give him the shilling. "Oh dear no, sir," he said, "I don't want the money, I want souls to be saved," and the earnestness and solemnity of the man confirmed his words. In half an hour he had washed himself, cried the preaching, and we were on the way to the Chipping, to preach. To human reason it seemed impossible to get any to preach to.

Just as we came outside the town, we were passing a gentleman's house on the right. The Spirit of God stopped me, and distinctly directed me to stand on that doorstep, and on that end of it nearest the town. By this time, perhaps, half a dozen people had collected, and came and stood before me. I gave out the hymn,

> *"Just as I am, without one plea*
> *But that Thy blood was shed for me*
> *And that Thou bid'st me come to Thee*
> *Oh, Lamb of God, I come, I come!"*

There were very few to hear, but I was much led out in showing the exceeding riches of the grace of God, in receiving the sinner just as he was, and that in perfect righteousness, through the accom-

plished work of Christ. That it was not so much the joy of the prodigal, as the great joy of the father, in receiving him.

I found afterwards that the master and mistress of the house hearing someone singing on their doorstep, had come into the passage behind me, and had heard every word.

When I closed, the gentleman, who was a doctor, begged me to go in, and see his aged mother, upstairs. He said, as tears of joy rolled down his face, "I never heard this before: I thought I had a great work to do before I could be saved, and now I hear it has all been done, and God has joy in receiving me, just as I am."

I found the aged, bedridden, mother had heard every word, her window being exactly over that end of the doorstep. The circumstances of this day had almost passed from my mind, when years after, I was preaching at Cheltenham, and a lady there told me that the Lord blessed the word that day, in the conversion of the doctor, his wife, and also the aged mother, through the chamber window. The doctor and his mother had both departed to be with the Lord.

Is it not true that "He has mercy on whom he will have mercy"? Up to that day the doctor had been enveloped in the dark cloud of ritualism. What a contrast when the gospel is heard for the first time. How blessed, when the Lord opens the eyes of the blind.

(Charles Stanley, *Incidents of Gospel Work*, Believers Bookshelf USA)

> *In what situations have you experienced the leading of the Holy Spirit in a concrete manner? What obstacles keep you from being led by the Spirit? What situations in the New Testament can you think of where the Holy Spirit led people, and what can you learn from these incidents? What might you need to empty yourself of so that the Spirit can fill you more?*

Notes:

....

....

....

....

....

....

....

....

....

....

....

....

....

....

Evangelise with Faith and Perseverance

"Cast your bread upon the waters, for you will find it after many days." (Ecclesiastes 11:1)

The fact that living faith has concrete effects on the actions of believers is made clear by the story of Noah: "By faith Noah, being warned by God concerning events as yet unseen, in reverent fear constructed an ark for the saving of his household" (Heb. 11:7). God informs His servant that a great flood will come upon the earth and tells him to build an ark. Noah takes God at His word—and for about 120 years he builds a ship on dry land, although there is no water to be seen far and wide!

How much mockery and incomprehension this man would have reaped from his fellow men during these many years for this act of faith! Instead of believing the "herald of righteousness" (2 Pet. 2:5) and helping him to build the ship, they simply carry on as before. For how long? Until Noah enters the ark, God closes it behind him and judgment falls (see Lk. 17:27). Countless souls who didn't believe the word of God are swept away in the following days by mighty floods of water.

This incident also speaks to our time. We know that very soon a terrible judgment will come upon this world. Peter writes, "What will be the outcome for those who do not obey the gospel of God?" (1 Pet. 4:17). Men will one day say to the mountains and rocks, "Fall on us and hide us from the face of him who is seated on the throne, and from the wrath of the Lamb, for the great day of their wrath has come, and who can stand?" (Rev. 6:16–17).

Now we preach Jesus as the Lamb of God who takes away the sin of the world. However, those who do not accept Him as Saviour will come to know Him as Judge—and will come under the terrible wrath of the Lamb. Now there is still time to warn people of the terror of the Lord and of their running towards the edge of a cliff (2 Cor. 5:11; Job 36:12). Soon it will forever be too late for many!

Faith based on the Word of God is always right—even if it sometimes takes a while until the fulfilment of God's promises becomes evident. Peter speaks of this very thing when he writes, "The Lord is not slow to fulfil his promise as some count slowness, but is patient toward you, not wishing that any should perish, but that all should reach repentance" (2 Pet. 3:9).

We can apply Noah's act of faith to ourselves in a very practical way: God may also tell someone to preach the gospel on the street, regardless of whether they see fruit or not. Many people will simply shake their heads at such a person, but the Lord can save souls through this that would otherwise be lost for all eternity. The Japanese evangelist Matzuzaki preached the gospel at the same place on the street for over 1000 days until the first soul was converted. With Noah it was even 120 years—and seven souls were saved.

Maybe God wants to send someone to a faraway land where there are countless souls who have never heard the name of Jesus. Often this requires learning a new language and

> **In the morning I pray for two hours that He may save souls. The rest of the day I help him answer my prayers.**
> (Dwight L Moody, translated from German)

other preparations that require energy and time. Perhaps God makes it clear to a young Christian that he should learn Chinese, even though he doesn't see any possibility of going to China anytime soon. What is to be done then? Trust God and act in faith! As Solomon aptly says, "Trust in the LORD with all your heart, and do not lean on your own understanding" (Prov. 3:5).

Even on the mission field it sometimes takes a long time to see fruit. John Paton, William Carey, Adoniram Judson, James Fraser and others laboured, in some cases, for many years without anyone being converted at all. However, God rewards the faithfulness with which we still serve Him, even if no fruit is visible for a long time. This is also made clear by the following story:

In Sydney, there once lived an old man who kept passing out tracts in a business district. As he did so, he asked the same question each time, "If you die this night, will you be in heaven?" Many people took the tract as they passed by, but most of them just put it in their jacket pockets.

One of them, a young man, read it on the flight back from Sydney to London. The following Sunday, he attended a sermon at a London Baptist church. Toward the end of the meeting, he reported to the pastor and asked, "Can I say a few words?" "Well, it's getting late," the pastor replied, but then said, "All right, but no more than three minutes". The young man related, "Last week in Sydney an old man pressed a tract into my hand. In doing so, he asked me if I would go to heaven if I died that night. I could not get this question out of my mind. The very next day after my arrival here in London, I visited a friend whom I knew to be a Christian. He explained to me the way to heaven. That's how I became a Christian."

This story impressed the pastor. Some time later, he attended a missions conference held in the Caribbean. He incorporated the young man's story into his sermon there. Following the talk, three missionaries approached him and excitedly declared, "We know that old man! During a visit to Sydney, we also received that tract and through it we started to reflect on life. We came to believe in Jesus and became missionaries."

Subsequently, the pastor had business in India, and in his talks he again told the story, and also what the three missionaries had told him. After the lecture, one Indian told him, "I was a government employee and had official business in Sydney. And there in George Street, an elderly man handed me a tract and asked me the question, 'If you die this night, will you be in heaven?' That question stuck with me. When I got back to India, I went to the people in the mission station at the end of my street. They prayed with me, I was converted and later became a missionary. That's my story."

Over time, the pastor kept meeting people who had come to faith in Jesus Christ through the man from Sydney.

Years later, the pastor himself had business in Sydney. Now he was eager to meet the old man himself. Another pastor showed him where he lived. Together they set out. An old, frail man opened the door for them. He asked them to take a seat on the old, worn sofa and looked at them expectantly.

> **"As for you, always be sober-minded, endure suffering, do the work of an evangelist, fulfil your ministry."**
> (2 Timothy 4:5)

The pastor from London began, "I have heard that you distribute these tracts. Have you ever in your life heard of people being converted by them?" The old man smiled, "No, never. I've passed them out, asked a question in the process, and then never heard from people again."

The pastor replied, "I have travelled the world and given many talks. Again and again I have come across people who have come to faith through your ministry. Quite a few have even become missionaries."

The old man looked at him steadfastly with moist eyes. Then he told how he had come to proselytise in this way: "As a young man, I was quite a 'tough guy' as they say. Then I came to faith. That changed my life completely. I was and am so grateful to God that I don't have to go to hell but know: 'I am going to heaven'. Out of this gratitude, I promised God to either tell ten people about Him or to give them a tract every day. And I have kept that promise, for forty years."

> *Have you perhaps not seen any fruit in evangelising for some time? Don't give up! If the Lord wants you to do things like book-table work, distributing tracts and calendars, or sharing the faith in other ways, keep doing it. God will reward faithfulness—and His Word will not return to Him empty (see Isa. 55:11)!*

Notes:

....

....

....

....

....

....

....

....

....

....

....

....

....

....

....

....

Energy of Faith and Experiences of Faith

An Important Principle

"According to your faith be it done to you." (Matthew 9:29)

God shows us His will through His living Word. This applies both to basic decisions that we need to make and to specific things for which we need direction. If we have a sincere desire to serve Him and ask Him to show us what to do for Him, He will make His will clear to us!

If I have recognised the will of God, then a very decisive question arises for me: With what energy of faith do I do what He wants me to do? Do I give myself completely to it or do I do it halfheartedly on the side? The Word of God makes it clear in several places that the experiences of faith in service for the Lord are often related to the trust and faith in action that we display. To the extent that we trust God, put forth energy in faith, and take steps of faith, we also experience Him!

The Lord Jesus once told two blind men, "According to your faith be it done to you" (Mt. 9:29)—a word we can still apply to ourselves today! To the Roman centurion, who believed great things of the Son of God, He said, "Let it be done for you as you have believed" (Mt. 8:13). But in His grace, God also more often gives answers to prayer, even though the expectations and practical faith of those who pray leave much to be desired (see Acts 12; Jn. 11:40).

Here is an example of a person who served the Lord with devotion and faith in action:

William Carey, a shoemaker from a poor family in England, had an ever-increasing burden on his heart after his conversion to take the message of the Bible to people in faraway lands who had never before come in contact with God's Word.

The words of the Lord Jesus: "God so loved the world" (Jn. 3:16) and "Go into all the world" (Mk. 16:15) were always before his eyes as he studied the map of the world he had made. That map, along with the verses, reflected exactly what was in his heart.

While serving as a pastor in a Baptist church, he also preached more and more on the subject of missions, which was burning on his soul. He saw that there were some interested listeners—but apart from listening they did nothing. Ultimately, he could not help but follow the Lord's command himself and set out as a missionary.

Despite great opposition, he went to India in 1793. His great motto in serving the Lord was, "expect great things from God; attempt great things for God." And that is exactly what he did. With great energy of faith, he set about studying Indian languages, with the result that God enabled him to translate the Bible, or parts of the Bible, into 36 Indian languages and dialects. The printing press he started enabled 300 million people to have access to the Word of God.

> **We can expect great things from God and attempt great things for Him.**
> (William Carey)

God stands by His word when we expect great things from Him and—in dependence on Him—also attempt great things for Him!

> *With what energy of faith and devotion do you fulfil the mission God has given you? Which examples show that this faith in action and experiences of faith are often connected with each other? What is the reason that we often only half-heartedly do what God shows us?*

Notes:

....
....
....
....
....
....
....
....
....
....
....
....
....
....

Empty Vessels

Elisha and the Widow

"Now the wife of one of the sons of the prophets cried to Elisha, 'Your servant my husband is dead, and you know that your servant feared the LORD, but the creditor has come to take my two children to be his slaves.' And Elisha said to her, 'What shall I do for you? Tell me; what have you in the house?' And she said, 'Your servant has nothing in the house except a jar of oil.' Then he said, 'Go outside, borrow vessels from all your neighbours, empty vessels and not too few. Then go in and shut the door behind yourself and your sons and pour into all these vessels. And when one is full, set it aside.'" (2 Kings 4:1–4)

What a hopeless situation this widow finds herself in! Her husband has died, she is in debt, and now the creditors are coming to take her two sons as slaves. What terrible misery! What does she do in her distress?

Instead of despairing or resigning, she goes to Elisha, the man of God. With every hardship that God allows in our lives, He intends to draw us closer to Himself. Difficulties and problems should, in fact, always drive us into the open arms of God, for "God is our refuge and strength, a very present help in trouble" (Ps. 46:1).

Elisha is also called the prophet of grace. Why? Because he encounters people from the most diverse social backgrounds—kings, soldiers, lepers, the poor—and responds to their needs each time. To each one he brings the blessing that God holds in His heart for that person. In this he is a wonderful foreshadow of the Son of God, from whose fullness we too receive to this day "grace upon grace" (see Jn. 1:16).

What does the man of God say to this woman? First of all, he asks her what she has in the house. He thus takes up what she already has. This is a divine principle that is still valid today: the Lord wants to use the little that we have to make blessings out of it. To do this, however, we must first find out what is available to us and/or what abilities God has given us. Perhaps they are inconspicuous gifts or talents that have no special value in our eyes, but it is precisely the weak and the despised that God uses to mightily show Himself (see 1 Cor. 1:26)!

Now, after the widow tells Elisha that she has only one jar of oil left, the prophet urges her to borrow vessels from her neighbours. He does not tell her how many to ask for—that is left to her faith—but says only that it should not be a few! Because Elisha knows his God, he knows that much grace can be counted on from Him!

As someone once aptly said, "Elisha does not say, 'Be careful not to borrow too many vessels,' because in 'God's bank' faith can never ask for too much credit. He who trusts in God has never brought to Him an empty vessel that He could not have filled."

They are to be empty vessels—for this reveals that the blessing is truly from God Himself. They are not to be few—this shows us that it is God's desire to respond to faith in abundant measure with blessings. His sources of help are inexhaustible! As David writes in the Psalms, "The river of God is full of water" (Ps. 65:9). We cannot expect too much from Him when we are in His will. It honours Him when we say with conviction of faith, "All my springs are in you" (Ps. 87:7)—and make abundant use of His grace!

To show how great and fitting God's sources of help are, here follows the experience of a poor woman who was also once in great need:

A missionary woman one day found herself utterly destitute among a pagan tribe, far from any food supply. In her great need, she appealed to God's promise that He would provide for her. She also felt very miserable health-wise. Then several large packages of Scottish oatmeal arrived from a businessman living far away. The missionary still had several tins of canned milk, so she was forced to live on this monotonous food for four weeks. In time, however, she felt noticeably better, and after the four weeks she felt completely well again.

> **Empty buckets are fittest for the well of grace.**
> (Charles H Spurgeon)

Later, when she told a group of people about her condition, a doctor who was present inquired with particular interest about the nature of her previous ailments. Then he said, "The Lord has heard your prayer and provided for you more faithfully than you can imagine; for the illness from which you have suffered, we doctors prescribe a four-week diet of oats. The Lord Himself prescribed it for you and saw to it that you got nothing else. It was just the right medicine for you!"

(Lettie B Cowman, *Alle meine Quellen sind in dir* [All My Springs Are In You], Gerth Medien)

"The river of God is full of water."

Psalm 65:9

> *What goes through your mind when you realise that God wants to challenge your faith and encourage you to expect much from Him? What abilities and talents has God entrusted to you? How can you use them to bless others?*

Notes:

....

....

....

....

....

....

....

....

....

....

....

....

....

....

....

Faith in Action Is Rewarded!

"So she went from him and shut the door behind herself and her sons. And as she poured they brought the vessels to her. When the vessels were full, she said to her son, 'Bring me another vessel.' And he said to her, 'There is not another.' Then the oil stopped flowing. She came and told the man of God, and he said, 'Go, sell the oil and pay your debts, and you and your sons can live on the rest.'" (2 Kings 4:5–7)

Try to put yourself in the shoes of this widow: She has almost no oil left in the house and yet she is supposed to go from door to door in her village asking for empty vessels. What should she answer if the neighbours ask her criticising questions?

By asking all over the place for empty vessels, she surely gives the impression to others that there is plenty of oil in her house or that there will be very soon. Doesn't she run the risk of losing face in the event that she has to return the jars unused? In a sense, she is being asked to go out on a limb. However, the order comes from the man of God—and that is what ultimately matters!

> **"The fear of man lays a snare, but whoever trusts in the LORD is safe."**
> (Proverbs 29:25)

Thus the widow needs faith to go around the neighbourhood, knocking on doors and asking for empty vessels. She is to trust the word of the prophet and show faith in action. In such a situation, doubtful questions may have arisen in her heart: "Aren't three vessels enough? Can I really dare to borrow five vessels? Isn't ten somewhat exaggerated? What will the people think of me? What if I get no oil or only a little?"

Such thoughts can also come to us when the Lord gives us a task to do and we wonder what intensity and faith in action we should apply to fulfil that task. When someone serves the Lord with devotion, he must take into account that he may be judged by people. At the same time, we mustn't forget that those who judge can usually only see the outward deeds but have not themselves experienced how the Lord has made His will clear in this matter and our motivation for the service.

Especially when someone serves with a lot of energy in faith and does things that are perhaps somewhat unusual, he must expect that catchwords such as "soberness" or "balance" will be expressed by others. They are often well-intentioned but frequently act like a fire extinguisher on burning hearts. When the ailing and old George Whitefield was urged to take a more sensible approach to his health, he replied only, "Better to burn than to rust!"

In some parts of Christendom today, people are virtually frozen in a false form of soberness, while in other parts there is a tendency to be effusive. We must beware of both—and be very careful about judging others who may show more devotion than we do ourselves!

Soberness in the sense of the Bible means, among other things, that we do not let ourselves be distracted from what really matters. We are to live our life in the light of eternity—and we may do this with devotion!

The widow then sets out and goes from house to house. Her faith now becomes outwardly displayed. Finally she returns with several vessels and closes the door behind her and her sons. Certainly the vessels had different sizes as well as shapes and were also in different condition—small, large, beautiful, worn or old. They had one thing in common though: they were all empty.

This is exactly where our lives come in to play, because in several places the Word of God refers to believers as vessels. Oil, on the other hand, is usually a picture of the Holy Spirit dwelling in believers. The first application of this story is therefore obvious: the more we are emptied of ourselves, the more the Holy Spirit can fill us and make us a channel of blessing for others.

Paul writes that we are not to be intoxicated with wine, but to be filled with the Holy Spirit (see Eph. 5:18). Furthermore, the Son of God said, "If anyone thirsts, let him come to me and drink. Whoever believes in me, as the Scripture has said, 'Out of his heart will flow rivers of living water'" (Jn. 7:38). He who drinks abundantly at the fountain can also give much to others!

Behind closed doors, the widow now begins to pour oil into the individual vessels with her sons. In the process, they experience the way the oil is miraculously multiplied. God's work often happens in stillness before it becomes outwardly visible. In order to be filled with the Holy Spirit, we need hidden contact or real communion with God. This happens, for example, when we quietly talk to God about His Word in prayer.

What is the result of this act of faith? The woman receives just as much oil as she in faith has asked for vessels from her neighbours. In other words, the blessing she receives is equal to the practical faith she summoned up to fulfil the prophet's commission.

The little jar, which before seemed inconspicuous and inconsequential, becomes the means by which God bestows miraculous salvation. He suddenly provides oil for every vessel. None remains empty or only half filled. How many more vessels could have been filled if they had been asked for in faith? The widow in no way exhausted the depths of God's resources!

> **Expect great things from God, and great things you will have. There is no limit to what He is able to do.**
> (George Müller)

The spiritual lesson for us is: the more practical faith we muster to fulfil the tasks God gives us, the more blessings we will also enjoy practically. God desires that we count on Him, expect much of Him, and draw abundantly from His infinite sources of help. He never tires of meeting our needs.

Dwight L Moody once learned an important lesson due to such an experience:

No one—absolutely no one—could fill up a Sunday school better than young Dwight Moody. All week long he worked as a shoe salesman for one of the biggest shoe companies in Chicago. (He was good at selling shoes, too, and he planned to make a lot of money.) But on Sunday, he walked through the streets rounding up as many kids as he could. He took them all to Sunday school. Once he got them there, though, Moody felt like his job was done. It was someone else's job to teach the Bible, wasn't it?

He was sure of it the day Mr. Hibbert was sick, and Moody was asked to teach his class of twelve-year-old girls. Those girls acted up during the whole lesson—even laughed in his face! Moody had to bite his tongue to keep from telling them to "get out and don't came back."

One day, Mr. Hibbert came into the shoe store and asked to speak to Moody. The man was middle-aged, but he was sick with a rattling cough. "How can I help you Mr. H.?" Moody said. "You look like you should be in bed." Mr. Hibbert nodded sadly. "My lungs are bleeding... doctor says I won't survive another winter in Chicago. So I'm leaving soon to go back home to my family—going home to die, I suppose. But..."

"But what, Mr. H.?" Moody asked. "I hate leaving my class," said the Sunday school teacher. "You see, not one of those girls has accepted Christ as her Saviour yet. If I leave them now..." Oh no! Thought Moody, He's not going to ask me to teach that class of horrible girls, is he? Quickly he said, "Why don't you visit them—you know, individually—and tell them how you feel." Mr. Hibbert's tired face lift up. "That is exactly what I want to do, Dwight. But... I don't know if I have the strength. Will you go with me?" Moody gladly agreed. The last he could do for the poor man was take him where he needed to go.

So each evening after work, Dwight Moody walked with Mr. Hibbert to each girl's house, helped him up the rickety stairs to the dingy apartments, and sat quietly while the teacher talked sincerely to each pupil. To Moody's amazement, first one, then another, then another girl accepted Christ as her Saviour. After ten days of visiting, every single girl in that class had given her life to Jesus. On the last day before Mr. Hibbert was supposed to leave, Moody picked up all the girls so they could say goodbye to their teacher. It turned into a regular prayer meeting, as each girl thanked God for her teacher and prayed for him.

Moody went to the train station the next day to see Mr. Hibbert off. To his surprise, all the girls showed up too, crying and waving as the train pulled out. Mr. Hibbert stood on the platform at the back of the train, a peaceful smile on his face. His finger pointed up toward heaven, where he would see each of his students again someday. Dwight Moody's heart was full nearly to the bursting point. "Oh, God!" he cried. "Selling shoes and making money don't seem very important compared to what I've seen in the last two weeks. Forgive me, Lord, for focusing on the wrong things. From now on, I want to tell boys and girls and men and woman about the Good News. I'm your man full time!"

(Dave & Neta Jackson, *Hero Tales*, Bethany House)

> *What does it mean to you to drink abundantly at the fountain and have hidden interaction with God? Why does Paul contrast drinking wine with being filled with the Holy Spirit, and what can you learn for yourself from this? What might wine represent in your life? What intentions of God to bless you do you see in Romans 15:13 and how can you come into greater enjoyment of that blessing?*

Notes:

....

....

....

....

....

....

....

....

....

....

....

....

....

....

....

The Energy of Faith—in Practice

"Go outside, borrow vessels ... and not too few." (2 Kings 4:3)

We've seen in the widow the connection between the energy of faith and experiences of faith. Paul speaks of the same principle in another context when he says, "The point is this: whoever sows sparingly will also reap sparingly, and whoever sows bountifully will also reap bountifully" (2 Cor. 9:6). Because so much for our practical life of faith and ministry depends on this principle, we'll look at some examples that will help us understand how we can put this all into practice.

If God has given you the mission to evangelise, take advantage of the opportunities you have and do it in the energy of faith. Don't stop when you have distributed five or ten tracts and people have maybe made fun of you. Sometimes you have to sow for a long time without seeing fruit until eventually the harvest comes. This is what the Lord Jesus, God's Sower, experienced. For three and a half years He saw almost no fruit from His labour; but how tremendous is the harvest that has now been reaped for almost 2,000 years. God's Word is alive and does not return to Him empty!

If you have the charge of practising hospitality, do not limit it to once or twice a year. We are to seek to serve others in our homes (see Rom. 12:13). Let the Lord show you opportunities and seize them. Remember Priscilla and Aquila, who often opened their homes to others and were a blessing to many as a result.

If God has shown you that you need to spend more time studying the Bible, try to set aside as much time as possible to do that. The more you prayerfully study the Word, the more blessings you will receive through it. God does not say how often you should do this, but rather, "Let the word of Christ dwell in you richly" (Col. 3:16). This also applies to memorising Bible verses or chapters. "Your words were found, and I ate them, and your words became to me a joy and the delight of my heart" (Jer. 15:16).

If you know you have a ministry to children or women, don't just do it on the side. Take time to consider how you can best magnify the Lord to them and advance them in the faith. Pray for each individual person you minister to. The Lord will show His faithfulness!

We can apply this to our prayer life as well: Our petitions (the empty vessels we bring before God) can never be too many. We may come as often as we like and bring as many vessels as our faith will allow—we will always experience that He has mercy and grace in store for us at the throne of grace. Therefore, "Open your mouth wide, and I will fill it" (Ps. 81:10) is also true for us!

> **Without the present operation of faith therefore, there can be no display of power through the servant, whatever his earnestness or zeal for the glory of God; whereas, on the other hand, if there be but the smallest degree of faith in exercise, divine power is so brought in that obstacles as large as mountains are removed, and all difficulties are victoriously surmounted.**
> (Edward Dennett)

When you become aware anew of the need for prayer, give yourself to prayer and dare to pray for things for which you may have lacked faith until now. James writes, "You do not have, because you do not ask" (Jas. 4:2). Jabez opened his mouth wide—and was blessed abundantly (see 1 Chron. 4:10).

A young Christian woman saw her mission from God as teaching Sunday school. While she was in charge of a Sunday school class for a while, one child after another was converted until finally all were saved. She was asked to give the Sunday school class to someone else and take over a new class.

Again the same thing happened: one child after another accepted Jesus Christ as their personal Saviour. After some time, she was again asked to give the Sunday school class to someone else and take a third class. It didn't take long, and the same results were seen: all the children converted and were saved.

After the death of this young Christian woman, her diary, which she had kept regularly, was found. In it were, among others, three special entries. The first read, "I have decided to pray every day for each of my Sunday school children by name".

A later entry added the words: "And I will fight for them in prayer". Finally, she had written down the following sentence: "I have resolved to pray for my Sunday school children every day, to fight for them in prayer, and to expect a blessing from God".

She ministered through faith in action and experienced that God stamped His blessing on it. We can do the same today: instead of doing the will of God casually (see Jer. 48:10), we should be abounding with determination in the Lord's work at all times, knowing that our effort is not in vain (see 1 Cor. 15:58).

Returning to the story in 2 Kings 4, the prophet finally tells the widow to sell the oil, pay her debts, and live from the rest with her sons. This is no sooner said than done. The oil she uses to pay off the debt is not only for the present removal of the shortage, but also for the future preservation of the whole family.

Applied to our lives, this means that the Holy Spirit not only gives us strength to serve the Lord, but He makes us abundant in hope—which thereby bubbles over to others as well—as we cling in faith to the promises of God (see Rom. 15:13).

The incident begins with a widow in poverty and ends with a family that has abundance. God's mercy is always greater than what we need. We see the same thing in the feeding of the 5,000: the Lord Jesus not only meets the needs of the crowd but makes sure that 12 hand baskets full of bread remain at the end. The grace of God triumphs! As Paul writes to the Ephesians, "Now to him who is able to do far more abundantly than all that we ask or think, according to the power at work within us, to him be glory in the church and in Christ Jesus throughout all generations, forever and ever. Amen" (Eph. 3:20–21).

> *What does it mean to be always abounding in the Lord's work (see 1 Cor. 15:58)? What ministry has the Lord given you and how can you do it with more practical faith?*

Notes:

....

....

....

....

....

....

....

....

....

....

....

....

....

....

....

....

....

....

....

....

....

....

Digging Pools of Blessing

"Make This Valley Full of Ditches"

"He said, 'Thus says the LORD: "Make this valley full of ditches." For thus says the LORD: "You shall not see wind, nor shall you see rain; yet that valley shall be filled with water, so that you, your cattle, and your animals may drink." And this is a simple matter in the sight of the LORD; He will also deliver the Moabites into your hand ...'. Now it happened in the morning, when the grain offering was offered, that suddenly water came by way of Edom, and the land was filled with water." (2 Kings 3:16–18, 20, NKJV)

When the Moabites turn away from the Israelites, the Israelites ally with Judah and the Edomites to fight Moab. But they have a big problem: there is no water for the soldiers or for their animals.

In this precarious situation, they go to the prophet Elisha to ask God through him. The LORD answers. He gives His servant a prophetic word and tells them to make ditch after ditch in the valley and that He Himself—without causing it to rain—will fill the holes with water.

Every ditch they dig increases the blessing gained for them and their animals when God sends the promised water. They are not told how many ditches to dig—that is left to their faith; but the expression "make this valley full of ditches" indicates that they are not to be few.

How can we dig ditches today—figuratively speaking—to receive the blessing God wants to give us? By humbling ourselves before the Lord. Just as water always gathers in the deepest place, God has the most blessings in store for those who sincerely humble themselves before Him. The deeper and more sincere the humility, the more blessings we will enjoy.

God loves to richly give us gifts. However, we must also be in the right condition to receive the blessings He wants to give us. For example, if we are proud and complacent, as is said of Laodicea, then we miss out on what God has intended for us, for "God opposes the proud but gives grace to the humble" (Jas. 4:6).

What does it actually mean in concrete terms to humble ourselves before God? How do we do it? This is an important question that is given far too little thought! One way to humble ourselves before God is to consciously express our dependence on God in prayer, admitting that we ourselves are unable to do anything.

Peter, who for a time trusted in himself and had to learn the above-mentioned truth in a bitter way, encourages us with the words, "Humble yourselves, therefore, under the mighty hand of God so that at the proper time he may exalt you" (1 Pet. 5:6). And how are we to do this? By "casting all [our] anxieties on him, because he cares for [us]" (1 Pet. 5:7)!

Humility, therefore, consists, among other things, in acknowledging that we cannot solve problems by our own wisdom, human strategy, or political string-pulling, but that we rely on God's help and are truly dependent on Him. Instead of hewing out cisterns that hold no water (see Jer. 2:13), i.e. seeking human aids that will get us nowhere, we should dig ditches that God can fill with blessings! Instead of trusting in ourselves and taking things into our own hands, we hand them over to the One who is mighty and able to take care of them.

Many will probably agree with this in principle, but the question is to what extent we actually put this into practice. For example, when a problem arises in a church community, how much time do we spend discussing it or looking for possible solutions, and how much time do we spend in prayer, in the knowledge that it is the Lord who must give deliverance? In reality, unfortunately, it is often the case that in such situations there is much more talking than praying.

> **God creates out of nothing. Therefore, until a man is nothing, God can make nothing out of him.**
> (Martin Luther)

The question is whether we are humble enough to admit to ourselves that without the Lord we can indeed do nothing (see John 15:5). It is one thing to speak of being unable to do anything without the Lord, and quite another to live it out in practice! If we are humble, then especially in times of crisis this will show itself through persistent prayer—and will most certainly be blessed by the Lord!

> *How much do you talk about or brood on problems and how often do you pray about them? Why is it sometimes so difficult for us to consciously surrender a need to the Lord and then stop worrying about it? When is the first time the Bible mentions that people prayed, and what can you learn from the context for your life of faith?*

Notes:

....

....

....

....

....

....

....

....

....

....

....

....

....

....

....

....

Humility, the Way to Revival

"And he said, 'Thus says the LORD: "Make this valley full of ditches." For thus says the LORD: "You shall not see wind, nor shall you see rain; yet that valley shall be filled with water, so that you, your cattle, and your animals may drink." And this is a simple matter in the sight of the LORD.'" (2 Kings 3:16–17, NKJV)

Humbling ourselves before God also means confessing our personal and collective failures to Him with a broken heart and sincerely repenting of them, i.e., consciously changing direction. God does not want us to just pay lip service, but to be genuine and true. As it is written, "rend your hearts and not your garments. Return to the LORD your God" (Joel 2:13) and "[She] did not return to me with her whole heart, but in pretence, declares the LORD" (Jer. 3:10).

If we do this, we will experience God's blessing and assistance afresh and have a greater consciousness of it: "For thus says the One who is high and lifted up, who inhabits eternity, whose name is Holy: 'I dwell in the high and holy place, and also with him who is of a contrite and lowly spirit, to revive the spirit of the lowly, and to revive the heart of the contrite'" (Isa. 57:15).

At the dedication of the temple, the LORD made a wonderful promise to Solomon that we can still apply to ourselves today: "If my people who are called by my name humble themselves, and pray and seek my face and turn from their wicked ways, then I will hear from heaven and will forgive their sin and heal their land" (2 Chron. 7:14).

This principle runs throughout the Scriptures: every time people have sincerely humbled themselves before God, He has responded with grace. Every time! This was the case even with Manasseh, who surpassed all previous kings in wickedness. "God opposes the proud but gives grace to the humble" (Jas. 4:6). Do we take God at His word on this issue as well and act accordingly? He has said, "But this is the one to whom I will look: he who is humble and contrite in spirit and trembles at my word" (Isa. 66:2).

We can be sure that even today God will give healing and revival if we humble ourselves before Him, call guilt by its name, confess our sins to one another and forgive one another's sins, and repent from wrong ways. In church history we read of times of revival when the floor was wet with tears because believers wept over their failures and confessed them before the Lord. God responded with magnificent blessing!

Perhaps you find that superficiality and indifference have increasingly crept into your personal walk of faith. Or maybe you feel the failure of Christianity in general and of the believers with whom you have to do. Then humble yourself before the Lord. Take time to confess things and start digging those ditches in the valley you're currently in! By the way, Daniel (Dan. 9), Nehemiah (Neh. 9) and Ezra (Ezr. 9), in their humility included themselves in confessing the sins of the people, even though they had not themselves committed them.

God has the power to make springs appear not only in the mountains but also in the valleys (Ps. 104:10). He rules over the springs of the deep and over the windows of heaven. He is indeed the Father of the rain (Job 38:28), from whom every blessing and every good gift comes. In the prophet Isaiah He says: "I will open rivers on the bare heights, and fountains in the midst of the valleys. I will make the wilderness a pool of water, and the dry land springs of water" (Isa. 41:18). The psalmist confirms this with the words: "He turns rivers into a desert, springs of water into thirsty ground" (Ps. 107:33).

It is therefore not surprising that God suddenly caused water to burst forth from invisible springs overnight, as was the case in the history of Israel. He can cause wonderful blessings to appear within a very short time—whereby His actions sometimes happen inconspicuously and not always in the manner we would imagine or expect.

We need faith that expects God to act even when we see neither wind nor rain. When ditches are furrowed and pits are dug, blessings also flow from supernatural sources!

Because the people dig the ditches, they experience the way God gives them victory and the enemy takes flight—since the enemy is powerless against obedient and humble hearts. In this context, by the way, it is very interesting that Joshua and

> **From the day of Pentecost, there has not been one great spiritual awakening in any land which has not begun in a union of prayers, though only among two or three. No such outward, upward movement has continued after such prayer meetings have declined.**
> (Arthur T Pierson)

337

the people were victorious every time they went into battle from Gilgal. Gilgal is the place of self-judgment!

Revival often begins with humbly admitting that we need revival—and then pleading intensely for it in prayer. We need deep roots downwards so that there can be fruit upwards (see Isa. 37:31)! When the Spirit of God then begins to work, further humility will surely follow, which always happens when people place themselves in the light of God.

Church history gives us many accounts of revivals that God has worked among believers. Here is an example. In the 1970s, a mighty work of God happened in Borneo, where a mission team prayed more intensely for revival.

The turning point came when a group of Bornean students spent the whole night in prayer and fellowship. In June 1972 the missionaries held a house party for the students and this led to an even greater desire for prayer. Two students began to pray each evening at 9:30 pm; gradually the group grew and then divided into two groups until a great wave of student prayer was reaching God for revival in Borneo.

In a simple letter to his friends in England, an elder in the church of Bario in Borneo revealed this change from tears of sorrow to songs of joy. He was writing on 7 November 1973, shortly after revival had come to the church there:

"The services are so different from what I have ever experienced before. When the Holy Spirit comes down upon the congregation, people begin to cry out loud wailing... after the sin problems have been dealt with by the Lord and forgiveness granted, then the ser-

vice goes on with loud singing and praises while tears of joy are still flowing down."

(Brian H Edwards, *Revival—A People Saturated with God*, Day One Publications)

> *Are there times in your life when you have sincerely humbled yourself before God? When was the last time you confessed your failures to Him and pleaded with Him for revival in your life and in the lives of your fellow believers? What examples can you think of in the Bible where God responded to humbleness? Do you long for new spiritual blessings? Dig the ditches, God will fill them!*

Notes:

....

....

....

....

....

....

....

....

....

....

Arrows of Victory

The Key to Victory

"Now when Elisha had fallen sick with the illness of which he was to die, Joash king of Israel went down to him and wept before him, crying, 'My father, my father! The chariots of Israel and its horsemen!' And Elisha said to him, 'Take a bow and arrows.' So he took a bow and arrows. Then he said to the king of Israel, 'Draw the bow,' and he drew it. And Elisha laid his hands on the king's hands. And he said, 'Open the window eastward,' and he opened it. Then Elisha said, 'Shoot,' and he shot. And he said, 'The LORD's arrow of victory, the arrow of victory over Syria! For you shall fight the Syrians in Aphek until you have made an end of them.' And he said, 'Take the arrows,' and he took them. And he said to the king of Israel, 'Strike the ground with them.' And he struck three times and stopped. Then the man of God was angry with him and said, 'You should have struck five or six times; then you would have struck down Syria until you had made an end of it, but now you will strike down Syria only three times.'" (2 Kings 13:14–19)

This story shows us again how important it is to act with energy in our faith if we want to experience victories of faith. Elisha challenges Joash to shoot arrows out of the window. Immediately afterwards, he explains to him what the arrows mean: salvation for the people! Now it becomes exciting! For now the prophet tells the king to take the arrows and strike the ground with them. But he does not tell him how many times he should strike—and therein lies exactly the challenge for his faith.

Although Joash knows that the arrows mean victory for Israel, he strikes only three times and pauses. The prophet is stunned. He rebukes the king for stopping after only three strikes. Why is he so upset about this? Because he knows that God actually wanted to give him much more, if only he had reached out for more. According to the king's faith, God gives Israel three victories against the Syrians. Had he fulfilled the prophet's instruction with more dedication and energy in his faith, the enemies would have been completely destroyed.

Because Joash acts halfheartedly, he falls short of the blessing God would have liked to have given him. What do we learn from this? When we do something for the Lord, let's do it with all our heart, with determination and with perseverance. He will be faithful and put the stamp of His blessing on it! Hezekiah is a good example in this regard. Of him it is said, "And every work that he undertook in the service of the house of God and in accordance with the law and the commandments, seeking his God, he did with all his heart, and prospered" (2 Chron. 31:21).

> **Wherever you are, be all there.**
> (Jim Elliot)

What can you do to earn more victories and blessings in your life of faith? Here are a few examples.

If you sow to the Spirit, you will reap eternal life (see Gal. 6:8). What does sowing to the Spirit look like in practical terms? It happens when you read the Word of God, keep Christ before your eyes, pray, and occupy yourself with heavenly things. The more you do this with energy of faith, the more you will experience what abundant life really means (see Jn. 10:10). This is not a pious theory but is rather a practical requirement for a fulfilled life.

The more you consciously go through your day in communion with God, drinking from the fountain so to speak, the more streams of living water will flow from you as a blessing to others (see Jn. 7:38). It is interesting, by the way, that in the story of Samson the effectiveness of the Spirit of God is explicitly mentioned exactly three times. God wanted to bring about great victories for His people through this man. But just as Joash struck the earth only three times, Samson fell far short of what the LORD could have worked through him for the blessing of others.

If you want to experience the God of peace, you must focus on the things Paul presents in Philippians 4:8–9. The more intensely you do this, the more you will gain the awareness that the God of peace is with you—keeping your heart in a peace that surpasses all understanding. Regarding this J N Darby aptly said, "The secret of inward peace and outward strength is to occupy yourself with good, to occupy yourself with good again and again". The "again and again" is a matter of energy in your faith!

The importance of intensive, faith-filled and persevering prayer, especially in this respect, is made clear by the following story, which took place at the beginning of the 20th century:

Revival had come to Charlotte Chapel in Edinburgh in 1905 and two years later the church was still in the full experience of it. The members had prayed urgently for revival when their pastor returned from Wales in 1905, and when it came, even that insistent prayer was transformed:

"What can I report about our Prayer meetings? Did ever anyone see such meetings? They used to begin at seven o'clock on Sunday mornings, but that was felt to be far too late in the day for the great business that had to be transacted before the Throne of the Heavenly Grace! The meetings now begin at six o'clock and go on for almost seven days a week, with occasional intervals to attend to business, household duties, and bodily sustenance!

> **That we work more than we pray—the presence and power of God are not seen in our work as we would wish.**
> (Andrew Murray)

Some of you who are strangers may smile—many of us did—but we don't now. It is that continuous, preserving, God-honouring weekly campaign of prayer that has moved the mighty hand of God to pour upon this favoured people the blessings of His grace in such rich abundance; and if ever you should be asked the secret of this church's great spiritual prosperity, you can tell them of the prayer meetings, and especially of the gatherings of God's people— forty to sixty strong—in the Upper Vestry every Sunday morning at six or seven o'clock—summer and winter, wet day and fine—to pray. Yes, that is the secret—the secret of our church's success and prosperity."

(Brian H Edwards, *Revival—A People Saturated with God*, Day One Publications)

"Let us insist on prayer in secret to the children of God, for it is a major requirement of the spiritual life! The Father sees in secret and will repay publicly. The greatest service is useless and fruitless if it does not have its origin and source in hidden prayer. Let each of us ask ourselves the question: Do I love the hidden place, that there I may commune with the Lord, renew my strength, wrestle with God, and conquer?" (John Nelson Darby)

> *To what can you apply the arrows of victory regarding your life of faith? How much effort do you put into doing things that you are sure will bring about blessing and spiritual victory (see, e.g., 2 Cor. 9:6; Mt. 7:7; Gal. 6:8)? Why is it that you may be doing some things halfheartedly, and what can help you to change that?*

Notes:

....

....

....

....

....

....

....

....

....

Being Devoted to Prayer—The Arrow of Victory!

"The LORD's arrow of victory... Take the arrows... Strike the ground with them. ... You should have struck five or six times." **(2 Kings 13:17–19)**

God has given us, figuratively speaking, a great arrow of victory in our hands to use with energy of faith: prayer! Every believer can understand the meaning of the following verses:

- "Ask, and it will be given to you; ... For everyone who asks receives." (Mt. 7:7–8)
- "If you ask me anything in my name, I will do it." (Jn. 14:14)
- "Whatever you ask in prayer, believe that you have received it, and it will be yours." (Mk. 11:24)
- "Let us then with confidence draw near to the throne of grace, that we may receive mercy and find grace to help in time of need." (Heb. 4:16)
- "The prayer of a righteous person has great power as it is working." (Jas. 5:16)

The means to victory is clear. The question is: With how much energy in your faith do you make use of it?

Prayer should characterise the life of every Christian. It was said of Paul shortly after his conversion, "Behold, he is praying" (Acts 9:11). But it is one thing to pray now and then, and an entirely different thing to do it with energy in faith and with devotion. The apostle, however, did just that, for he writes, "as we pray most earnestly night and day" (1 Thess. 3:10). God wants us, figuratively speaking, not to stop doing this after praying once, twice, or three times, but to keep "striking the earth".

No man (of God) is greater than his prayer life.
(Leonard Ravenhill)

The Lord has said, "knock, and it will be opened to you ... and to the one who knocks it will be opened" (Lk. 11:9–10). If the door doesn't open immediately, then we are to keep knocking. How long? Until the door opens! The believers in Jerusalem are an example to us in this. When Peter was in prison, they prayed until God opened the prison door and their brother finally stood before them again. How often do we behave like "knock and run" players who knock briefly on the door and then run away?

The faith of Joash trusts God for only three victories. Abraham strikes, figuratively speaking, more often on the earth. When he prays for Sodom and Gomorrah, he pleads with the Lord six times, until out of 50 righteous he arrives at ten righteous. Couldn't he have asked a seventh time for the cause? Most certainly! God would certainly have answered that as well.

Elijah prays seven times until finally a cloud the size of a man's fist appears on the horizon. Because He doesn't stop pleading with God to open the windows of heaven, at some point he hears not only a light splashing, but also the rushing of a mighty rain (see 1 Ki. 18:41).

How did the Son of God encourage His disciples to bring a matter before God in prayer with perseverance, over and over again? He presented them with the case of a helpless widow who would not stop pestering an unjust judge until he eventually provided justice and gave her what she asked for.

We are to learn from this the importance of "praying through"—and not stopping halfway. Epaphras struggled in prayers in his devotion to other Christians and is held up as an example by Paul (see Col. 4:12). The apostle himself urges the believers in Rome to strive for him in their prayers (see Rom. 15:30). Have you ever fought on your knees? At the Judgment Seat we will one day see how many blessings we have missed because of a lack of energy in our faith.

> **We can never draw nigh to God in believing prayer, but the answer will be more than we had grace to hope for. Expectation from God is a precious fruit of prayer.** (Robert C Chapman)

When God brought about a revival among the Moravian Church almost 300 years ago, one result was that a so-called hourly prayer was started. The Christians at that time decided to pray around the clock for one hour at a time. This created a chain of prayer that lasted not just a few weeks, but 120 years!

In their simple-minded faith, they had based their prayers on the following verses of God's Word: "On your walls, O Jerusalem, I have set watchmen; all the day and all the night they shall never be silent. You who put the LORD in remembrance, take no rest, and give him no rest until he establishes Jerusalem and makes it a praise in the earth" (Isa. 62:6–7). By the way, God responded wonderfully to the

Moravians' devotion to prayer. Several hundred missionaries, some of whom willingly allowed themselves to be enslaved to reach captives with the gospel, were sent out into the harvest at that time.

> **"Put me to the test, says the LORD of hosts, if I will not open the windows of heaven for you and pour down for you a blessing until there is no more need."**
> (Malachi 3:10)

What reactions would there be today if Christians started a prayer chain or encouraged more private prayer meetings? Unfortunately, one must then reckon with statements such as: "Stay rational", "Don't go into a false euphoria", or "You can't organise a revival". Of course revival cannot be 'organised', but we may ask God persistently and intensely to work revival in hearts. Moreover, this should not stop us from spurring one another on to love and good works—and this includes prayer!

If the Lord has responded to prayer for revival so many times in church history, why would He not do so again today? We may be spurred on to test God anew by the faith and devotion of Christians who have gone before us. However, if we are satisfied with our spiritual condition and do not reach out for revival in our surroundings and do not long for it with yearning, we need not be surprised if everything continues as before.

Do we try to pressure God when we bring a matter before Him again and again in prayer with perseverance, or doesn't He rather want this perseverance? What does it mean that Paul pleaded beyond measure? Why do we often fail to take full advantage of the promises God has given us in connection with prayer? What needs to happen for revival to happen locally today?

Notes:

....
....
....
....
....
....
....
....
....
....
....
....
....
....
....
....

Faith Tested

Everything on the Altar?

"The Scripture was fulfilled that says, 'Abraham believed God, and it was counted to him as righteousness'—and he was called a friend of God." (James 2:23)

How tremendous is the faith of Abraham! For 25 years he waits for the birth of his son Isaac, through whom God would bring to fulfilment His promises made to him. Finally, the son of promise is born. What a joy it is for Abraham to see him grow up. Then one day Abraham suddenly hears the voice of God telling him, "Take your son, your only son Isaac, whom you love, and go to the land of Moriah, and offer him there as a burnt offering on one of the mountains of which I shall tell you" (Gen. 22:2). What a tremendous test of faith!

How does the patriarch respond to this challenge? Although it must have been heart-breaking for him as a father, he does not hesitate for a moment and sets out early in the morning in obedience born of faith to do what God has told him to do. How brightly his obedience of faith shines forth in this situation! He is actually willing to offer to God on the altar the most precious thing he has—his unique son, on whom all his hope rested. Wonderful devotion!

Yet at the same time, the "friend of God" is firmly convinced that God keeps what He promises. The Almighty had said that He would give Abraham a great posterity through Isaac. What does faith conclude from this? That if Isaac is to be sacrificed, God will raise him from the dead!

That is why Abraham says to his servants when he goes off to sacrifice his son, "Stay here with the donkey; I and the boy will go over there and worship and come again to you" (Gen. 22:5). The Epistle to the Hebrews says, "By faith Abraham, when he was tested, offered up Isaac, and he who had received the promises was in the act of offering up his only son, of whom it was said, 'Through Isaac shall your offspring be named.' He considered that God was able even to raise him from the dead, from which, figuratively speaking, he did receive him back" (Heb. 11:17–19).

Charles H Mackintosh has very aptly said in this connection:

> **It is only when we are really put to the test that we discover what God is. Without trial we can be but theorists.**
> (Charles H Mackintosh)

It is deeply interesting to mark here how Abraham's soul is led into a fresh discovery of God's character by the trial of his faith. When we are enabled to bear the testings of God's own hand, it is sure to lead us into some new experience with respect to His character, which makes us to know how valuable the testing is. If Abraham had not stretched out his hand to slay his son, he never would have known the rich and exquisite depths of that title which he here bestows upon God, that is, "Jehovah Jireh" [which means, 'The Lord will provide']. It is only when we are really put to the test that we discover what God is. Without trial we can be but theorists.

(Charles H Mackintosh, *Notes on the Pentateuch: The Book of Genesis*)

It is in times of testing that we come to know God in a very special way. That is why Paul was able to say, "Not only that, but we rejoice in our sufferings" (Rom. 5:3). The question that arises to test us is whether or not we will willingly accept them from God. Only when we have a "yes" to the ways of God will we grow spiritually.

When Jonathan and Rosalind Goforth were serving the Lord as missionaries in China, their 18-month-old son suddenly became terminally ill. After several days of fighting for their child's life, they realised one evening that the time of his death had come near.

Rosalind began to rebel against God in her soul and to quarrel with Him, as she could see nothing but terrible injustice in this illness and the death of the child. Her husband implored her to surrender her will and her child to God. After a long and bitter struggle, she finally managed to place her child in the hands of God. Then they both knelt down at the child's bedside and committed the little one's soul to God's mercy.

As Rosalind prayed, she noticed the child's rapid, heavy breathing had ceased. Thinking that her son had died, she quickly fetched a flashlight. But as she looked at the child's face, she realised that he had fallen into a deep sleep, that then lasted for most of the night. The next day, the boy was almost completely cured of the dangerous disease.

Looking back, Rosalind realised that the Lord had tested her faith to the last moment. After she was willing to give Him her beloved treasure and thus give God first place, He had given her back the child.

(Rosalind Goforth, *How I know God answers prayer,* Harper & Brothers Publishers)

"Blessed is the man who remains steadfast under trial"!

James 1:12

> *Why did God put Abraham's faith to such a test? In terms of tests of faith that God allows in your life, what can you learn from Abraham? What does it mean to you to lay the dearest thing you have on the altar of God?*

Notes:

....

....

....

....

....

....

....

....

....

....

....

....

....

....

Answer to Prayer at the Last Second

"Let us then with confidence draw near to the throne of grace, that we may receive mercy and find grace to help in time of need." (Hebrews 4:16)

Sometimes God hesitates to answer our prayers in order to test our faith and make salvation all the greater. Especially in situations where we are running out of time, we are to trust that He has everything under control.

If we trust God, then we will not be stressed when time is also short in a test of faith. Isaiah writes, "Whoever believes will not be in haste" (Isa. 28:16; see the footnote in the New Translation—"shall not hasten with fear").

When George Müller and his wife once wanted to travel by ship from Quebec to Liverpool, he had prayed intensely beforehand that a deck chair for his wife would arrive in time before their departure from New York. Mrs. Müller suffered from seasickness, so the chair was extremely important to her.

Her husband was full of confidence that God had heard his prayer. About half an hour before the escort boat was to take the passengers to the ship, officials alerted him that no chair had arrived and could not possibly arrive in time for departure. Yet he was not persuaded by anything to buy another one at a nearby store.

"We have asked our heavenly Father so specially to get it for us. We want to trust Him to do it," was his reply. Then he went aboard, absolutely sure that his trust was not misplaced and would not be dashed.

Just before the escort boat was about to leave, a furniture truck pulled up. At the head of its load—George Müller's chair. It was quickly brought on board and placed precisely in the hands of the man who had told George Müller to buy another one! When he handed it over to Mr. Müller, the latter did not express any astonishment, but quietly took off his hat and thanked his heavenly Father. For this man of God, such an answer to prayer was not surprising, but natural. God allowed this delay in order to magnify His faithfulness and thereby also encourage us to trust Him. For we would never have heard of this incident without this delay.

> **You do not lose time when you wait for God.**
> (Corrie ten Boom)

The following is another example from India, as reported by T E Koshy in his biography of Bakht Singh:

Several times during his travels, Bakht Singh went by faith, trusting in the Lord to find a seat on a plane or train and the Lord amazingly honoured his faith. In the early 60s, he came to Bombay with a missionary couple. The lady had had a hip operation and therefore was in a cast from the hip down and was using crutches.

Just about two hours before the departure of the Bombay–Hyderabad Express train, Bakht Sigh came to the author and said he would like to have three sleeping berths, and one of which should be a lower berth for the missionary lady on crutches. The author looked at him in dismay and told him it would be impossible to get three sleeper berths, particularly a lower berth that late, as normally these are booked weeks and even months in advance.

But Bakht Singh said he had prayed, and the Lord assured him that He would provide him with three berths on the same train, so he asked me to enquire with the station master. On enquiry, he said that no berth was available. Then half an hour before the departure of the train, the station master said that even the VIP seats were given out.

Hearing that, Bakht Singh said, "No, God will provide." The author suggested he should try to go the following day, but Bakht Singh was very sure that the Lord would help them to travel on that particular train and on that particular day. A few minutes prior to departure, the station master came and informed us that it was a miracle that someone came and cancelled three sleeping berths and one was a lower berth.

Bakht Singh looked at the author, and said, "You see, the Lord will never fail." Throughout his life and ministry he thus demonstrated that one can live by faith and prove the faithfulness of God.

(T E Koshy, *Brother Bakht Singh of India*, OM Books)

**"We should never forget that God is our Father,
but neither should we forget that our Father is God."**

William Kelly

> *Why is it so valuable to God when faith stands the test? Has the Lord ever put you in a situation where you experienced His help at the last minute? Why do such experiences strengthen your faith? God's help comes at the latest just on time!*

Notes:

....

....

....

....

....

....

....

....

....

....

....

....

....

....

....

....

....

....

....

God's Miraculous Salvation

"For there is no other god who is able to rescue in this way."
(Daniel 3:29)

When God speaks into our lives by giving us a personal promise, things initially may turn out quite differently than we hope and expect. Joseph, for example, first had to be sold into Egypt and even spend two years in prison there before God's promise to him was fulfilled. During this time in prison, his adherence to God's promises was put to the test, for regarding this time it is said, "The word of the LORD tested him" (Ps. 105:19).

Moses had received a promise from the great "I Am" that he would one day lead the people of Israel out of Egypt. On the way to the fulfilment of this promise, however, there were a lot of headwinds and resistance. But because Moses had the Giver of the promise before his eyes, he didn't crumble or buckle under the tremendous pressure: "By faith he left Egypt, not being afraid of the anger of the king, for he endured as seeing him who is invisible" (Heb. 11:27).

David also had to wait a long time for what God had foretold about him to come to pass. After Samuel anointed him king, the man after God's heart had to flee from Saul and go through severe trials in the years that followed. Only after he had finally lost literally everything did God see to it that he was made king of Judah and Israel.

The following example from church history shows that God stands by His word even when all seems lost in the meantime:

During the Boxer Rebellion in China at the beginning of the 20th century, many missionaries were murdered in cold blood. But God miraculously preserved some—and even announced it beforehand! The story of Jonathan and Rosalind Goforth, who survived this time in China, shows this in an impressive way:

God works in our faith so that this does not cease. He does not take away the difficulties, but He gives strength, so that we can withstand them!
(Hendrik L Heijkoop)

Just when Rosalind Goforth was about to travel to China with her children to meet her husband, who had travelled on ahead, a telegram arrived from there with the message that some missionaries had been cruelly killed. Many asked her to wait a little longer before leaving. However, she had the impression that she should start the journey immediately anyway.

Shortly before the train left the station in Toronto, a woman suddenly stepped up to the window of the train and said, "You don't know me, but I have been praying for the Lord to give me a promise for you. This is what I would like to pass on to you; please accept it as coming from the Lord: 'No weapon that is fashioned against you shall succeed'" (Isa. 54:17).

Rosalind then prayed and asked the Lord to fulfil this promise to her and those close to her. As she prayed, she received a firm assurance that the Lord had answered her prayer.

Finally, in the summer of 1900, a tremendous persecution broke out in China. The Goforths and their four children were repeatedly in great danger at their mission station. Finally, they were forced to leave the city of Chang Te early one morning. At the first major town they came to, an attempt was immediately made to break into their lodging. However, as they were praying, the crowd dispersed. As they started on their way again, Mr. Goforth jumped down from the wagon to get fresh water. Meanwhile, many people gathered together, threatening him and shouting "Kill, kill!" over and over again. But the Lord preserved him.

A short time later, fleeing again, they reached an inn where they sought refuge. However, it was not long before many people gathered outside, throwing stones at the house. The gate was barricaded. Inside, fear grew that soon the house would be stormed, and everyone would be cruelly murdered. In this distress, the Goforths and their associates gathered in a room for prayer.

Jonathan pulled a small book from his pocket and read aloud the Bible verses that immediately jumped out at him:

"The eternal God is your dwelling place, and underneath are the everlasting arms. And he thrust out the enemy before you and said, 'Destroy.'" (Deuteronomy 33:27)

"The God of Jacob is our fortress." (Psalm 46:7)

"You are my help and my deliverer; do not delay, O my God!" (Psalm 40:17)

"I will strengthen you, I will help you, I will uphold you with my righteous right hand. ... For I, the LORD your God, hold your right hand; it is I who say to you, 'Fear not, I am the one who helps you.'" (Isaiah 41:10, 13)

"If God is for us, who can be against us?" (Romans 8:31)

"So we can confidently say, 'The Lord is my helper; I will not fear; what can man do to me?'" (Hebrew 13:6)

The impact these verses had at that moment was indescribable. It was clear to all that God was speaking to them through His Word. The panicky fear had to give way to the divine peace that suddenly filled their hearts.

After the prayer time was over, they jumped on their carts and went into the densely populated street. They were amazed at how well they made their way through the crowds. As they approached the city gate, they saw several hundred men waiting for them, fully armed. No sooner had they passed the city gate than the men started throwing rocks at them and maiming the animals, some of them even killing the animals.

Jonathan Goforth jumped from the cart and shouted, "Take everything, but don't kill." He had hardly finished speaking when a man holding a sword with both hands gave him a heavy blow. But the Lord wielded it in such a way that he was struck with the blunt side of the sword, which, though it left clear marks on his neck, did not wound him further. Had the sharp side struck him, he would have been decapitated on the spot. His thick helmet was smashed to pieces—while he himself escaped unscathed.

Then he was hit by several blows that nearly knocked him unconscious. As he fell to the ground, he seemed to hear a voice, saying, "Fear not, they pray for you." As Rosalind watched her husband lying on the ground covered in blood, she thought he had died. But the Lord held His mighty hands over His servant. Rosalind and the children also miraculously escaped what should have been certain death.

It would go beyond the scope of this article to give all the details of this moving story. But the Lord's preservation of them until the moment when they were finally all safe is very moving.

(Rosalind Goforth, *How I know God answers prayer*, Harper & Brothers Publishers)

> **How do you handle it when the Lord gives you a personal promise through His Word, but shortly thereafter circumstances turn out quite differently than you had hoped? How does God purify us through His Word? What is the connection between living faith and the likelihood that something might happen?**

Notes:

....

....

....

....

....

....

....

....

....

....

....

In the Fiery Furnace

Someone once aptly said, "Genuine faith always increases when opposition comes, while false confidence only perishes as a result". George Müller writes to this effect: "Trials, obstacles, difficulties and sometimes defeats, are the very food of faith".

Faith that stands the test is more precious to God than all the gold in the world! Peter makes this clear when he writes, "In this you rejoice, though now for a little while, if necessary, you have been grieved by various trials, so that the tested genuineness of your faith—more precious than gold that perishes though it is tested by fire—may be found to result in praise and glory and honour at the revelation of Jesus Christ" (1 Pet. 1:6–7).

Shadrach, Meshach and Abednego trusted in God by transgressing against the word of the king and being willing to die rather than serve an idol. With great firmness they said to Nebuchadnezzar, "If this be so, our God whom we serve is able to deliver us from the burning fiery furnace, and he will deliver us out of your hand, O king. But if not, be it known to you, O king, that we will not serve your gods or worship the golden image that you have set up" (Dan. 3:17–18). They didn't know if they would survive. But they trusted that the LORD was above the circumstances and would rescue them from the hand of the king. This trust resulted in a powerful testimony that was to the glory of God (see Dan. 3:28).

Such stories give courage to be faithful in hard times. Here there was a 'happy ending'. Yet what would have happened if there had been no 'happy ending'? Even then, the faith of the three friends would have glorified God. There are many examples of God allowing tests of faith in which the humanly hoped-for salvation fails to materialise because He has a higher purpose.

In Hebrews 11:35–38 we read, "Some were tortured, refusing to accept release, so that they might rise again to a better life. Others suffered mocking and flogging, and even chains and imprisonment. They were stoned, they were sawn in two, they were killed with the sword. They went about in skins of sheep and goats, destitute, afflicted, mistreated— of whom the world was not worthy—wandering about in deserts and mountains, and in dens and caves of the earth."

> **Learning what God wants to teach us through adversity is more important than getting out of it.**
> (James Hudson Taylor, translated from German)

These heroes of faith trusted God in terrible sufferings and some died martyrs' deaths. However, it's precisely their faithfulness and trust in the Lord during this time of torment and trials that have inestimable value in the eyes of God. Therefore, they will also receive the crown of life that God has promised to those who love Him (see Jas. 1:12).

Jan Hus was a 15th century Bohemian theologian and reformer who put some truths of God's Word on the lamp stand in a new way, thereby rebelling against the papacy. For this he was burned at the stake by the Catholic Church.

It's very impressive to see the confidence born of faith and the determination of this man who was ready to die for Christ and the truth. During the last hours of his life, he kept his gaze firmly fixed on his Lord. When he was stripped and denounced by his tormentors, he prayed for them, saying, "Lord Jesus Christ, forgive my enemies for your mercy's sake".

In an elaborate ceremony, Hus was stripped of his priesthood. This ritual culminated in seven bishops taking the communion cup from his hands while declaring, "O accursed Judas ... we take away from you the cup of salvation". Hus was not impressed by this and calmly said: "I trust God".

He was then insulted with curses while being excommunicated from the church. The ritual ended with the bishops declaring: "We deliver your soul to the devil". But Hus was not shaken even by these words. He continued to keep his gaze firmly on the Lord and answered, "I give my soul to Jesus Christ".

When this faithful man saw the pyre before him, he said firmly, "I am ready to die for the gospel of Christ". After being tied to the wood, a rusty chain was placed around his neck. So he stood there, half-naked, facing death.

Two wagon loads of wood were unloaded and piled up to his chin. Then the executioners put straw and pitch on top of it—now came the moment of truth. The grand marshal encouraged Hus one last time to recant in order to save his life.

Eyewitnesses said that Hus barely paused when he said aloud, "God is my witness that the focus of my preaching was to turn people away from sin. In the truth of the gospel, I am ready to die today with joy."

Now that it was clear to everyone that absolutely nothing could turn this man from his faith, the pyre was set on fire. Until the last breath of his life, Hus kept his gaze fixed firmly on Jesus, his Lord. His last words were, "Christ, Son of the living God, have mercy on me".

What faith and steadfastness shine forth from the life of this man! This applies to us: "Consider the outcome of their way of life, and imitate their faith" (Heb. 13:7).

> *Why are temptations, oppositions, difficulties and sometimes even defeats the very nourishment of faith? Why does faith not depend on a supposed "happy ending" here on earth? How can you glorify God in suffering? "Let him who walks in darkness and has no light trust in the name of the LORD and rely on his God" (Isa. 50:10).*

Notes:

....

....

....

....

When Peace like a River

"You are good and do good." (Psalm 119:68)

God is good—and at all times! He gives us the promise that all things work together for good to those who love Him (see Rom. 8:28). This also applies to the difficult paths and trials He allows in our lives. Often we can glorify Him most by honouring Him in dark days through trust, and without rebellion, accepting from His hand whatever He sends.

When George Müller lost his wife, he decided to do the preaching himself. He chose the text, "You are good and do good" (Ps. 119:68). In his sermon he said, "The Lord was good and did good: first, in giving her to me; second, in so long leaving her to me; and third, in taking her from me".

When we trust in the Lord, it does not always mean that we will be spared from external dangers and sufferings. After the many impressive examples of victories of faith that are presented in Hebrews 11 come the

> **In order to realise the worth of the anchor we need to feel the stress of the storm.**
> (Corrie ten Boom)

moving words beginning with, "Others ..." (Heb. 11:35–36). There were also quite a number of believers who trusted God and yet went through much suffering—because they were faithful unto death. In this sense, they did not experience salvation from external circumstances, but they were allowed to experience God carrying them through—and this is often greater than being spared from suffering!

This is also true in the life of Adoniram Judson. After losing his wife and several children on the mission field, he said meaningfully, "If I didn't know that God's infinite love and mercy was carrying me and He had planned everything just so, I would have given up long ago".

The Apostle Paul also went through a great deal of suffering. This sometimes went so far that he and his co-workers despaired of life. But God pursued a good plan with all the suffering he allowed.

Over many centuries, believers have received comfort and encouragement from reading the Psalms. Many of these songs were written under great suffering. When David was hunted like a partridge on the mountains, the sound of his harp was most beautiful. Songs born in pain help us overcome sadness and turn our eyes back to heaven!

Horatio Gates Spafford was a successful and very wealthy lawyer who lived in Chicago in the 19th century. He was married and had four daughters. When the "Great Chicago Fire" broke out in 1871, it destroyed Spafford's property and caused him great financial loss.

He was a Christian who truly had a heart for the Lord. In the fall of 1873, Spafford planned to travel to England with his family. He intended to assist his friend, evangelist Dwight L Moody, in his evangelistic work there while his wife and daughters were to take a vacation.

But Spafford was delayed in Chicago on urgent business and decided that his family should go ahead. So the mother and her four daughters boarded a French steamer to cross the Atlantic.

On November 22, 1873, the passenger ship was rammed by an English container ship in the middle of the Atlantic Ocean. Spafford's four daughters: Anna (11), Maggie (9), Bessie (5) and Tanetta (2) were washed overboard and the ship sank in a very short time. 226 passengers drowned in this accident.

Spafford's wife was one of the few who survived. The last thing that she could remember was her young daughter Tanetta being torn from her arms by the force of the water. She herself was rescued by a sailor and taken to Wales. To her husband she sent the heart-breaking telegram, "Saved alone."

Upon hearing this terrible news, Spafford immediately sailed off to England with a heavy heart to assist and comfort his suffering wife. Bertha Spafford-Vester, the later fifth daughter of Horatio Spafford, wrote about his crossing in her book "Our Jerusalem":

"Father was convinced that God was good and that he would see his children again in heaven. This thought calmed his heart ...

On the voyage across the Atlantic, the captain, Mr. Goodwin, asked my father into his private cabin: 'A careful calculation has been made,' he told him, 'and I believe we are now in the area where the "Ville du Havre" went down.'

Father wrote to Aunt Rachel, 'On Thursday we were over the spot where the ship went down in the middle ocean; the water is three miles deep. But I don't think of our loved ones there. They are safe and secure in the arms of the Good Shepherd and—not for long— then we will be there, too. In the meantime, we thank God and still have opportunity to serve HIM and praise HIM because of His love and grace toward us.'"

After this conversation with Captain Goodwin, Spafford wrote down in his cabin at night the words of the song that is now well over 100 years old and which has been a blessing to millions:

When peace, like a river, attendeth my way,
When sorrows like sea billows roll;
Whatever my lot, Thou hast taught me to say,
It is well, it is well with my soul.

Chorus:
It is well with my soul,
It is well, it is well with my soul.

Though Satan should buffet, though trials should come,
Let this blest assurance control,
That Christ hath regarded my helpless estate,
And hath shed His own blood for my soul.

My sin—oh, the bliss of this glorious thought!—
My sin, not in part but the whole,
Is nailed to the cross, and I bear it no more,
Praise the Lord, praise the Lord, O my soul!

For me, be it Christ, be it Christ hence to live:
If Jordan above me shall roll,
No pang shall be mine, for in death as in life
Thou wilt whisper Thy peace to my soul.

What confidence of faith! With the peace of God that surpasses all understanding in his heart, this man was able to write this won-

derful song. He had not become bitter because of the suffering, but found his refuge and consolation in God.

(F Müller, *Wenn Friede mit Gott* [When peace like a river], VdHS)

> **What does it mean when a soul is blessed in the Lord? How attached are you to your life here in this world, and to what extent can you say with Paul, "For to me to live is Christ, and to die is gain" (Phil. 1:21)? What is the key to experiencing the peace of God in a tangible way?**

Notes:

....

....

....

....

....

....

....

....

....

....

....

....

....

What a Friend We Have in Jesus

"God my Maker, who gives songs in the night." (Job 35:10)

Some of the songs we sing today have a very moving history. In part, they were written under great suffering. That is precisely what makes them so valuable, because living faith that clings to God in adversity can be seen in them.

God enabled Paul and Silas to sing hymns and praise Him in the dungeon at midnight with their feet in the stocks. Throughout church history, He has also given those who have trusted Him songs of praise at night! An example of this is Joseph Medlicott Scriven.

Faith is always stronger and more glorious when affliction and temptation are greatest.
(Martin Luther)

The day before his wedding, his bride crossed a bridge on her horse. Scriven was waiting for her at the other side. However, she was caught by a gust of wind, fell into the river, and he had to watch as she drowned in front of his eyes.

After this terrible suffering, he asked God to guide him further. Finally, at the age of 25, he emigrated to Canada. He did so with the hope of being able to forget the suffering he had encountered in Ireland. After some time, he met a woman named Eliza Roche and became engaged to her.

Yet again, great suffering awaited him. A few weeks before their wedding, his bride caught a cold, from which pneumonia and a high fever developed. She died a short time later at the age of 23. Scriven was devastated. But in faith, he clung to Jesus Christ, who had saved him and to whom he had surrendered his life.

So what happened next? Instead of becoming discouraged or giving up, Scriven decided to devote himself to ministering to widows and sick people. As a result, many of them gained hope—especially because of his life, which reflected the love of God.

After many years, a neighbour visited him and found the poem "What a friend we have in Jesus" lying on a table next to his bed:

What a friend we have in Jesus,
All our sins and griefs to bear!
What a privilege to carry
Everything to God in prayer!
Oh, what peace we often forfeit,
Oh, what needless pain we bear,
All because we do not carry
Everything to God in prayer!

Have we trials and temptations?
Is there trouble anywhere?
We should never be discouraged—
Take it to the Lord in prayer.
Can we find a friend so faithful,
Who will all our sorrows share?
Jesus knows our every weakness;
Take it to the Lord in prayer.

Are we weak and heavy-laden,
Cumbered with a load of care?
Precious Saviour, still our refuge—
Take it to the Lord in prayer.
Do thy friends despise, forsake thee?
Take it to the Lord in prayer!
In His arms He'll take and shield thee,
Thou wilt find a solace there.

Blessed Saviour, Thou hast promised
Thou wilt all our burdens bear;
May we ever, Lord, be bringing
All to Thee in earnest prayer.
Soon in glory bright, unclouded,
There will be no need for prayer—
Rapture, praise, and endless worship
Will be our sweet portion there.

The visitor was impressed by the poem and asked Scriven if he had written it. His reply was, "The Lord and I wrote it together". It had come out of fellowship with the Lord. He wanted to use these words to comfort his sick mother, who was very sad because her son was suffering so much. The trust that radiates from this song has already strengthened the faith of thousands of Christians—and continues to do so!

"Out of the eater came something to eat. Out of the strong came something sweet."
(Judges 14:14)

(F Müller, *Tatsachenbericht von Joseph Medlicott Scriven* [Report on Joseph Medlicott Scriven], VdHS)

> *Why does faith glorify God more in difficult times than in times when there are no problems? How can one best honour the Lord in sorrow and suffering? What can help you not to give up when God allows suffering in your life?*

Notes:

....
....
....
....
....
....
....
....
....
....
....
....
....
....
....
....
....
....
....
....

Boldness in Faith

Jonathan

"Jonathan said to the young man who carried his armour, 'Come, let us go over to the garrison of these uncircumcised. It may be that the LORD will work for us, for nothing can hinder the LORD from saving by many or by few.'" (1 Samuel 14:6)

Jonathan is an encouraging example of someone who went forward in faith with boldness—and he was richly rewarded by God for it. What was going on? The people of Israel were under attack by the Philistines, who far outnumbered them. Fear and despair became increasingly widespread.

But faith, which sees everything in connection with God, cannot bear to see the people of God oppressed by the enemy and the LORD thereby dishonoured. And it is exactly this faith that we see here in Jonathan. Although the situation seems hopeless, he trusts in God and in His unfailing faithfulness to His people.

This characterises faith: not only does it acknowledge that God is great, but it also contemplates the unbreakable bond between God and His people. Jonathan sees the Philistines as uncircumcised, that is, as having no relationship with God and therefore no power. The people of Israel, on the other hand, were the apple of God's eye and could, in faith, count on His assistance.

Because faith does not depend on circumstances, Jonathan does not worry about the number of enemies. God is almighty, so it makes no difference to Him to effect salvation through many or through few. Thus Jonathan does not rely on natural means, but his expectation comes from the living God, for whom nothing is impossible!

King Asa, in great distress, once expressed it similarly in prayer: "O LORD, there is none like you to help, between the mighty and the weak. Help us, O LORD our God, for we rely on you, and in your name we have come against this multitude. O LORD, you are our God; let not man prevail against you" (2 Chron. 14:11).

Gideon liberated Israel with only 300 men, without weapons and with only trumpets, pitchers and torches (Judges 7). About 2,000 years ago, when a few men went about preaching the gospel, it was said of them, "These men who have turned the world upside down" (Acts 17:6).

Jonathan rejoices in having a fellow soldier in the faith in his armour-bearer. But beyond that, he seeks no other help. His courage of faith and his confidence are also shown in that he doesn't involve his father Saul or anyone else from the people in this undertaking. He thus does not consult with flesh and blood—with other people—but trusts exclusively in the LORD and boldly goes forward with Him.

Unfortunately, it is often the case that, by their doubting deliberations, those who lack faith only hinder and discourage others who want to go forward courageously in faith. We should be very thankful when God provides likeminded believers to help us, as the armour-bearer did for Jonathan here. It takes a lot of determination and energy in faith to take steps of faith in dependence on the Lord and to not be held back by paralysing influences.

Jonathan's step of faith first caused a small victory—measured against the overwhelming power of the enemy. But God honours the faith of His servant by revealing Himself, and the terror of the LORD seizes the enemies. Therefore, they fall before the man who was driven to action by his faith. God has thus multiplied the victory.

Moreover, Jonathan's act of faith produced two other unexpected effects: First, the Hebrews who had defected to the Philistines came back "to be with the Israelites" (1 Sam. 14:21). Secondly, those who had hitherto hidden themselves despairingly and fearfully in the mountains of Ephraim now boldly pursued the Philistines in battle (see 1 Sam. 14:22).

The faith and boldness of one man were used by God in a mighty way to bless many. This can still happen today.

> **Faith is led confidently to expect what reason would never suggest.**
> (Charles H Spurgeon)

There is no hindrance for the Lord—neither in terms of strength to overcome nor in terms of restoration and encouragement of individuals!

An impressive example of what it can still mean today to move forward with boldness in faith is the story of Ray Lentzsch, who has preached the gospel in many countries around the world.

He was present at a prayer night where several Christians prayed for the Muslim world. Ray had heard that the highest-ranking man in the Muslim world was the Prince of Mecca. This man was in charge of the shrines and the holiest place for the Muslims. Therefore, Ray prayed, "Lord, send someone to take the gospel to the Prince of Mecca. You said, 'Go into all the world and proclaim the gospel to the whole creation' (Mk. 16:15). That includes Him. If you want me to go—I know it could cost my life—I am willing to go."

Some time later, he was travelling in North Africa, and he considered going to the Saudi embassy to try to find a possible way to travel into Saudi Arabia. But there he was told the only way into the country was to get an invitation from a high-ranking person in Saudi Arabia. He then took a cab towards Cairo to try again.

On the way to Cairo, they stopped at an oasis where they met a young motorcyclist. The latter had lost his way and asked them if he could follow them when they continued on their way. So it came to be that this motorcyclist sat next to Ray and the two talked.

In the conversation Ray learned that this young man was from Saudi Arabia. Ray told him about his intentions to travel there and his problem with not being able to get into the country without an invitation from a significant person. The young motorcyclist said, "Okay, I'll write you a letter of invitation."

It turned out that the head of the security unit of the Prince of Mecca was the father of the motorcyclist. When Ray arrived in Cairo, he went to the Saudi Embassy, presented the letter of invitation, and immediately he received his visa. Next, he bought a beautiful Bible to give to the Prince of Mecca. He put it in his suitcase, not knowing how to get this Bible through the border control into Saudi Arabia, because normally the Bible would be confiscated immediately if someone found it.

Then, when he arrived at the boat that would take him to Saudi Arabia, he again encountered the young motorcyclist who had issued him the letter of invitation. The man was a little embarrassed that he had not suggested to him earlier that they travel together. So Ray got on the motorcycle behind him, and they drove off. At the border, the man only had to give a hand signal, which allowed them to enter the country without any problems and without a border inspection.

At the home of the head of the security unit, Ray received a very warm welcome. The next morning he set off with the Bible to the palace to meet the Prince of Mecca. When he got there, a man from security told him that the prince was not there because it was currently Ramadan and he was staying in a tent city in the desert during that time.

However, the man agreed to issue Ray a passport that would entitle him to visit the tent city. Ray therefore went there, showed his passport that was issued by the palace security personnel, and was let in.

As he walked across the courtyard, a man asked him what he was doing here. Ray replied that he had come to meet the Prince of Mecca. The man asked if he spoke Arabic, to which Ray answered with "No". "But the prince speaks only Arabic," replied the man. "However, I am an interpreter for the ambassador, and I will translate for you".

They then arrived at the prince's tent where the royal family and mullahs (Islamic legal and religious scholars) were gathered. As Ray walked toward the prince, everyone fell silent. Everyone in the room wondered who the stranger was and what he wanted.

Although Ray did not speak Arabic, he immediately noticed that the interpreter was not translating what he was trying to tell the Prince of Mecca. When he asked him why he was not translating him correctly, the latter replied that he did not want to embarrass the prince.

Ray then turned to those gathered and said, "Surely there is someone here who can translate me. Even though it may cost me my life, I would like to explain why I am doing all this."

Then he presented the Bible to the Prince of Mecca, saying that this was the most valuable gift he could ever give him (in the meantime a new translator had been found). Thereupon the prince asked him why he was risking his life with it.

"For by you I can run against a troop, and by my God I can leap over a wall." (Psalm 18:29)

Ray replied that Jesus Christ had changed his life and he had to tell everyone how wonderful Christ is. The prince still did not understand why he was willing to throw his life away to do such a thing.

Ray asked, "If I had the cure for cancer and you were sick with cancer, but I didn't tell you about the cure, what would you think?"

"That would be terrible!" the prince replied.

Ray countered that the prince had something much worse than cancer: "Cancer will kill your body, but sin will damn your soul if you don't have a Saviour."

For the next 15 minutes, Ray was able to preach the gospel to these leaders of Saudi Arabia. When he finished, he turned to leave the tent—certain that someone would demand his arrest. But nothing of the sort happened.

He left the tent, went back to his hosts' house, packed his things, and was taken by the young motorcyclist to the main road from where he would catch a bus to leave Saudi Arabia.

As they sat on the side of the road watching the sunset, the young man told them that he had spent the last year studying in a university in the West where he had a Christian as a roommate. The contact had shaken his faith, as he realised that his roommate had something better than he did.

But he also knew that his father would kill him if he became a Christian. Therefore, he said, he had tried to forget what his roommate had told him through wild partying. But as he sat next to Ray at that oasis, he said the latter had picked up where his roommate had left off. Ray did not know if this young man converted that day, but apparently his younger brother did.

(J B Nicholson, Uplook Ministries)

"Who through faith conquered kingdoms, enforced justice, obtained promises, stopped the mouths of lions, quenched the power of fire, escaped the edge of the sword, were made strong out of weakness."

Hebrews 11:33–34

> *With what eyes do you see the people of God and the many people who are on their way to eternal damnation? To what extent does your faith depend on circumstances or on the greatness of God? How can you today, in dependence on God, be a blessing to others through steps of faith?*

Notes:

....

....

....

....

....

....

....

....

....

....

....

....

....

....

....

....

....

David

"David said, 'What have I done now? Was it not but a word?' And he turned away from him toward another, and spoke in the same way, and the people answered him again as before. When the words that David spoke were heard, they repeated them before Saul, and he sent for him. And David said to Saul, 'Let no man's heart fail because of him. Your servant will go and fight with this Philistine.'" (1 Samuel 17:29–32)

A shepherd boy confronts a giant who is about ten feet tall and heavily armed and says, "You come to me with a sword and with a spear and with a javelin, but I come to you in the name of the LORD of hosts, the God of the armies of Israel, whom you have defied. This day the LORD will deliver you into my hand, and I will strike you down and cut off your head. And I will give the dead bodies of the host of the Philistines this day to the birds of the air and to the wild beasts of the earth, that all the earth may know that there is a God in Israel" (1 Sam. 17:45–46).

That is boldness! How does a young man come to have such courage and to face such a powerful enemy with such assurance? Because he knows God. David had experienced the way the LORD had helped him in great dangers and had saved him from dangerous animals. That is why he said to Saul, "The LORD who delivered me from the paw of the lion and from the paw of the bear will deliver me from the hand of this Philistine" (1 Sam. 17:37). These were not empty words; there was a firm conviction of faith behind them.

He could really say with certainty: "The LORD is my shepherd; I shall not want" (Ps. 23:1)!

What do we learn from this? The experiences we have with God strengthen our faith and give us the boldness to take courageous steps of faith. We see this also in Paul: he had been rescued from the lion's jaws and could therefore say with conviction of faith, "The Lord will rescue me from every evil deed and bring me safely into his heavenly kingdom" (2 Tim. 4:18). Faith measures every difficulty by the power of God, and thus the mountain becomes a plain.

What drove David to take this mighty step of faith? The zeal for the glory of the LORD! Goliath had mocked and ridiculed the people of God. In doing so, he got into direct conflict with God Himself. Because David loved the LORD, he could not bear to see His name so publicly dragged through the mud. He saw in the Philistine's provocation a mandate to fight for the glory of God. Moreover, he realised that he could certainly count on God's assistance in taking on this giant who was terrifying and terrorising the people.

David's outward appearance as a young man at that time did not give the impression that he could take on this giant. He was not even able to walk in Saul's armour. But God had already said to Samuel: "Man looks on the outward appearance, but the LORD looks on the heart" (1 Sam. 16:7).

> **"For the eyes of the LORD run to and fro throughout the whole earth, to give strong support to those whose heart is blameless toward him."**
> (2 Chronicles 16:9)

With God it doesn't depend on outward appearance nor on age. That is exactly why Jeremiah, when God called him to the ministry, was not to say he was too young—and why Paul also told Timothy, "Let no one despise you for your youth" (1 Tim. 4:12).

Spurgeon aptly commented, "Therefore let us contend boldly against the enemy, as David contended against the Philistine. The Lord has been with us. And He is with us now. He has said, 'I will not fail thee, nor forsake thee.'

All God's giants have been weak men who did great things for God because they reckoned on God being with them.
(James Hudson Taylor)

Why do we tremble? Was the past a dream? Remember the dead bear and lion! Who is this Philistine? True, he is neither bear nor lion; but God is the same, and it is a matter of His glory in one case as in the other. He did not save us from the wild beasts to have us killed by a giant. Let us be of good cheer!"

When John Paton wanted to go to the New Hebrides (a chain of islands in the South Pacific) to take the gospel to the people there—some of whom were cannibals—many tried to stop him.

A certain Mr. Dickson exploded, "The cannibals! You will be eaten by cannibals!"

The memory of Williams and Harris [men who had been killed] on Erromanga was only 19 years old. But to this Paton responded:

"Mr. Dickson, you are advanced in years now, and your own prospect is soon to be laid in the grave, there to be eaten by worms; I

confess to you, that if I can but live and die serving and honouring the Lord Jesus, it will make no difference to me whether I am eaten by Cannibals or by worms; and in the Great Day my Resurrection body will rise as fair as yours in the likeness of our risen Redeemer."

(John Piper, *Filling up the Afflictions of Christ*, Inter-Varsity Press)

> **What experiences that you have had with God in the past encourage you to trust God for great things in the future and to take steps of faith in dependence on Him? In what way is the glory of God being dragged through the mud today and how can you stand up for it with boldness in faith? What giants are there in your life that you want to defeat with God's help? What does it mean to steadfastly resist the devil in faith (see 1 Pet. 5:9)?**

Notes:

....

....

....

....

....

....

....

Elijah

"Elijah the Tishbite, of Tishbe in Gilead, said to Ahab, 'As the LORD, the God of Israel, lives, before whom I stand, there shall be neither dew nor rain these years, except by my word."
(1 Kings 17:1)

As if from nowhere, Elijah appears before the powerful King Ahab and announces to him that there will be no more rain in the next few years unless he himself says so. This is boldness 'par excellence'. How can someone have such certainty? And how does one get the courage to announce this conviction to someone who is not likely to be very pleased about it and who also has the power to have people killed instantly?

The answer is: through persistent prayer and a conscious of living in the sight of God. What Elijah did came out of intense supplication and a lived-out communion with the living God. Both are possible only through faith.

James writes, "The prayer of a righteous person has great power as it is working. Elijah was a man with a nature like ours, and he prayed fervently that it might not rain, and for three years and six months it did not rain on the earth" (Jas. 5:16–17). Elijah not only prayed intensely; he also had a firm assurance that God had answered his prayer.

Why was he so sure of this? Because his sole concern was the glory of God and because he knew that his prayer was in accordance with the will of God. God Himself had said that He would withhold the rain if His people turned away from

Him (see Deut. 11:17). For such cases, Solomon had also prayed at the dedication of the temple (see 1 Ki. 8:35–36). And now that's exactly what had happened, since the people of Israel, under the reign of Ahab, had begun to worship Baal, the rain god.

Because Elijah was a prophet, he had the task of bringing the people to repentance and back to God. But how could this be done? The skies had to be shut up so that the people would become aware that there is only one true God in heaven—the Father of the rain (see Job 38:28).

In other words, Elijah prayed for God to chastise His people and thereby move them to repentance. And so that it is clear in advance that this act is from the living God, the prophet announces it to the king of Israel right at the beginning.

What courage Elijah needed to perform this act of faith! The later story makes it very clear that Elijah was indeed not an overachiever, but a man of the same sensibilities and feelings as we are. He knew ups and downs in his walk of faith. Yet this very fact should encourage us to take bold steps of faith when God gives us a task to fulfil.

> **Elijah could stand before the wicked king because he had knelt before the living God!** (Hamilton Smith)

Elijah's boldness goes even further. On Mount Carmel, he takes on 850 false prophets. He mocks Baal because his followers fail to make fire fall from heaven. When it is up to him to call upon the LORD to send fire from the sky, Elijah first has everything poured over with water so that God's victory will shine out all the more clearly. How many of us would have called out to the man of God at that time: "Why do you always have to be so extreme? You have to remain sober. God has given us reason too, you know."

Of course, God has also given us a mind, which is often very useful. But when that mind, which is often characterised by purely rational thinking, goes against what God wants, we must apply the following: "Trust in the LORD with all your heart, and do not lean on your own understanding" (Prov. 3:5).

What does Elijah do? He knows his God and is zealous for the glory of the LORD—and that is exactly what God commits to. Fire falls from heaven, 850 prophets are slain, and the people cry out with a loud voice: "The LORD, he is God; the LORD, he is God" (1 Ki. 18:39).

Then comes the crowning moment: although it hasn't rained for 3½ years and there is not a cloud on the horizon far and wide, Elijah tells Ahab, "Go up, eat and drink, for there is a sound of the rushing of rain" (1 Ki. 18:41). Why was he so sure that a mighty rain would come? Because he knew his God and took Him at His word! God had promised that He would hear from heaven and heal the land if they would turn to Him (see 2 Chron. 7:13–14).

Seven times the prophet puts his head between his knees and prays for God to fulfil His promise. What was the result? "Then he prayed again, and heaven gave rain, and the earth bore its fruit" (Jas. 5:18).

The story of Elijah is certainly unique. Nevertheless, church history shows us that God has always responded in a special way to courageous faith when His glory has been at stake. Here is an example from the life of Bakht Singh following a revival:

For several weeks following the revival, about seventy young people who had a deep love for the Lord and compassion for souls went from village to village preach-

"With God we shall do valiantly."
(Psalm 108:13)

ing the gospel. The moving of God began to spread to about 35 to 40 villages. From Martinpur, they set out with 70 young people to Sialkot, which was about 150 miles away.

They went singing and praising the Lord, trusting Him for their every need. They stopped in every village along the way, singing, sharing their testimonies, and proclaiming the gospel to those who came to listen. They ate whenever someone gave them food, and slept wherever they were given shelter.

When they went to Malwall, a Sikh village, they had a big open-air meeting. Bakht Singh told the people there that they were Christians and they talk to God; they do not pray as non-Christians do. One old man then got up and said, "You say you Christians know how to pray. Please pray for rain." They had not had rain for some time.

Bakht Singh accepted the challenge, then he knelt down and said to the Lord, "Lord, the old man says he wants rain, please send rain." After he got up from his knees his friend, Mr. Chandy, the customs officer from Karachi, said to him, "Brother, you made a mistake. If rain comes we have no umbrellas. We have to go to the next village for the next meeting, and we will all get wet."

Bakht Singh said that he could not change his prayer. After a while the rain did come: it just poured. As a result they did have to walk in the rain to the next village for meetings.

(T E Koshy, *Brother Bakht Singh of India*, OM Books)

> **"Would that the saints of God tried themselves by this test: 'How much do I believe?' instead of 'How much do I know?'"**

Robert C Chapman

> *What does it mean that Elijah was a man with a nature like ours? What promises in the Bible encourage us to expect great things from God and test Him in a positive way? What is the difference between boldness in faith and folly or recklessness?*

Notes:

....

....

....

....

....

....

....

....

....

....

Moses

"There has not arisen a prophet since in Israel like Moses, whom the LORD knew face to face, none like him for all the signs and the wonders that the LORD sent him to do in the land of Egypt, to Pharaoh and to all his servants and to all his land, and for all the mighty power and all the great deeds of terror that Moses did in the sight of all Israel." (Deuteronomy 34:10–12)

The story of Moses is very impressive. God turns a broken, fearful shepherd into a man who stands with great courage before the most powerful man in Egypt, leads a nation of at least two million people out of captivity, and speaks face to face with the eternal "I Am".

His secret? Moses was a prayer warrior! There is hardly anyone in the Bible of whom it is so often said that he prayed, called out to the LORD, or even cried out. But not only that! Because he had such intimate dealings with God, he also learned to pray in accordance with God's will—and already while praying, or even before, he gained the conviction that his prayer would be answered.

Who among us would have dared to say to Pharaoh, "Be pleased to command me when I am to plead for you and for your servants and for your people, that the frogs be cut off from you and your houses and be left only in the Nile" (Ex. 8:9)? When someone speaks like this, he must be quite sure that his prayers will be answered.

What was the secret of this faith? Moses was zealous for the glory of God. When Pharaoh told him to pray the next day, Moses replied, "Be it as you say, so that you may know that there is no one like the LORD our God. The frogs shall go away from you and your houses and your servants and your people. They shall be left only in the Nile" (Ex. 8:10–11). Shortly thereafter it says, "Moses cried to the LORD about the frogs, as he had agreed with Pharaoh. And the LORD did according to the word of Moses" (Ex. 8:12–13).

> **We should be honouring God by praying for great things.**
> (William MacDonald)

Joshua apparently learned from Moses. He prayed in public, before the eyes of Israel: "'Sun, stand still at Gibeon, and moon, in the Valley of Aijalon.' And the sun stood still, and the moon stopped, until the nation took vengeance on their enemies" (Jos. 10:12–13). Only someone who knows how the heart of God beats can pray so daringly.

With what boldness did Jabez pray, did Achsah ask for springs of water, did the daughters of Zelophehad struggle for an inheritance, and did the four friends of the paralytic uncover the roof of a house! God responded wonderfully each time. Would He not still do so today, if we prayed fearlessly and with the right motivation, reaching out for spiritual growth?

"Ask what I shall give you."

1 Kings 3:5

> *How can a broken, fearful shepherd like Moses was, become such a courageous man of prayer? What other incidents can you think of where people in the Word of God have shown boldness in their faith? What passages come to mind that encourage the sharing experiences of faith with others?*

Notes:

....

....

....

....

....

....

....

....

....

....

....

....

....

....

....

....

....

Final Thoughts

To Trust in God or in Man?

"It is better to take refuge in the LORD than to trust in man. It is better to take refuge in the LORD than to trust in princes." (Psalm 118:8–9)

Self-reliance and reliance on God are completely opposed to each other. They cannot coexist. Either we lean on God, or we lean on our own abilities.

The same applies to the question of whether we trust in people or in God. Do I rely on human help, or do I really depend on God's help? The prophet Jeremiah uses very clear words when he says: "Cursed is the man who trusts in man and makes flesh his strength, whose heart turns away from the LORD. ... Blessed is the man who trusts in the LORD, whose trust is the LORD" (Jer. 17:5, 7). Of course, the Lord can also use people to help us; but we are to see God, who works all things, behind everything, and to put our trust in Him alone in this regard. People disappoint but God never disappoints us!

It is said of Hezekiah, "He trusted in the LORD" (2 Ki. 18:5). The king of Judah didn't seek help from the Egyptians in his battle against the Assyrian as his father had done. Instead, he put his trust solely in the living God. Because he did so, he was able to encourage the people and say, 'Be strong and courageous. Do not be afraid or dismayed before the king of Assyria and all the horde that is with him, for there are more with us than with him. With him is an arm of flesh, but with us is the LORD our God, to help us and to fight our battles.' And the people took confidence from the words of Hezekiah king of Judah" (2 Chron. 32:7–8).

That these were not empty words is made clear by his actions: immediately afterwards he demonstrates his faith concretely by crying out to heaven together with the prophet Isaiah—whereupon the LORD gives a miraculous salvation!

With Asa we see the exact opposite. He trusted in men instead of the LORD and therefore had to hear the judgment of God: "Because you relied on the king of Syria, and did not rely on the LORD your God, the army of the king of Syria has escaped you. ... For the eyes of the LORD run to and fro throughout the whole earth, to give strong support to those whose heart is blameless toward him. You have done foolishly in this, for from now on you will have wars" (2 Chron. 16:7, 9).

> If to wait on God be worship, to wait on the creature is idolatry; if to wait on God alone be true faith, to associate an arm of the flesh with him is audacious unbelief.
> (Charles H Spurgeon)

Especially in trials of faith, there is also a great temptation for us to seek our help more from men than from God. We often don't do this in obvious ways but rather indirectly. Sometimes it occurs by pulling others' 'heartstrings' to get them to act, but then subsequently attributing the action to God. In such cases, it becomes very difficult to distinguish what is truly worked by the Lord and what is the result of emotional pressure.

Preparations for sailing to China were at once taken up. About this time, I was asked to give a lecture on China in a village not very far from London, and I agreed on condition that there should be no collection and this should be announced on the posters. The gentleman who invited me and who kindly presided as chairman said he had never had that condition imposed before. He accepted it, however, and the posters were issued accordingly for the second or third of May. With the aid of a large map, the extent and population and deep spiritual need of China was presented, and many were evidently impressed.

At the close of the meeting, the chairman said that by my request it had been announced on the posters that there would be no collection, but he felt that many present would be distressed and burdened if they did not have the opportunity of contributing to the proposed good work. He trusted that since the proposition originated entirely from him and expressed, he felt sure, the feelings of many in the audience, I should not object to it.

I begged, however, that the condition agreed to might be carried out. I pointed out, among other reasons for making no collection, that the very reason cited by our kind chairman was, to my mind, one of the strongest for not making it. My wish was that each one should go home burdened with the deep need of China and ask God what He would have them do, not that those present should be relieved by making a contribution that might there and then be convenient under the influence of a present emotion.

If, after thought and prayer, they were satisfied that a monetary contribution was what He wanted of them, it could be given to any Missionary Society having agents in China, or it might be posted to our London office. In many cases God might not want a mon-

ey contribution, but rather personal consecration to His service abroad or the giving up of a son or daughter—more precious than silver or gold—to His service.

I added that I thought the tendency of a collection was to leave the impression that the all-important thing was money, but no amount of money could convert a single soul. What was needed were men and women filled with the Holy Ghost to give themselves to the work, for the support of such would never be lacking. As my wish was evidently very strong, the chairman kindly yielded to it and closed the meeting. He told me, however, at the supper table that he thought it was a mistake on my part, and in spite of all I had said, a few persons had put some little contributions into his hands.

Next morning at breakfast, my kind host came in a little late and acknowledged not having had a very good night. After breakfast, he asked me to his study and gave me the contributions handed to him the night before. He said, "I thought last night, Mr. Taylor, that you were wrong about a collection; I am now convinced you were quite right. As I thought in the night of that stream of souls in China ever passing onward into the dark, I could only cry as you suggested, 'Lord, what wilt Thou have me to do?' I think I have obtained the guidance I sought, and here it is."

He handed me a check for five hundred pounds, adding that if there had been a collection, he would have given a few pounds, but now this check was the result of having spent no small part of the night in prayer.

(J Hudson Taylor, *A Retrospect (Updated Edition): The Story Behind My Zeal for Missions*, Aneko Press)

> *What can be indications that someone is putting their trust in the Lord alone and not in people? What can keep you from making people your arm? Ask the Lord to help you let go (anew) and expect everything from Him alone!*

Notes:

....
....
....
....
....
....
....
....
....
....
....
....
....
....
....
....
....
....
....

Claiming God's Promises

"Do as you have spoken, and your name will be established and magnified forever." (1 Chronicles 17:23–24)

This word expresses an important element of true prayer. David asks God to do what He has promised him. He demands, so to speak, in faith that the promise will be fulfilled. Incidentally, Solomon did this at least twice (see 2 Chron. 1:9; 6:17).

Sometimes we ask for things that are not clearly promised in God's Word. Therefore, we are not sure whether these requests are in accordance with God's intentions or not—unless, perhaps, after prolonged prayer, He gives us peace or deep assurance about them.

But there are also situations—as we see here in the life of David—in which we are firmly convinced that our requests are in accordance with God's will.

> **"I am watching over my word to perform it."**
> (Jeremiah 1:12)

We feel urged to claim a promise of Scripture for ourselves, under the special impression that it contains a message for us personally. At such times we say in confident faith, "Do as you have spoken!"

We, as Christians, are never as strong, sure, and unshakable then when we put our finger on a promise in the Bible and claim it in faith.

Spurgeon aptly said on this subject:

I believe in business prayers. I mean prayers in which you take to God one of the many promises which He has given us in His Word, and expect it to be fulfilled as certainly as we look for the money to be given us when we go to the bank to cash a cheque.

We should not think of going there, lolling over the counter chattering with the clerks on every conceivable subject except the one thing for which we had gone to the bank, and then coming away without the coin we needed; but we should lay before the clerk the promise to pay the bearer a certain sum, tell him in what form we wish to take the amount, count the cash after him, and then go on our way to attend to other business.

That is just an illustration of the method in which we should draw supplies from the Bank of Heaven.

(*The Kneeling Christian*, Zondervan Publishing House)

Paul often received promises from the Lord upon which he could rely on during his ministry. These promises gave the apostle courage to continue. When he was in Corinth, the Lord said to Him, "Do not be afraid, but go on speaking and do not be silent, for I am with you, and no one will attack you to harm you, for I have many in this city who are my people" (Acts 18:9–10). Paul took God at His word and acted on it, for immediately following it says, "And he stayed a year and six months, teaching the word of God among them" (Acts 18:11).

Later, when the apostle was in captivity, the Lord encouraged Him, saying, "Take courage, for as you have testified to the facts about me in Jerusalem, so you must testify also in Rome" (Acts 23:11). These words surely gave Him confidence on the long journey that still lay ahead of Him and was fraught with many trials. The Lord made good on His promise, for when Paul eventually was in prison in Rome, he wrote: "All the saints greet you, especially those of Caesar's household" (Phil. 4:22).

He himself was not afraid to confess in public what the Lord had spoken to him in secret. On the unforgettable boat trip in Acts 27, during which he and the other prisoners faced death on several occasions, he said aloud in front of everyone after God had given him a promise: "So take heart, men, for I have faith in God that it will be exactly as I have been told" (Acts 27:25).

We are thus to trust God to keep what He promises. Why? Because by doing that we take Him seriously and show that we consider Him to be trustworthy! When He gives us a mission, He will also pay for the costs associated with it. Give His kingdom first place, and you will see Him give you everything you need to live.

After Watchman Nee gave his life to Christ, he got a strong urge to preach the gospel. In the process, he experienced in an impressive way how God cared for him:

> **God's promises are better than a cheque and bank notes. When you have used them fifty times, you can present and use them again for the fifty-first time.**
> (James Hudson Taylor)

"Are you sure God wants you to quit school to preach the gospel?" the English missionary asked the young Chinese man who had come to see her.

Watchman Nee nodded. Since he had given his life to Jesus, the way he looked at life had changed. The things he was studying at the university no longer interested him. He had only one passion: to preach the Word of God. "But if I don't go to school, I lose my college scholarship," he admitted to his friend. "I don't know how I will take care of myself."

Miss Barber smiled. "I worried about money, too, when I first became a missionary. But a dear Christian friend told me, 'If God sends you, He must be responsible.' And God has met every need."

Watchman carried Miss Barber's words in his heart. *If it's God's responsibility*, Watchman told himself, *then I don't need to tell other people about my needs. God knows what they are.*

As Watchman Nee was preaching in his hometown of Foochow, he got a letter from a former classmate, also a Christian. "Please come to Chien-O to preach at some evangelistic meetings," said the letter.

Watchman felt his heart stir. He very much wanted to go. But Chien-O was 150 miles upriver, and the fare by motorboat was eighty dollars! Watchman counted his money: thirty dollars. "But if God is sending me, then God is responsible," he reminded himself.

The day before he was to leave on his trip, Watchman heard about a friend who badly needed money. God seemed to be urging to help his friend. Watchman gulped. Could he trust God to take care of him if he shared his money with someone else? His faith felt shaky, but he sent twenty dollars to his friend.

As he headed toward the river dock the next day, Watchman had only ten dollars in his pocket. "Oh Lord," he prayed, "I'm not asking you for money. Only a way to get to Chien-O."

At the dock, the owner of a small boat yelled at him, "Are you going to Yen-ping or Chien-O?"

"Chien-O," Watchman yelled back.

"I'll take you then—only seven dollars," said the man, taking Watchman's bags and putting them on his boat. In amazement, Watchman learned that someone else had hired this boat to take some cargo to Chien-O, but the boatman still had room for one passenger.

Watchman Nee preached for two weeks in Chien-O with only $1.20 in his pocket. As he prepared to leave, one of the English missionaries said, "You have helped us so much. Can we help you with your expenses?"

With only a few coins in his pocket, Watchman had no idea how he was going to get home. But he said, "There is no need. All is fully taken care of."

As he walked back to the dock, however, he felt anxious and worried. "Oh, God," he prayed, "You got me here; You'll have to get me back!"

Just then a messenger caught up to him with a note and some money. It was from the grateful missionary. "Even though you have someone to pay your fare," the note said, "please accept this gift, and let me play a small part."

Now Watchman knew this was how God was meeting his need. And there was the same boat, willing to take him back to Foochow for only seven dollars.

(Dave & Neta Jackson, *Hero Tales Volume 2*, Castle Rock Creative)

> *How do you handle it when in your quiet time God shows you a promise in His Word through which He speaks to you? With what expectation do you lean on what God has said, and how does that expectation manifest itself?*

Notes:

....

....

....

....

....

....

....

....

....

....

....

....

....

....

....

....

....

....

....

....

God Rewards Trust

"Because you have made the LORD your dwelling place—the Most High, who is my refuge—no evil shall be allowed to befall you, no plague come near your tent." (Psalm 91:9–10)

The Word of God shows in many places that God rewards trust. The following three examples make this very clear:

"The men of Judah prevailed, because they relied on the LORD, the God of their fathers." (2 Chron. 13:18)

"So Daniel was taken up out of the den, and no kind of harm was found on him, because he had trusted in his God." (Dan. 6:23)

"And when they prevailed over them, the Hagrites and all who were with them were given into their hands, for they cried out to God in the battle, and he granted their urgent plea because they trusted in him." (1 Chron. 5:20)

David, the man after God's own heart, is a great example as far as trusting God is concerned. From him comes the precious Psalm 62, in which trusting in God alone is emphasised over and over again. When we place our hope exclusively in God, it means at the same time that we do not have a plan B or a parachute in our luggage. It means letting go and throwing ourselves into God's mighty arms.

> **When we look back on a past life, we realise that it is for the trials that we have most to be thankful.**
> (John Nelson Darby)

Amy Carmichael once found herself in a position where she had to spend 100 rupees to save a Hindu child from being sold to a tem-

407

ple woman. She questioned whether she was justified in spending so much money on a child when she could have helped many girls with such a sum.

She then had a time of prayer, asking God to send her exactly the even sum of 100 rupees if it was His will that she should spend it now on the one Hindu child. The money came—the exact amount! The sender noted that she had sat down to write out a check for an uneven amount, but that she had felt forced to make it exactly 100 rupees instead.

That happened fifteen years ago, and since that time the same missionary has tested God again and again. He has never let her down.

Looking back, she could testify that during those fifteen years a bill never went unpaid, nor did they have to tell anyone when they needed help, plus there never was a lack of any good thing. Once, as if to show them what was possible if it had to be, twenty-five pounds came by telegram. Sometimes it even happened that an unknown man would emerge from a shouting crowd at a railroad station, slip a needed gift of money into their hands, and disappear again into the crowd before the giver could be recognised.

Often, Amy was tempted to let others know of her financial need, but she always received the inner assurance, like the voice of God, telling her that He knows and that is enough. How could it be otherwise? God was glorified. During the critical times of war, even the pagans used to remark that their God feeds them. It was known throughout the land that their God answers prayers!

(F Houghton, *Amy Carmichael von Dohnavur,* Brockhaus Verlag)

What other examples are found in the Bible that show us that God rewards trust? In this context, how can we understand that throughout church history there were many believers who died martyrs' deaths despite their trust? In what ways does God reward trust?

Notes:

....

....

....

....

....

....

....

....

....

....

....

....

....

....

....

....

....

How We Should Trust God

In many places the Word of God calls us to trust God. We can do this in a variety of ways, as the following verses make clear:

"Trust in the LORD with all your heart" (Prov. 3:5)—we are not to trust Him halfheartedly, but fully: "For the eyes of the LORD run to and fro throughout the whole earth, to give strong support to those whose heart is blameless toward him" (2 Chron. 16:9).

"For God alone my soul waits in silence; from him comes my salvation" (Ps. 62:1)—it is always more excellent to place our trust exclusively in God and not in man: "It is better to take refuge in the LORD than to trust in man" (Ps. 118:8).

"Trust in him at all times" (Ps. 62:8)—our trust should not be occasional but continuous: "I have set the LORD always before me; because he is at my right hand, I shall not be shaken" (Ps. 16:8).

"Trust in the LORD forever" (Isa. 26:4)—it is not just about a certain period of life, youth or old age, but our whole life as believers should be characterised by trust in God. For He has said, "Even to your old age I am he, and to gray hairs I will carry you. I have made, and I will bear; I will carry and will save" (Isa. 46:4).

"Blessed is the man who trusts in the LORD, and whose trust is the LORD!" (Jer. 17:7)—we are to make God the centre and focus of our trust. We expect everything from Him and accept eve-

rything as coming from His hand: "For God alone, O my soul, wait in silence, for my hope is from him" (Ps. 62:5).

Trusting God also means asking Him for help and direction, and then counting on Him to act. As David says in Psalm 37:5, "Commit your way to the LORD; trust in him, and he will act". Church history is a powerful testimony to God's faithfulness—also in view of this wonderful verse.

> **Just as we must learn to obey God one choice at a time, we must also learn to trust God one circumstance at a time. Trusting God is not a matter of my feelings but of my will.**
> (Jerry Bridges)

Paul Gerhard was a man who trusted God in a time marked by suffering. Yet despite the great hardship, his faith rose above the circumstances and enabled him to write a song that has become a source of comfort for thousands of Christians. It is based on Psalm 37:5 and is known by the title, "Thy Way and All Thy Sorrows".

There are various stories connected with this song that are vouched for as true. For example, in a Polish village not far from the city of Warsaw there lived a small farmer named Dobry. He was of German origin and an honest, truly pious, God-fearing man. There came to be hard times in the country, and the farmer often didn't know where to get food and clothing for himself, his wife and their many children.

In the winter of 1708 he found himself in increasing distress, for his debts had multiplied through various afflictions, and the creditors were preparing to drive him and his entire family from their house and farm. There was much weeping and lamenting among his wife and children, but he spoke to them comfortingly as a God-fearing fa-

ther and husband, and called upon his family to sing with him the aforementioned glorious song of faith and consolation. So they sang:

> Thy way and all thy sorrows,
> Give thou into His hand,
> His gracious care unfailing,
> Who doth the heav'ns command;
> Their course and path He giveth
> To clouds and air and wind;
> A way thy feet may follow,
> He too for thee will find.

And even while these words were sung from moved hearts, help was already coming. A raven, to which the family had given shelter every winter for years, knocked on the window and demanded to be let in. After the song ended, the black guest was allowed in. And what did it bring with him? A flashing, valuable ring, which, as the honest Dobry found out, belonged to no less a person than King Stanislaus.

The king richly rewarded the honest man and thus made it possible for him to pay his debts and rebuild his dilapidated house. Above the new door, however, the grateful father had a raven engraved and, in addition, the lines from the song they had sung that evening in prayer before God:

> Thy way is ever open;
> Thou dost on naught depend;
> Thine act is only blessing,
> Thy path light without end.

(E Dönges, *Das Leben von Paul Gerhard* [The Life of Paul Gerhard], Verlagsgesellschaft Dillenburg)

> *Why does God present us with so many different aspects of trust in His Word? Psalm 62 says on the one hand: "For God alone my soul waits in silence; from him comes my salvation" (Ps. 62:1), and on the other hand: "For God alone, O my soul, wait in silence, for my hope is from him" (Ps. 62:5)—what is the difference for our practical life of faith?*

Notes:

....

....

....

....

....

....

....

....

....

....

....

....

....

....

....

Go Forward with Boldness

"Every place that the sole of your foot will tread upon I have given to you ... Have I not commanded you? Be strong and courageous. Do not be frightened, and do not be dismayed, for the LORD your God is with you wherever you go." (Joshua 1:3, 9)

Perhaps at the end of this book, you will ask yourself the question as to how you can experience God and the fulfilment of His promises more fully. The answer is: take Him at His word and go forward boldly in faith—even if that means 'letting go' and that you aren't able to see the consequences. Dare to take steps of faith!

> **God is waiting to pour out His richest blessings on you. "Go forward" with bold confidence and take what is yours.**
> (Lettie B Cowman)

When the people of Israel were about to enter the promised land of Canaan, they stood before the Jordan River which seemed to block their way. But God told them, "When the soles of the feet of the priests bearing the ark of the LORD, the Lord of all the earth, shall rest in the waters of the Jordan, the waters of the Jordan shall be cut off from flowing, and the waters coming down from above shall stand in one heap" (Jos. 3:13).

The Levites were really brave. Why? Because they carried the Ark of the Covenant straight into the river. The water parted only when they dipped their feet in, not before (see Jos. 3:15). God had promised the same—and today He still rewards living faith that looks only at the promise and goes forward boldly!

We can imagine how the Israelites watching might have said, "I wouldn't take that risk! This is madness! The ark will be washed away!" But that's exactly what didn't happen: "The priests bearing the ark of the covenant of the LORD stood firmly on dry ground" (Jos. 3:17).

L B Cowman aptly commented, "*So even the ark of God did not move itself but was carried. When God is the architect, men are the bricklayers and labourers. Faith assists God. It can shut the mouths of lions and quench the most destructive fire. Faith still honours God, and God honours faith. Oh, for the kind of faith that will move ahead, leaving God to fulfil His promise when He sees fit! Fellow Levites, let us shoulder our load, without looking as though we were carrying God's coffin. It is the ark of the living God! Sing as you march toward the flood!*"

(Lettie B Cowman, *Streams in the Desert: 366 Daily Devotional Readings*, Zondervan)

Maybe you have wishes about what you would like to do for God. Don't be disappointed if He leads you differently than you thought. Do what He puts before your feet with an active faith and with confidence that He can use even unimpressive ministries to bring great things out of them. An example of this is the story of Edith Hayward:

Edith Hayward's dream in life was to go to India as a missionary. But the Lord had other plans for her. She married John, had children, and ministered faithfully to those in her community in Winnipeg, Canada. The Lord never gave her the opportunity to go to the country she longed to reach for Christ.

Yet by opening her home to an unknown, lonely international student and working with her husband to invest in that student's spiritual growth, she helped prepare a man who would go on to bear more spiritual fruit than any other Indian in history. Of course, she didn't realise what was happening at the time. Nor could she imagine how her family's investment would pay off as God anointed Bakht Singh and used him so mightily. But what a wonderful testimony and what a wonderful model for us.

By faithfully doing something small and doing it well, John and Edith Hayward did something big. By investing in just one, they blessed many—and helped change the spiritual destiny of millions

(Joel C Rosenberg & T E Koshy, *The Invested Life: Making Disciples of All Nations One Person at a Time*, Tyndale House Publishers Inc.)

**"For our heart is glad in him,
because we trust in his holy name."**

Psalm 33:21

> *Maybe you know you're supposed to take a step of faith, but you're afraid because you don't feel up to the situation. The moment you step forward with faith in dependence and trust in the Lord, you will experience that He stands with you in the battle! It is He who makes you an overcomer and a channel of blessing to others.*

Notes:

....

....

....

....

....

....

....

....

....

....

....

....

....

....

....

....

By the same author:

Dependence in the Life of Christ

Encouragement and Challenge to True Discipleship (123 devotions)

How can a born-again Christian lead a fulfilled life, honouring God and producing fruit for eternity? What do these words of the Lord Jesus, "Abide in me, and I in you... for apart from me you can do nothing" (Jn. 15:4–5), mean in this context? What helps and tools are available to us to live in dependence on God—and how can we best use them?

These are important questions that every true disciple of Christ who has the desire to live a life devoted to God should ask themselves. The devotions in this book are meant to be a help to find answers to these questions, and to be an encouragement to faithfully follow in the footsteps of our Lord and Master.

The "founder and perfecter of our faith" has shown us through His example what it practically means to live in dependence on God on a daily basis. We should learn from Him. His wonderful life encourages and motivates us to true discipleship. At the same time we are challenged to reconsider our own lives—and when necessary to correct them!

388 pages, £8.90, ISBN 978-1-913232-44-3

Distributors:

USA
Believers Bookshelf Inc.
PO Box 261
Sunbury, PA 17801
www.bbusa.org
Email@bbusa.org

Kenya
Christian Library And Help Services (CLAHS)
PO Box 41234
Mombasa — Kenya
kenyaclahs@gmail.com

Malawi
Christian Aid & Literature Africa
PO Box 30809
Lilongwe 3
calamalawi@gmail.com
www.biblecenter-mw.com

Nigeria
Echoes of Truth
KM 16 Ojodu-Ijoko Road,
Nepascoop Estate Bus Stop
Olajumoke Akute, Ogun State
Echoes_of_Truth@yahoo.com

Rwanda
Diffusion de la Bible et de Traités Chrétiens au Rwanda (DBTCR)
PO Box 539, Kigali
PO Box 528, Kamembe
fon.dbtcr@gmail.com

Sierra Leone
Christian Literature for Sierra Leone
christianliteraturesl@gmail.com

South Africa
Christian Library And Help Service (CLAHS)
60 Bram Fisher Drive
Blairgowrie
Johannesburg
PO Box 2048, Pinegowrie 2123
clahsbooks@gmail.com

Uganda
Promotion Of Christian Literature & Aid Services (PCLAS)
PO Box 32036
Kampala
pclas.ug@gmail.com
PO Box 460
Kasese
pclas.kasese@gmail.com

India
Spiritual Truth Communications
Flat #208, DRK Orchids
Opp: KGK Kalyanamandapam
DL Puram, Kakupalli BO
Nellore — 524 346, A.P.
joseph_stc2000@yahoo.com

Notes:

....
....
....
....
....
....
....
....
....
....
....
....
....
....
....
....
....
....
....
....
....
....
....
....
....
....
....
....
....
....

Notes:

....
....
....
....
....
....
....
....
....
....
....
....
....
....
....
....
....
....
....
....
....
....
....
....
....
....
....

Notes:

Notes:

Notes:

Notes:

....
....
....
....
....
....
....
....
....
....
....
....
....
....
....
....
....
....
....
....
....
....
....
....
....
....
....
....

Notes:

Notes:

....
....
....
....
....
....
....
....
....
....
....
....
....
....
....
....
....
....
....
....
....
....
....
....
....
....
....

Notes:

Notes:

....
....
....
....
....
....
....
....
....
....
....
....
....
....
....
....
....
....
....
....
....
....
....
....
....
....
....
....

Notes:

Notes: